JOSEPH HONE

The Book Forger

The True Story of a Literary Crime that Fooled the World

VINTAGE

3 5 7 9 10 8 6 4 2

Vintage is part of the Penguin Random House group of companies

Vintage, Penguin Random House UK, One Embassy Gardens,
8 Viaduct Gardens, London SW11 7BW

penguin.co.uk/vintage
global.penguinrandomhouse.com

First published in Vintage in 2025
First published in hardback by Chatto & Windus in 2024

Copyright © Joseph Hone 2024

The moral right of the author has been asserted

Penguin Random House values and supports copyright. Copyright fuels creativity, encourages diverse voices, promotes freedom of expression and supports a vibrant culture. Thank you for purchasing an authorised edition of this book and for respecting intellectual property laws by not reproducing, scanning or distributing any part of it by any means without permission. You are supporting authors and enabling Penguin Random House to continue to publish books for everyone. No part of this book may be used or reproduced in any manner for the purpose of training artificial intelligence technologies or systems. In accordance with Article 4(3) of the DSM Directive 2019/790, Penguin Random House expressly reserves this work from the text and data mining exception.

Printed and bound in Great Britain by Clays Ltd, Elcograf S.p.A.

The authorised representative in the EEA is Penguin Random House Ireland,
Morrison Chambers, 32 Nassau Street, Dublin D02 YH68

A CIP catalogue record for this book is available from the British Library

ISBN 9781529931440

Penguin Random House is committed to a sustainable future
for our business, our readers and our planet. This book is made
from Forest Stewardship Council® certified paper.

Praise for *The Book Forger*

'This is an absolutely fascinating literary detective story. Real-life audacious crimes uncovered by the most intrepid amateur detectives, investigated all over again a hundred years later here, in delicious forensic detail, by Joseph Hone. A must-read for anyone enthralled by the value and integrity of books. A page-turner about page-turners'
Janice Hallett, author of *The Mysterious Case of the Alperton Angels*

'This book has a great story to tell and Joseph Hone narrates it brilliantly . . . Hone makes a page-turning narrative of their detective work'
Literary Review

'Spies, detectives, forgers and The Case of the Kernless "f". Another superb piece of narrative scholarship from the best storyteller in book history'
Dennis Duncan, author of *Index, A History of the*

'Hone is a dexterous guide and an astute contributor to the long tradition of writers gripped by the connection between bibliography and crime'
Times Literary Supplement

'An extraordinary story, meticulously researched and beautifully written. Utterly enthralling'
Shaun Bythell, author of *The Diary of a Bookseller*

'Joseph Hone's hugely entertaining new account shows how this "Moriarty of the book world" met his match in a duo of intrepid young book dealers ... *The Book Forger* unfolds as a propulsive if unlikely thriller and also a useful reflection on literary forgery in general, which speaks to our own era of post-truth and deepfakes ... Unexpectedly gripping'
London Review of Books

'Criminally sophisticated skulduggery ...
A thoroughly enjoyable romp through an infamous moment in book history'
Oliver Darkshire, author of *Once Upon a Tome*

'Fascinating ... For all the thrills and shenanigans, the forensics and meticulous detail, this is a curiously moving book'
Scotland on Sunday

'I loved this elegant untangling of a real-life literary mystery. With a cast stretching from Robert Browning to Dorothy L. Sayers, it's the perfect piece of armchair detection for any book lover'
Ruth Ware, author of *The Woman in Cabin 10*

'Meticulously researched ... *The Book Forger* is delightfully and unapologetically bookish, offering glimpsed portraits of significant behind-the-scenes literary figures'
Spectator

'Intriguing, well written and impressively researched, *The Book Forger* tells a great story that is truly stranger than fiction'
Martin Edwards, President of the Detection Club

JOSEPH HONE

Joseph Hone is a writer and academic specialising in the history of the book. He studied and taught at Oxford, before holding fellowships at Cambridge, Harvard and Yale. In 2022 he was awarded the Philip Leverhulme Prize in Languages and Literatures.

To the booksellers

The detection of types is one of the most elementary branches of knowledge to the special expert in crime.

SHERLOCK HOLMES

Contents

Prologue — 1

1. Innocent Fancy — 3
2. Communism with Bibliography — 21
3. Forging Ahead — 37
4. Birrell and Garnett — 53
5. Nothing Surreptitious — 65
6. The Biblio Boys — 79
7. Making a Market — 95
8. A Book We Don't Much Care For — 113
9. The Moral Position — 125
10. The Kernless f and the Curious ? — 141
11. Sticky Fingers — 157
12. Chemical Wood, Traces of Rag — 171
13. Putting on the Ritz — 183
14. From Pillar to Post — 199
15. Giving Yourself Away — 211
16. Wisecracking — 221
17. A Delicate Mission — 233
18. What a Lot of Books — 245

Epilogue — 259
Further Reading — 265
Acknowledgements — 271
Notes — 273
Index — 307

Prologue

This is the story of perhaps the most sensational literary scandal of the last hundred years. In the summer of 1934, forty-six of the most coveted and valuable first editions of the Victorian age were revealed to be worthless fakes. By the year's end, that number had risen to above fifty. Of each of these fake first editions there were many dozens of copies: more than a thousand individual forgeries fluttering about the rare book world. Since the end of the nineteenth century, these books had been listed in the pages of auction catalogues and reference bibliographies and sold for high prices from the glass-fronted cabinets of antiquarian bookshops. They could be found on the shelves of private collections and in august public institutions, from the British Museum in London to the Huntington Library in California.

The case was cracked by a pair of young London booksellers: one of them an impossibly debonair habitué of Mayfair, the other a dishevelled communist with a sideline in espionage. Although what follows is a true story—the events and dialogue reconstructed from a variety of published and unpublished sources—the details of their investigation can sometimes seem worthy of fiction. That is because they were themselves inspired by fiction. This was the golden age of the detective story. When the forgeries first began to trickle onto the market, Sherlock Holmes was making his debut in *Beeton's Christmas Annual*. By the time the forger was unmasked, fictional detectives such as Hercule Poirot and Lord Peter Wimsey were household names, untangling the knottiest of crimes through a combination of deductive reasoning and the latest methods in forensic science. When it came to tackling the puzzle of the bogus first editions, our two young booksellers viewed themselves as the natural successors to those fictional sleuths. They were Poirots of the library, Holmeses of the book world, bibliographical detectives rooting out suspicious discrepancies with their fastidious eyes for fonts and printings.

When published, the results of their investigation shook the literary establishment to its core, for their chief suspect was himself an establishment figure: a self-made man who had, by the dawn of the twentieth century, assembled what was widely considered the greatest private library in the English-speaking world. He was a former president of the Bibliographical Society of London, an honorary graduate of the University of Oxford, and a member of the Roxburghe Club, the oldest and most exclusive assembly of bibliophiles in the world. For more than fifty years he had cultivated a reputation as a bookhunter of extraordinary skill and tenacity. 'Great collectors, like great poets, are born, not made', observed one admirer, and this man was perhaps the greatest collector of them all. He was a pugnacious burster of bubbles, a pioneer of modern firsts, a scourge of fools and double-dealers, a figure of unquestioned and unquestionable authority. He was also a liar, a thief, and a forger.

His name was Thomas James Wise.

I

Innocent Fancy

THE Shelley Society met on the second Wednesday of the month. Though it had no formal home, the society would usually congregate in the lecture theatre of University College London, on Gower Street in Bloomsbury, from October through to June. There its members were regaled with long, meandering papers about the poetry of Percy Bysshe Shelley and his circle.

The society's founder and unofficial leader was Dr Frederick James Furnivall, a sturdy, cheerful old fellow with an unruly beard and a long, wispy mane. At Cambridge, he had been a first-class oarsman, though never more than a second-class student. Instead of dreary academics, his talents lay in his ability to organise a crowd and enliven a discussion. He was a flirt, a dabbler, and a dandy. People liked him and he liked them.

One chilly December afternoon in 1885, while out on one of their Sunday walks across Hampstead Heath, Dr Furnivall and his friend Henry Sweet began discussing the merits of Shelley.

'Why not found a Shelley Society?' Sweet asked his friend. After all, Dr Furnivall was known throughout the land for his relentless energy in founding literary societies. Until recently, he had been an editor of the new *Oxford English Dictionary*. For this and other work, he had received honorary doctorates from Oxford and Berlin—a fact of which he was rather proud. At first Dr Furnivall seemed taken aback by the suggestion. He had previously founded societies for the study of historical masters such as Chaucer and Shakespeare. But he had also recently founded one for the study of Robert Browning, who was not only alive but a good friend. So why not one for Shelley? The old man drew in his breath and gave Sweet a quizzical look, eyebrow cocked, before letting out a sharp exclamation.

'By Jove! I will,' he barked, slapping his companion on the back. He saw 'no good reason why it should not be established, and several good reasons why it should'.

The next morning, Dr Furnivall called on William Michael Rossetti at his Bloomsbury townhouse. Brother of the famed painter and sonneteer Dante Gabriel and the poet Christina, Rossetti was a celebrated writer and critic in his own right. He was also a firm admirer of Shelley's, having edited his poems for publication in 1870 with a revised and much expanded edition following in 1878. Once Dr Furnivall had explained his plans over tea, Rossetti was firmly on board. This would not be an exclusive intellectual affair like the Society of Antiquaries. Nor would it be a political dining club with literary pretensions, as the Johnson Club had become under the influence of William Gladstone. Rather, Dr Furnivall and Rossetti decided that the Shelley Society would be an egalitarian association, open to men and women of all stripes, so long as they could afford the annual subscription fee of a guinea.

That same afternoon, the pair got to work recruiting a small core of patrons. The following morning Dr Furnivall drew up a prospectus for forming the society, outlining its aims and rationale. Though he had founded literary societies before, those were, for the most part, respectable and scholarly organisations. They produced neat and utilitarian editions of obscure manuscripts which attracted little interest beyond the chalky philologists and bibliophiles who haunted the reading room of the British Museum like the unquiet spirits of the long-dead authors they studied.

A Shelley society was an altogether riskier proposition. Dr Furnivall was resolute that contemporary literature, no less than the great books of bygone centuries, merited serious and sustained reading, but he was ahead of his time. No respectable gentleman thought of English literature as a subject fit for academic study. Such books were a hobby to be pursued in one's spare time, the subject of casual discussion at the tea-table. At university, one may have read Shakespeare or Dryden or Pope for pleasure; but one studied Virgil and Horace and Homer. During the long and acrimonious debates about whether English literature ought to be admitted to the curriculum at Oxford, the grouchy Regius Professor of Modern History, Edward Augustus Freeman, cautioned against a slippery slope. 'We cannot examine tastes and sympathies', he argued. What measures would be put in place to ensure this new discipline would entail 'the study of great books, and not mere chatter about Shelley'?

The statement speaks volumes about Shelley's reputation. Since his death in 1822, the poet had been denounced for his atheism, for his political radicalism, and for what the critic Matthew Arnold euphemistically called his 'irregular relations'. For tightly buttoned readers, knowledge of Shelley's scandalous biography tarnished the allure of his poems. Ever an arbiter of public taste, Arnold dismissed Shelley and his writings as 'not entirely sane . . . The Shelley of actual life is a vision of beauty and radiance, indeed, but availing nothing, effecting nothing. And in poetry, no less than in life, he is a beautiful and ineffectual angel, beating in the void his luminous wings in vain.' In Arnold's judgement, it was simply impossible to admire the writings of man who led such an unpalatable life. The popular press was more succinct, describing the poems and plays as 'the foul and unnatural ravings of a diseased and morbid imagination'.

How shocking, then, that Dr Furnivall would consider forming a society devoted to this 'ineffectual angel' of English poetry. As far as he was concerned, though, 'chatter about Shelley' was anything but 'mere'. Nor did he believe that Shelley's life tainted his writings; quite the opposite. As he explained in the prospectus, 'Next to the love of Shelley's poetry comes the love of Shelley himself.' And like the great man, any members of the society must be willing 'to assert and promote liberty and independence of opinion' against the priggish sensibilities of critics like Arnold. To those with a certain cast of mind, it was an attractive proposition. Within three months, Furnivall was collecting subscriptions for one hundred and forty-four members. By the year's end, the membership had swollen to above four hundred.

The Shelley Society's inaugural meeting took place in the Botany Theatre at University College London on the evening of 10 March 1886, Ash Wednesday. When asked about it the following morning, most were inclined to agree the event was a resounding success. Hundreds of people from all walks of life had crammed into the theatre. There were the usual Bloomsbury housewives with time on their hands and literary men from the British Museum; but among the familiar faces was a scattering of wild, radical types, such was Shelley's appeal. The German-born poet and biographer Mathilde Blind was present, chatting away with her friends and mentors. A few rows along sat the bushy-bearded F. S. Ellis, a keen-eyed antiquarian bookseller and publisher of works by William Morris and the Pre-Raphaelites. There was the actress Alma Murray, whose startling looks and exquisite voice—'bright, melting, ringing, or thrilling, at command', according to Robert Browning—set her apart from the throng. At the back of the theatre could be spied Edward Bibbins Aveling, a well-known biologist and, somewhat controversially, common-law husband to Karl Marx's youngest daughter, Eleanor. Aveling, the hot-headed translator of *Das Kapital*, founder of the Socialist League, and vice-president of the National Secular Society, was as seductive to radicals in the room as he was repellent to the usual assemblage of philologists and bibliographers.

Mingling at the centre was the mischievous young Irishman George Bernard Shaw, described by another attendee as a 'tall lank figure in grey flannels, with a flaming head and beard'. Dr Furnivall was fond of Shaw, who was, in his own words, an 'inveterate public speaker, and could always be depended on to enliven a discussion'. On this occasion, Shaw was gleefully introducing himself to the 'pious old ladies whose subscriptions kept the societies going' by announcing that, 'as a good Shelleyan', he was 'a socialist, an atheist, and a vegetarian', pausing for dramatic effect after each statement. 'Three damned good reasons why he ought to be chucked out', grumbled

Henry Arthur Jones, a few seats away. Two prim ladies resigned their membership in shock. Over the coming months, the newspapers would latch on to this odd array of 'snobbish swellish supercility in early summer suits, enthusiastic votaries of the poet, shabby dramatic parasites, a few angular blue stockings with the indispensable *pince nez*, and one or two real artists' who attended the society's gatherings.

Hushing the crowd into silence before introducing the inaugural speaker, Dr Furnivall took a moment to explain the aims of the society. They were threefold. First, it would endeavour to increase public knowledge of Shelley's life and works, which had been much besmirched in recent years. Second, it would stage his unperformed plays for the first time. Third, it would reprint in facsimile the rare first editions of his works, which all members would receive as part of their subscription. Enthusiastic muttering rippled across the theatre at that last piece of news. Everybody in the audience loved books, especially rare books. First editions were so difficult to find; these facsimiles were the closest many would get to owning the real thing.

The Rev. Stopford Brooke, notable Shelley enthusiast and preacher of some repute, used his address to reflect on the aims outlined by Dr Furnivall. Joining such a society will, he suggested, bring us 'face to face with those persons who, while they really care for poetry, do not care for Shelley's poetry. I can imagine Mr Matthew Arnold, who is such a person, being even distressed in mind, or perhaps contemptuous, when he hears of this society.' While he used much of his lecture to attack Arnold's philistine sensibilities, the real object of the Rev. Brooke's enthusiasm was the programme of facsimile printing set out by Dr Furnivall: 'it pleases us to have facsimiles of the first editions of Shelley, and other bibliographical curiosities', he admitted.

> I do not say that this is a very high ambition, nor that it has anything to do with love of poetry; yet it is a harmless and innocent fancy, and just as good as the little fancies other folk may have about great men for whom they care. A lover likes everything that puts him in mind of his mistress, even a picture of the room she dwelt in, and we may like to see how Shelley clothed his books. For in this case there is a distinct

interest. Shelley looked after the 'get-up' of many of his poems and pamphlets himself, above all those that were printed in Italy, and we seem to touch his personality in these examples.

To touch his personality. Inhabiting the mind of the poet through his writings was all well and good, but nothing could match the sensory thrill of skin against paper. As the Rev. Brooke spoke those words about the allure of Shelley's books, a serious-looking young man at the front of the auditorium appeared to shuffle in his seat: in his twenties, neatly dressed in dark worsted, a pair of little round spectacles perched on his nose and a bowler hat in his lap, dancing nervously upon his knees. His name was Thomas James Wise.

According to whom you asked, Wise went either to one of the established public schools or to the City of London School, a modern but academically excellent institution on the banks of the Thames. From their meetings at various Shelley Society events, George Bernard Shaw recalled he was 'slim, well-proportioned, well-dressed, and passed as a university graduate', though precisely where he had studied remained a mystery. He said little about his family but, at rare candid moments, claimed descent from the ancient Irish line of Wyse. Apparently, his grandfather's cousin, Sir Thomas Wyse, a diplomat and distinguished MP, had been a friend to Shelley during the poet's residence at Dublin in his teenage years. It was a charming anecdote. 'Rather a distant relationship certainly; but it is a bit interesting to myself to reflect that a Thomas Wise was supporting Shelley upon the platform upon the occasion of his first appearance as a public man, whilst a Thomas Wise is among the warmest of Shelley's admirers today.' As Wise later explained, his grandfather had changed the spelling of the name and that 'simpler form' was continued by his own father and by Wise himself.

The truth was rather different. At the time of that first Shelley Society meeting, Wise was lodging with his father and youngest brother on Devonshire Road in Holloway, in a snug terraced house a short walk east of Finsbury Park. For the past decade, since his sixteenth birthday, he had been working as a humble clerk at Herman Rubeck and Co., a modest firm trading in colonial goods: tea, coffee, sugar, herbs, spices, essential oils, and the like. There is no record of any connection to Irish aristocracy. There is no record of him attending university. There is not even any record of his schooling besides the later claims of his brother that ill health had prevented Wise from receiving a formal education, and that he was taught at home, away from the other boys.

When Wise's mother died of consumption in 1871, Thomas was aged just twelve. Her influence lived on in his love of books. As a boy, Wise would read to his mother in her sickbed, particularly poems by her beloved Shelley. After her death, he began to pick up odd and occasional pamphlet editions of the poems over which he and his mother had bonded, reminders of a stolen future. Not until he began working at Rubeck and Co. did collecting become a full-time occupation. Instead of catching the morning omnibus, Wise would set off early and walk the four miles to work, saving his pennies for the way home, when he would riffle through the untidy stacks in the second-hand barrows propped up along Farringdon Road. Among the street-side fruit traders and bric-a-brac men, Wise started to assemble the foundations of his library.

The same commercial instincts that saw him excel in his day job came in very useful while prowling for bargains. Once he plucked up the courage to step through bookshop doors and explore the hidden worlds within, Wise soon discovered his niche. He recognised that he would not be able to afford any of the rarer sixteenth- or seventeenth-century books: works by the likes of Shakespeare and Milton were far too expensive for a junior clerk, even in poor condition, and older books were scarcer still. He learned that there was little demand for damaged or incomplete titles, no matter how rare, and resolved to stop buying books that were not in perfect condition.

He did, however, sense a small, growing market for good copies of more recent titles, little pamphlet poems that did not look like much but were first editions or from small, private print runs of minor works by popular authors of the day. 'The true book-hunter considers himself a discoverer rather than a purchaser,' wrote John Herbert Slater a few years later, 'and it is the essence of his skill to find value in those things which in the eye of the ordinary possessor are really worthless.' Wise possessed this skill in spades. He bartered and bought from the cheaper stalls and, when occasion demanded, sold at a small profit some of the rarities he discovered. Nobody could hope to get rich by freelance bookrunning, but it helped make a potentially expensive habit a little bit more affordable.

Bookshops became a haven to Wise, a welcome escape from his dingy quarters in Holloway. His favourite haunt was the modest but well-curated shop of Bertram Dobell, on the Queen's Crescent in Kentish Town. Dobell and his fellow booksellers were only too happy to entertain this thoughtful teenager, with his questions about bindings and watermarks and rare editions and private sales. When he wasn't asking questions, Wise was skulking behind shelves, thumbing through copies of nineteenth-century poems and listening to the booksellers as they gossiped about the market and who sold what to whom for how much. Sometimes they would chuckle at the misfortunes of a dealer who let a rare edition slip through his fingers; sometimes they would sigh and whistle over another who bought valuable works at a bargain price. Here he received an education that far outstripped his informal schooling. The more he learned, the more eagerly he bought and sold and reinvested in his growing library.

It would be no exaggeration to call young Wise an addict, for books very quickly became the air he breathed, a way of masking childhood grief and projecting a bold new vision of himself to the world. By his eighteenth birthday, the allure of the beaten-up editions lining his room in the family home had begun to fade. He was ready to start investing in big ticket items. His first such purchase was a job lot: a substantial twenty shillings for first editions of Thomas Moore's novella *The Epicurean* and Shelley's unperformed tragedy *The Cenci*. If Wise sought to 'touch the personality' of Shelley through his books, as the Rev. Brooke put it in his inaugural address, this first edition of *The Cenci* was an opportunity too good to pass up—printed in Livorno under the supervision of Shelley himself during his Italian tour, in a limited run of only two hundred and fifty copies.

By the age of twenty-five, the determined young bibliophile was hunting down mint copies of desirable books and buying them for record sums with his hard-earned money. He invested £45 in a pristine copy of Shelley's elegy for John Keats, *Adonais*, one of a hundred printed at Pisa and wrapped in decorative cobalt papers. Soon thereafter he bought another pair of Shelley first editions from the Scottish booksellers Kerr and Richardson for £40, both in fine condition and in the original wrappers: precisely the sort of detail that Wise had learned to look out for and to treasure.

For a young man on a budget, Wise quickly made a name for himself among London's booksellers. Because his ambitions as a collector outstripped his means, Wise spent much of his spare time bartering and selling items from his library. At weekends and in the evenings, he would trudge from shop to shop, building relationships with all the dealers in town, from the humble barrow-men to the titans of the West End. Touring the choice establishments, he also began to encounter his rivals: wealthy gentlemen who bought up all the rarest and most valuable materials before Wise could even make an offer. As his tastes became ever finer, Wise found himself in the awkward position of not being able to afford exciting new books for his collection, of becoming embarrassed by the imperfect volumes he had once proudly foraged from the streets of Farringdon. If he wished to expand his library—and he wished for nothing more—he would need to look beyond overpriced Mayfair dealers to pastures new. And surely the most fruitful territory, he rationalised, would be the untapped boxes of letters and manuscripts kept by the poets, their friends, and their descendants.

If Wise hoped to track down those materials, he would need to make connections. So he masked his sharp cockney accent as best he could, paid his guinea subscription fee to the Browning Society, and, through its activities, was introduced to Dr Furnivall. Ever the kindly gentleman scholar, and perhaps sensing that Wise was not quite as well-connected as he liked to make out, Dr Furnivall took the young collector under his wing. After a few months he introduced this latest protégé to Browning himself. When the pair called on the poet one morning in the spring of 1886, they discovered him in the front room. Cobwebs clinging to the cuffs of his shirt, he had a dusty leather trunk open before him, bursting with old papers and pamphlets, handfuls of which he was blithely tossing into the fire.

Wise was distraught, much to the amusement of Dr Furnivall, who had known this lion of the literary establishment for many years and long since given up trying to sway his foibles. And then something quite extraordinary happened. They saw Browning pull out a pair of unassuming, slim pamphlets from the case, bound in drab cardboard with white paper labels pasted to the covers: two copies of his earliest printed poem, *Pauline*. Furnivall said nothing but Wise paused, heart thumping against his ribs, tongue stuck to the roof of his mouth. It was an exceedingly rare book. In all his years of searching, he had never so much as seen a copy before. Now there was not one but two within his grasp. 'Had I upon the instant asked Browning for one of them, I am convinced he would have given it to me,' he later recalled. 'But delicacy forced me to hesitate, and I allowed the opportunity to pass.' He said nothing, and the book slipped through his fingers.

A few days later, still kicking himself for his lack of initiative, Wise was invited to dinner by a rival collector, James Dykes Campbell, at his flat in Kensington opposite the park. They were joined by Browning. After dinner, Campbell and Wise sat in the study smoking and discussing bookish topics, with music from the bandstand floating through the window. Meanwhile, Browning strolled around the room, arms behind his back, perusing the contents of the bookcases which lined two of the walls.

'I see you have everything of mine, Campbell,' he nodded approvingly.

'No,' Campbell replied after a moment. 'I still lack *Pauline*.'

'Oh, that gap can soon be filled,' the poet responded airily: 'the other morning I happened upon two copies of it; one of them shall be sent to you tomorrow.'

Wise could not believe his ears. 'Here was an opportunity for me to ask for the other copy,' he reminisced. 'But once more modesty restrained me, and again I allowed the moment to pass.' Truthfully, it was more than modesty restraining Wise. He was held back by a potent cocktail of shame, anxiety, and fear. All this time he had been lying about his background, lying about his education, lying about the depth of his pockets. His passion for books had carried him this far. But begging for a copy of *Pauline* was hardly the behaviour of a gentleman. There was always the possibility that it would mark him as the outsider he truly was. The risk was too great. Once again, Wise held his tongue and looked on at Campbell with envy.

After a restless night's sleep, though, Wise could not stop thinking about the book. Had he not been there when Browning unearthed the copies? Was he not more deserving of it than his rival Campbell? Something needed to be done. Swallowing his nerves, Wise marched over to his little desk, whipped out his pen and a small sheet of paper and began to compose a letter. Dr Furnivall had already suggested to Wise that he write a simple note to Browning, asking for the pamphlet in return for a generous donation to charity. No gentleman could refuse such an offer, Furnivall had said. But the old poet's reply, when it came a few days later, was filled with regret. Alas, Browning explained, having already given one of the copies to Campbell, he was now keeping the other as a memento for his son.

Although this came as a bitter disappointment for Wise, on reflection all was not lost. It dawned on him that while he had failed to secure this particular volume, he had caught a glimpse of the gems that awaited tenacious collectors who ventured off the beaten track. And more importantly still, his humble origins had not been discovered. His chance would come.

When the decision was made to found the Shelley Society, young Thomas James Wise was naturally one of Dr Furnivall's first recruits. He quickly secured responsibility for the society's facsimile reprints of rare editions, a subject close to his heart. Under the auspices of the Browning Society, Wise had already overseen a facsimile reprint of the same *Pauline* edition that Browning had kept from him, producing four hundred copies for members and, in the process, creating a makeshift plug for the gap in his own collection. But it was very clear that Browning was uncomfortable with the reprint, and consented to it only as a 'concession to the whim of the more than friendly members of the society'. No further reprints would be allowed.

There was to be no such meddling with the Shelley Society's reprints, for the object of their veneration was dead. Besides the sporadic intervention of Shelley's son, Sir Percy, who asked the society not to reproduce some of the more scandalous writings, Wise would be free to print whatever he saw fit. He started immediately. Within a month of Dr Furnivall's fateful stroll on Hampstead Heath, Wise had drafted an introduction for a reprint of *Adonais*. He showed it to the society's founder on 6 January and, at his recommendation, sent it the following morning to Harry Buxton Forman for further comments.

Wise had been aware of Forman for some time, but had only met him recently: a sober, serious fellow, though generous; slow to smile, though quick to offer encouraging words to a novice. Little did Forman know that, in the following decades, this novice would become the domineering figure in his own field. Early on, the two of them had been rivals at Dobell's bookshop, the senior collector snapping up all the finest items before Wise could get a look in. From the talk of the town, Wise understood that Forman, who had recently completed his own multivolume edition of Shelley's works, was now compiling a catalogue of rare Shelley editions. At the end of his letter, Wise added a postscript. 'By the way Dr Furnivall told me that you had very kindly expressed your willingness to shew me sundry of your Shelley treasures. I need hardly tell you I should appreciate such kindness most highly.'

Four days later he received a reply. 'The line you have taken in your introduction is the right one,' Forman began. But the details, he thought, were slapdash. Wise needn't be so hasty in his writing, he explained: 'the first principle of our society should be to issue nothing that has not received the sanction of the committee. Accuracy, good taste, and finish, are of infinitely greater importance than hurry. In fact there *is no hurry*.' The truth of the matter is that Wise was eager to get to work. There was much he wished to accomplish.

For his edition of *Pauline*, Wise had employed Richard Clay and Sons. A well-known printing firm with a massive range of equipment and typefaces, they proved more than capable of producing the pamphlet in facsimile. 'In all respects save the paper, which it has been found absolutely impossible to match exactly, the present reprint may be considered a very good and precise representation of it,' Wise boasted of the Browning volume when it was delivered to subscribers. At this stage he knew little about the mechanics of printing, but he learned fast.

Clay and Sons proved adaptable, proficient, and, most importantly, willing. Wise would stick with the firm for his new series of Shelley reprints. Despite his injunction to slow down, Forman's revisions were quickly incorporated into the introduction for *Adonais*. In the week following the inaugural Shelley Society meeting, Wise spent all his free time poring over the proof sheets and correcting them against his copy of the original edition. He was meticulous. A margin increased by a sixteenth of an inch here; a capital letter made a point or two smaller there. No detail was too minute. All the work paid off. Within the month, three hundred copies of the finished book were ready for subscribers, who received the volumes with glee.

This was only the beginning. With the sort of energy that only the young and ambitious can muster, Wise set about printing facsimile editions of two more Shelley titles: *Alastor* and *Hellas*, the second of which Wise proudly claimed was 'as exact a representation as it has been found possible', with each 'printer's error, dropped letter, or other peculiarity of the original being carefully retained'. Besides the facsimile reprints, he was supervising the production of other Shelley Society titles, including Forman's bibliography and an edition of *The Cenci* to accompany the society's once-in-a-lifetime production of the play at the Grand Theatre in Islington. With the enchanting Alma Murray in the lead role, the occasion drew an audience of nearly three thousand. In Browning's own words, it was 'perhaps the most distinguished and critical' audience 'that an actress has ever played to, completely representing as it did the intellectual *élite* of the time'. And there, among the great and the good of literary London, within spitting distance of Oscar Wilde, Robert Browning, and George Bernard Shaw, sat the awkward young clerk from Holloway.

Printing these facsimile volumes must have seemed innocent enough at first. They hurt nobody and made some rare and expensive books accessible to hundreds of enthusiasts. Had they been available in his boyhood, Wise would doubtless eagerly have snapped them up. But that innocence was not to last. In the autumn of 1886, while hard at work on a reprint of *The Necessity of Atheism*, one of Shelley's most provocative tracts, Wise received word that Sir Percy, worried about a potential scandal, had requested he abort the edition. The news came as a severe blow. Much of the cost of printing came from the process of typesetting, which was already complete. His aim had been to print off three hundred copies for members of the Shelley Society, which would now be impossible without Sir Percy catching wind of it. Strictly speaking, Wise ought immediately to have sent word to the printer to break the type and forget all about the job. But what harm could there be in running off a single copy, Wise thought, purely for his own collection? Or perhaps two or three? Nobody would ever need to know.

Perhaps it was only ever intended as a one-off. Perhaps he justified his action as a cheerful act of defiance against Shelley's censorious son and heir—very much in the spirit of the poet himself. And yet, when the next legitimate facsimile was scheduled for the press, in another limited run for members of the society, Wise succumbed once again to temptation. Without telling his friends, he slipped across to the print shop and asked the workmen to run off a few extra copies on upmarket paper and vellum, removing any mention of the Shelley Society from the imprint and replacing it with the enigmatic notice 'PRINTED FOR PRIVATE CIRCULATION'. He rationalised that the type had already been set up and, as he was supplying his own paper for the extra copies, it barely cost the Shelleyans a penny. He could then wait a few months before selling these additional copies to subsidise his own collection.

Although Wise was not strictly doing anything illegal, his behaviour could hardly be described as honest. Such petty moral scruples never seemed to bother him. Maintaining his obsession was in his eyes a simple matter of calculus. He wanted to expand his library. To do so, he needed more money. He was prepared to tell a few white lies and act a little ruthlessly to earn that additional cash, which he could then plunge back into his collection. Perhaps more significantly, though, Wise had been accepted, if not embraced, by this strange corner of the literary world. And with every fibre of his being Wise wanted to belong. He knew his position was precarious, grounded in his capacity to buy and barter interesting copies of desirable books. Without money, his ability to ferret out rare editions would amount to nothing. If his reputation as a book-hunter fell away, so too would his access to Browning and the refined literary community that surrounded him. He could not afford to let that happen.

For someone who so desperately sought the approval of others, though, Wise could be extraordinarily pig-headed. At the first annual general meeting of the society, he was duly praised for his enthusiastic service in the print shop. 'He has had control of all the society's printing work, and has edited three of its reprints, and has, moreover, rendered most useful and highly valued aid,' agreed the committee. But relations soon began to sour, with the ambitious young bibliophile proving increasingly difficult for Dr Furnivall and his fellow Shelleyans to control. Matters came to a head in 1887, with the curious case of Shelley's *Poems and Sonnets*. The previous November, the Irish critic Edward Dowden had produced a new biography of Shelley, wherein was printed for the first time a series of unpublished poems from a newly unearthed manuscript. Wise thought these verses ought to be printed independently of Dowden's biography, for which he received a tacit nod of approval from Rossetti and Forman. But they also suggested that he ask Lady Shelley before he proceeded, who, in Wise's own words, 'expressed dissent', scuppering the plan.

And so he cooked up a new scheme. Instead of publishing the poems under his own name, he would publish them under the guise of 'Charles Alfred Seymour', a fictitious member of the equally fictitious Philadelphia Historical Society. The printers at Clay and Sons had learned not to ask too many questions. When Wise instructed them to alter the imprint to state that *Poems and Sonnets* was printed in Philadelphia, they did so without dissent. The request may have raised one or two eyebrows, but it was ultimately a small leap from printing facsimile books with earlier dates on them to printing a book with a false place of origin on the title page. Maybe Wise reassured them that the book was to be a facsimile of a supposed Philadelphian original. Maybe he claimed the books were going to be shipped over to America and sold there. In the end, Wise was a loyal customer and if Clay's did not print the book somebody else surely would. Why not take the money and be done with it? Unbeknownst to the printers, the preface and texts of the poems had been copied wholesale from Dowden's biography, much to the Irishman's annoyance. Wise even had the cheek to send him a copy of the plagiarised book, to which Dowden replied with a sarcastic letter: 'When a gentleman of the road makes you stand and deliver, and then courteously hands you back your purse, you can do no less than make a bow and say that he has the manners of a prince.' Quite simply, for all his veneer of cordiality, Wise had behaved like a highwayman.

The degree to which Wise began to attract and dispense contempt was a good measure of his standing in the literary world. As he became more comfortable in his position and networks of influence, allowing his affected upper class tones to shake off his cockney vowels, he found it increasingly easy to sever friends and make enemies. Dowden was merely the first. Rossetti followed in 1888, after Wise produced an unsanctioned edition of Shelley's unpublished correspondence. The letters in question belonged to a lawyer and collector called Henry J. Slack, who had granted Rossetti exclusive permission to reproduce them in some future publication for the Shelley Society. Wise had never been a patient man and refused to wait for approval. Under false pretence he borrowed Rossetti's transcriptions and, without his knowledge, copied them up for the printers. It was an outrageous, insolent deception and so, once again, Wise told his printers to supply a false imprint, this time stating that the book had been printed in New York.

Rossetti eventually found out, of course, when Wise tried and failed to buy the original letters. Wise protested that the publication of such documents was part of the core mission of the Shelley Society. Rossetti had been sitting on the transcripts and so, as a good scholar and Shelleyan, Wise had decided to take matters into his own hands. The older man was not amused. But he could do very little other than grumble to anyone who would listen, which few collectors were inclined to do. To Rossetti, Wise was an irritating flea. The only way to prevent him biting again was to crush him with a slap. The collectors saw Wise very differently: more songbird than pest. This brash young bibliophile may not have the most orthodox approach, they reasoned, but he was also responsible for making all those bijoux facsimiles and reprints which they liked so much. Few people had done more in recent years to slake their thirst for literary curiosities. What would be the point of clipping his wings now?

The printing shop was a place of many temptations. By the indulgence of his kindly mentor Dr Furnivall, young Wise had become the golden boy of the Shelley Society. He had been thrust into a position of trust—trust which he did not deserve. So far, his crimes had been limited to printing off odd copies and sidestepping inconvenient issues of consent and permission. But he had also spent his time absorbing every detail of how books were made, in the process discovering how easy it was to manipulate his fellow collectors and how credulous they were, how eager to get their hands on facsimile copies of terribly rare books they could never dream of owning. It was here, working with the printers at Clay's, tinkering with the details of fonts and paper, that the seed of an idea planted itself deep in his mind.

2
Communism with Bibliography

In the winter of 1921, just down the road from Christ Church, Oxford, there was a little bicycle shop. The building was a converted medieval house. It had a workshop at the back for repairs and, up a narrow staircase, two rooms and an ample kitchen. To supplement his modest income, the shop's owner, Mr Howes, had the idea of letting out the upstairs rooms, while he would lodge with his sister, a confectioner who lived across the road.

A tight-knit group of respectable-looking undergraduates responded to his advertisement, requesting the set. They were willing to pay the full sum and Mr Howes asked no questions. At first, they were quiet enough. College food left much to be desired and so this group paid a cook to prepare their meals. But because pubs were technically off-limits to undergraduates, drinking had to be done in private, and before long the rooms above the bicycle shop had become a secret drinking den. And then it was not so secret. The sounds of laughter and music, of popping corks and smashing glass, were waking up the neighbours. Crates of champagne and a new set of flamboyant young men, in silk shirts and loud outfits, drew glances and mutters.

They called themselves the Hypocrites Club, for their motto was 'water is best', from one of Pindar's odes, when their preferred drinks were wine, beer, and gin. While Mr Howes was growing exasperated by his tenants, they were recruiting new members. One of the founders was Terence Greenidge, a louche, tousled classics student at Hertford College. In 1922, it was Greenidge who inducted a young

Evelyn Waugh into the club, where he grew close with those disreputable aesthetes Harold Acton, Robert Byron, and Alastair Hugh Graham. In his memoirs, Waugh would recall the club as 'notorious not only for drunkenness but for flamboyance of dress and manner which was in some cases patently homosexual'. When Waugh dragged his former schoolmate Tom Driberg to the ramshackle quarters above the bicycle shop, Driberg enjoyed an evening of dancing while Waugh and another friend rolled around on a battered old chesterfield, 'their tongues licking each other's tonsils'.

Years later, when writing of his own time as a Hypocrite, the novelist Anthony Powell observed two distinct groups within the club: 'The premises, reputed to be Tudor, were certainly very rickety. The membership, equally irregular, was in process of changing from shove-halfpenny playing bohemians to fancy-dress wearing aesthetes.' Waugh and his showy friends belonged to the latter camp, presenting themselves as the standard bearers of a vibrant post-war generation. At the time of his matriculation, Waugh observed, 'the last of the ex-service men had gone down and the first of the puritanical, politically minded had either not come up or, at any rate, had not made himself noticed'. He and his fellow bright young things set out, in the words of the slightly older Maurice Bowra, 'unashamedly to be aesthetes and to revive some glories' of the *fin de siècle*. Had Waugh bothered to look a little harder, he would have found several 'politically minded' young men in his midst. Among them was Terence Greenidge's cousin, Henry Graham Pollard, one of those 'shove-halfpenny playing bohemians' at whom Waugh and Powell liked to sneer.

In many ways, Pollard—Graham to his friends—was an outsider among the Hypocrites. He had not gone to Eton and, in his politics at least, staunchly opposed the wanton excess of his contemporaries. That Pollard should fall in with such a wayward crowd would not have come as a surprise to any of his former schoolmasters. Though admitted to Shrewsbury School on a scholarship, and naturally shy of character, Pollard had been a troublesome student. 'One can only continue to express one's upsets at his attitude', ran one typical report, 'and to give him occasional unheeded exhortations on the subject.'

The margins of his exercise books are packed with juvenile doodles running alongside his Latin declensions.

Aged sixteen, his behaviour had become so poor that his housemaster at Shrewsbury, Mr Oldham, was forced to write a letter to his father, the eminent Tudor historian Albert Frederick Pollard: 'I am sorry to say Graham's work has become and remained so extraordinarily and unnecessarily bad,' Oldham explained. 'We came to the conclusion the only thing to do was for the headmaster to tell him he would be thrashed if his work did not improve. As it actually got worse, the headmaster thrashed him.' None of the teachers at Shrewsbury could induce young Pollard to apply himself. Although he read widely and enjoyed history and English literature and writing poetry, he saw little purpose or appeal in his school lessons. In Oldham's words, 'he will work at what he likes, but will do nothing at what he does not care for'.

Professor Pollard had studied at Oxford and expected his son to follow in his footsteps. After a disastrous scholarship examination for Balliol College, this path seemed unlikely. Feedback on his poetry essay damningly classed him as 'too voluble, and a fraud'. He came across in his interview as an 'ingratiating humbug' who would need 'plenty of vigorous criticism' before he was ready for undergraduate study. The fellows of Professor Pollard's former college, Jesus, proved more amenable. Going into his examinations, young Pollard was not confident. 'I do not think that I have a chance of a scholarship on my classics,' he confessed to his father; 'my only remote chance of getting one would be a brilliant star turn on the English or General Paper'.

The dreaded examinations went about as well as expected. But during his interview, one or two dons spotted Pollard's raw talent and the breadth of his reading. Graham received the news on New Year's Day, and immediately wrote to inform his father. 'I regret to say that I have been elected to an open scholarship at Jesus,' ran his letter, 'so I am afraid there is not much hope of getting out of it.' One might assume an ironic edge, were it not for an agonising subclause: 'I hope you might find some way out.' The senior bursar at Jesus was less downcast. He wrote to Professor Pollard to express his delight: 'we elected him rather on promise and general knowledge than on his actual historical work. We are very pleased to have the son of his father!'

Between Shrewsbury and Oxford, Pollard underwent a year of intensive historical study under his father's supervision at University College London, in a building adjoining the theatre where in bygone decades the Shelley Society had convened its lectures. The intention was to bring his work up to scratch. He would live with his parents in their ample home at Barnes—'Branksea'—just off the common, where his doting mother could keep an eye on him. Still Pollard proved himself incapable of settling into a scholarly routine. It was difficult to make friends in class, not least because his father was the instructor. But there was one group of students, outspoken and radical in their politics, who accepted him. Among their number was a girl: pretty, with short hair, mischievous eyes, and an energy quite unlike anything Pollard had ever encountered at Shrewsbury.

Her name was Kathleen Beauchamp, though friends called her Kay. Pollard was immediately smitten. Kay had come up to study in London from the quaint village of Midsomer Norton in Somerset, where her father was a gentleman farmer. Her mother had died while Kay was still very young, leaving her older sisters, Joan and Muriel, to school her in the ways of the world. Joan had been a prominent suffragette and anti-war campaigner all through her twenties, and had raised Kay to have the same independence of thought. Pollard found this irresistible, and Kay saw in him a kindred spirit.

It was difficult for Graham's father to approve. He had observed the pair's flirtation at first hand and did not wish to see his son led astray by such a disreputable companion. When Kay invited Graham to spend a week at the farm after the Easter break, Professor Pollard organised a family trip to visit his own elderly father, who lived in retirement on the Isle of Wight. Graham was not so easily discouraged. Over several long, tedious days staying with his grandfather, he plotted his escape. One morning, a little after six o'clock, with dew still fresh on the lawn, he snuck out with his bicycle and his father's tennis racquet, leaving behind only some luggage and a short but formal note addressed to his parents:

My dear Daddy and Mother,

I am going to Somerset today: I shall have breakfast at Cowes; catch the 8 o'clock boat to Southampton, have lunch at Salisbury, tea at Frome, and dinner at Midsomer Norton.

I have left all that I want taken back to London on the dressing table, and I shall be back at Branksea probably on Tuesday evening. I shall write more fully when I get to Somerset. Please do not worry about me at all as I shall be quite all right; the fact that most nearly prevented my going was Grandpa's and your illness last night but it has been no easy decision to come to; and the invitation which I am accepting is the occasion and not the cause of the present difficulty.

I am now, and I hope I shall always remain your affectionate, loving, and reverent son,

H. Graham Pollard.

By the time he arrived at the Beauchamps' gorgeous old farmhouse in the late afternoon, Pollard had cycled more than seventy-five miles along the edge of the New Forest and across the downlands of Cranborne Chase. After a welcome night's rest and a solid breakfast of thick-cut bacon and fried eggs, he composed another letter to his father: a lengthy outpouring of teenage angst, fired by a fierce independence of spirit. 'I am sure that both mother and you are conscious of the fact that not knowing many people in a sort of social intercourse, has driven me into myself a lot,' he wrote. 'You think that the remedy is in sympathy; that I had found that sympathy in Kathleen.' But nothing could be further from the truth. The plain fact was that young Pollard had grown to despise the grand redbricks and privet hedges of Barnes, the veneer of politeness that coated their middle-class existence there. The 'lack of good fellowship' from his father had been the final straw. 'I know that circumstances have made it necessary for you to have two servants, a suburban house, and not to entertain anyone much,' he explained, 'but I do not think that I am bound when it is not a question of economics to entirely accept this mode of life.'

In sharp contrast to the coolness of his father at home, Pollard's weeks in Midsomer Norton with the Beauchamps were warm and happy ones. He learned to milk the cows and clean the stalls and plough the fields and make cheese. He and Kay wandered up the sides of hills and through orchards, picking the first of the season's apples. They played tennis in the afternoon sun and read Boccaccio, Machiavelli, and, under the gaze of Kay's older sisters, Marx. Of those authors, it was the last who had the most enduring influence. Life at the farm was simple and communal in the best sense. The stark contrast between his parents' genteel life in the suburban outskirts of London and the Beauchamps, with dirt under their fingernails and laughter at their dinner table, affected him profoundly.

By the time Pollard arrived at Oxford in autumn, his transformation from naughty schoolboy to shaggy bohemian was almost complete. At the start of term he wrote wistful letters to his mother, asking her to send on items left at home: cushions, pictures, his tennis racquet, and foodstuffs including bread and ginger cake and eggs, with which he enjoyed making 'splendid onion omelettes' in the mornings. If lectures started at nine, he would cycle up to the parks around seven and bathe in the river with the dons, before returning to college for breakfast, prepared by his scout, who was a 'thoroughly good fellow'. He spoke in debates at the Oxford Union, and his speeches received decent notice in the student newspapers. When one of the editors muddled Pollard's college, calling him a Balliol man, he publicly challenged the culprit to a duel—'water pistols at two inches distance'—though explained warmly to his mother that the editor was, in truth, 'a charming person who is always teasing me about my hair'. Like most undergraduates, he tried rowing for one term but gave it up after Christmas.

In spring, Pollard began exploring the surrounding countryside in earnest. His favourite spot was the Trout, a handsome sandstone pub perched on the river at Godstow, on the far side of Port Meadow. He discovered the place in March, after a picaresque accident on the river. Taking a canoe from the college boathouse, Pollard had paddled his way upstream for a couple of hours in search of a quiet spot to moor up and do some reading. When he set off the air was still. But the breeze had been freshening all through the morning and, as he rounded a difficult bend by the pub, an unexpected gust hit the bow of his canoe, sending him 'spinning across the river' into the reeds on the opposite bank. In his panic, and with an almighty splash, he toppled over the side.

'I was done,' Pollard reported in his weekly letter home. Fishing his sodden things out of the river, he waded over to the Trout, where the kindly proprietor, one John Crawford Flitch, gave him some dry clothes and a warming lunch. As Pollard gleaned from their first encounter, Flitch was a great collector of paintings and old books. But he was an even greater traveller, having published memoirs of his voyages about the Mediterranean and across Spain, on what he loftily called his 'Goya pilgrimage'. The walls of the Trout were richly adorned by French impressionists and other 'perfectly magnificent' paintings that Flitch had acquired on his travels: 'worth thousands I should think,' Pollard told his mother. Over the coming months, Pollard made the Trout a home from home. Flitch was immensely generous with his books and, whenever he could, helped Pollard with his weekly essays. If lectures did not start until ten o'clock, he would get up at six and cycle out to Godstow. It was only a quarter of an hour's ride at that time in the morning, so he could bathe in the river, get an hour's work done, eat a hearty breakfast with Flitch, and cycle back with plenty of time to spare.

Outside his studies, much of Pollard's time was taken up by politics. Under Kay's guidance he had become a keen admirer of Marx and wished to contribute to the coming revolution in whatever way he could. The Oxford University Labour Club had been founded in 1919 and, in the following year, a scattering of local socialist parties had merged into the Communist Party of Great Britain, which urged its members to involve themselves in the labour movement. Pollard needed no encouragement and, by the end of his first term, was being dispatched to London as the local Labour Club delegate to the general meeting of the Young Communist League. Among his fellow students reading *literae humaniores* Pollard found others who sought to play their part, not least the historian Richard Pares, with whom he founded the Labour Club's new periodical, the *New Oxford*, and a young A. L. Rowse.

Already a promising scholar and dyed-in-the-wool socialist, in February 1923 Rowse was invited by Pares and Pollard to discuss the possibility of contributing essays to the *New Oxford*. He recorded the event in a vivid diary entry:

> I was asked to breakfast by Graham Pollard and Richard Pares at the Hypocrites Club. This place, the haunt of aesthetes and sub-aesthetes, had rather an unsavoury reputation to my innocent mind. I went with some trepidation to the tumble-down house in St Aldate's, up a tortuous staircase and along twisting passages to a room still filled with the atmosphere of beer, stale smoke and the nameless goings-on of the night before: it quite came up to my expectations of wickedness. Not for me membership of such an establishment. However, the meal provided the interest of a tremendous argument between Pollard and an American called Edwards, 'about the economic basis of the working classes' discontent', while Pares and I talked about poetry and the *New Oxford*, of which he wished me to join the editorial board next term.

Rowse was a good deal more efficient than Pollard, who found his editorial duties taxing. He hated trundling around Oxford trying to 'bamboozle tradesmen' into placing advertisements in the paper. But he was intrigued by the day-to-day business of the printing house. Often his busy schedule forced him to rush the job at the Holywell Press. 'I had only from about 8.30 to 11.30pm on Friday to see the paper put in type and to get the proof corrected so that there are a good many mistakes in the setting up,' he would complain to his mother. And yet that did not stop him from supervising every last process, nor from taking on new tasks and challenges whenever they were presented.

Unsurprisingly, Pollard cultivated an air of bohemian insouciance. In an age of sharply cut tweeds and cream flannels, his scruffiness helped him stand out. He was known, famously, as 'the Jesus man who introduced corduroy trousers to polite society'. For at this time corduroy was seen as the cloth of farmhands and country vagabonds, not of aspiring scholars or gentlemen. 'I have bought another pair of corduroy trousers that fit me beautifully for ten shillings. I got them at a public auction in the cattle market,' he told his despairing mother, 'and they will never, never wear out or at least I hope not.' Rowse, always a natty dresser, was quite appalled by Pollard's dishevelled looks. He recorded one morning when, having made an appointment to discuss *New Oxford* business, Pollard turned up late and 'in a most disreputable state, dirty red handkerchief around his neck, slovenly coat and trousers, heavy knapsack of books on his back, slouchy soft hat, untidy hair and unshaven face'. Quite clearly, he hadn't been to bed the night before. Asked about his sloppy appearance, Pollard responded simply that he had become engrossed in a 'gorgeous edition of the *Arabian Nights*' and 'just couldn't find time to undress and go to sleep'.

If Pollard learned only one thing from his time at Shrewsbury, it was probably his love of books. His housemaster, Mr Oldham, was the school's librarian and a distinguished bibliographer in his own right. He was likely responsible for first encouraging Graham to pursue the hobby as a teenager. At Oxford it developed into a more serious pastime. He somehow found the hours to juggle his studies and political activism with relentless and energetic book-hunting. Pollard felt at home surrounded by old books, as he was in the library or at the Trout. And it was his bookishness, no less than his political ardour or his scruffy attire, for which he became famous among his fellow students. Looking back on those halcyon undergraduate days, Evelyn Waugh recalled Pollard only as Terence Greenidge's 'tousled, corduroyed cousin in Jesus who combined communism with bibliography'.

Oxford was fertile ground for an ambitious young collector. Opposite the new buildings of Brasenose College, at 104 High Street, was

Chaundy's bookshop. The local photographer Henry Taunt had worked there as boy, some seventy years earlier, and 'learned here some of his book lore'. Even then it was 'an old shop', but it had more recently 'been extended much farther back and made three times the size to accommodate the vastly increased number of books. An immense stock of second-hand books will be found, with many remainders, and the proprietor, Mr F. W. Chaundy, lays himself out to secure scarce books or others required.' Among loyal customers of old, Chaundy counted Gladstone, Ruskin, and William Morris, to name but a few.

On Broad Street, just round the corner from Jesus College, stood another trio of well-respected bookshops: Thornton's, Parker's, and Blackwell's, the last of which would be taken over by the celebrated Basil Blackwell in 1924. These seasoned booksellers knew their stock intimately, so there were few bargains to be had. For less well-charted book-hunting territory, Pollard needed only to walk a hundred yards down Turl Street, where Parker kept his unsorted and disregarded stock in a musty basement, opposite Lincoln College. Here Pollard would rummage through piles of beaten-up quartos and thumb his way through loosely bound volumes, carefully probing for previous signs of ownership or any bibliographical oddities. Whenever he found something to his liking, he would give the shop assistant a non-committal shrug, as though the book was a worthless thing and he was doing the shop a favour by asking him to add it to his account.

Not long before Pollard arrived at university, the Warden of Wadham College had remarked that the 'old buildings combine with a dignity a millionaire could not surpass a standard of material comfort which in some respects is below that of an up-to-date workhouse'. Pollard was lucky. Despite the lack of running water, his digs over the gateway to Jesus College were comfortable enough: amply proportioned with a pleasant view down Turl Street from one window, and across the first quad from the other. There was plenty of shelf space for his growing collection. In his student diary, Rowse described it as a 'big room', looking 'more like a bookseller's shop' than an undergraduate set. He thought it a pleasant den for chatting *New Oxford* business and for reading 'poems out of the 1651 edition of Cartwright and equally early editions of Habington and Carew'. 'He has a glorious collection of books', Rowse added, as though to underscore the fact.

Book-hunting was a common enough pursuit in the university. Most Oxford collectors had a donnish interest in scholarly titles, to be either consulted in the day-to-day business of research or else put on the shelf and forgotten about. But from the start Pollard was a canny trader. His fellow students looked on in a mixture of admiration and bemusement. According to Anthony Powell, Pollard was 'already earning a living while an undergraduate by selling rare books'. Another student wistfully observed that Pollard would 'cull seventeenth-century books good chepe from the disregarded basement of Parker's, a hundred yards away along the Turl, and take them down to London to sell'. Early on, Pollard was confiding to his mother about the prices he had paid for books and begging for additional allowance so that he could have some of his paper-wrapped books bound in boards, which he could have done 'well and cheaply at a place I know here'. Once bound, he explained, the volumes would be worth three or four times what he had originally paid. He would of course pay her back in full.

Pollard's letters to his father, previously cool and forbidding, soon brimmed over with excitement and energy for his new hobby. 'I bought a good clean second edition of Gibbon's *Decline and Fall*, 1789,' he explained in one summer dispatch, plus a first edition of his autobiography and his six-volume *Works* of 1795 for under sixpence a volume. 'The great trouble is of course that the covers of all the volumes are off or nearly so. But still it was rather a bargain.' 'I have just made a find,' reported another letter: 'good clean folios' of Francis Bacon's *Sylva Sylvarum* and his *New Atlantis* at only five shillings the pair. He had found the seventeenth-century books tucked away at the back of Blackwell's, stuffed behind more recent stock. 'They must have been there for ten years at least. I don't know their exact worth but easily £1 I should think.' And, in his third year: 'I am rather elated now because I have sold one of my Beaumont and Fletcher folios 1679

(8/8/-) my 1598 Chaucer (5/5/-) and various other books altogether over £20 today. And I have also stumbled on about £3 worth of bargains in Oxford bookshops.' At last it seemed the mischievous student had learned to apply himself.

Much of Pollard's business was word-of-mouth. But he also used the columns of the *New Oxford* to advertise his wares, often at very competitive prices undercutting the major London dealers. As one example among many:

> Donne's *Poems*. 1654. Sm. 8vo. There is no portrait in this copy: some of this edition issued with and some without. Pickering & Chatto catalogue this at £6/6/- This copy in clean condition, £2. – Apply Box 1, c/o New Oxford, Holywell Press.

He started contributing a bibliographical column for the newspaper, reporting on some of the more noteworthy items scattered across Oxford's bookshops: 'There is in Blackwell's a copy of Charles Cotton's *Poems*, 1689, at £2 10s., which is not dear, as its Bond Street price is about five guineas. It is a wonderful volume too.' Digging around at Parker's, he came across the 1668 edition of Thomas Randolph's *Poems*, printed in Oxford, and the 'first and only collected edition in folio of Sir William Davenant's *Plays and Poems*', though he thought the price rather steep: '£5 seems a little too much, considering that we purchased a copy of the same book with only the additional defect of a mounted title-page for £3 at another shop in Oxford last term.'

For all its charms, Oxford could not contain Pollard's ambitions for long. He subscribed to catalogues from all the London booksellers. Their contents entranced him. 'I have not seen a recent catalogue with so many interesting books priced as low as they are here,' he remarked of one sample from Dobell's of Bond Street. Hodgson's auction room on Chancery Lane, opposite the grand Public Records Office, particularly captured his imagination. In his last year as a student, he began spending more and more time in London. 'I am coming up to town tomorrow to see about some books,' he told his mother in the spring of 1923, 'and I shall come home and leave some clothes in a bag and then I must rush off to Hodgson's.' Though close to graduating, Pollard was not yet a worldly man, more suited to roaming Cotswolds villages on his bicycle than to metropolitan life. His journeys to the city caused him no end of bother, though he thought the rewards worth the hassle. Asked about his old friend, Peter Quennell remembered a day 'when a railway strike happened to coincide with an important London book sale' putting young Pollard in the terrible dilemma of either missing the sale or crossing the picket. In the end, he took the train.

On another unfortunate occasion, en route back to Oxford after a fruitful auction at Hodgson's, Pollard stumbled onto a bus clutching his walking stick, overcoat, and a hefty bundle of old books tied loosely with string. To his dismay, the entire bus was packed with 'fat old ladies' spilling into the aisle. He carefully nudged his way towards the back, only for the bus to hit a pothole and lunge violently. Stick, coat, and books all went flying, as did Pollard himself, landing squarely in the lap of a particularly fearsome dowager. By the time he had managed to apologise, gather all his things, and squeeze into a seat 'between two of their frowns', the bus was halfway to Oxford. If the occasional passer-by chuckled at this clumsy young man, with his unkempt hair and baggy corduroy trousers and Marxist politics and parcels of antique folios, who could blame them? He was a little ridiculous. Beneath the fogeyish manners, though, a penetrating intelligence thrived.

By the start of his final year at Oxford, Pollard's prodigious collection had become the common gossip of the university's bibliophiles. He received admiring letters from his fellow undergraduates and even some of the more senior academics, hoping to examine his books. Some days, visitors would call unannounced, asking to look at this volume or that, at his rare editions of Donne or Bacon or Gibbon.

One such admirer was Cyril Wilkinson, a literary scholar based at Worcester College who was currently editing the poems of Richard Lovelace. Still in his thirties, Wilkinson was fast developing a reputation as 'one of the most legendary of Oxford's modern book-collectors'.

Alongside such academic luminaries as Sir Walter Greg, David Nichol Smith, and Percy Simpson, plus Falconer Madan and Strickland Gibson from the Bodleian, Wilkinson was a shining light of the new Oxford Bibliographical Society, formed in 1922 to encourage bibliographical research across the university and its colleges.

Wilkinson recognised the scholarly significance of Pollard's growing library early on, particularly his collection of rare works by the eighteenth-century poet George Crabbe. In 1775, aged twenty-one, Crabbe had published his first long poem with the Ipswich bookseller Charles Punchard, a feisty satire called *Inebriety*. The print run had been very small and Crabbe went to great lengths in later life to suppress all copies, embarrassed by his youthful pretensions. Consequently, it became a very rare book. Only three copies were known to exist, two of which were in America. The third, Pollard discovered in 1922, was tucked away in an unassuming corner of Dobell's bookshop on Bond Street. This copy had seen better days: at some point the title page had come loose and was now missing. But its value to scholarship was massively enhanced by an unnoticed manuscript note in the author's hand. 'Pray let not this be seen,' Crabbe had written; 'there is very little of it that I'm not heartily ashamed of.' At two guineas it was a bargain.

Pollard was proud of his find and received due praise from Wilkinson and the Oxford bibliophiles for his doggedness in seeking it out. In the summer of 1924 Pollard received a note from Wilkinson asking if he might bring round a distinguished guest to view the Crabbe pamphlet and other books. Surely Pollard was nervous about the encounter. His visitor was eminent indeed: a successful businessman, President of the Bibliographical Society, and, with Wilkinson's support, soon to be an Honorary Fellow of Worcester College.

On his arrival at Pollard's rooms, the guest was pleasant enough, shaking hands and nodding graciously at some prize tomes. He was a portly man in his sixties: short, pink-faced, bald-headed, and friendly in his manner. Pollard reminded him a little of himself, he said, back in his youthful collecting days when he too had been forced to pan for gold. But when shown Crabbe's *Inebriety* of 1775, with its missing title page and scribbled manuscript note from the author, his brow furrowed. He looked at Pollard severely through his little round spectacles and reproved him for buying this clearly damaged book. Such a volume did not belong in any serious collection, he explained, and Pollard ought to get rid of it. The visitor's name was Thomas James Wise.

3
Forging Ahead

It is difficult to counterfeit an old book. For the most part, this is due to equipment rather than skill. To undertake that sort of work, one requires access to a range of authentic early lead type, worn and heavy but in decent condition and not too broken up by hard use over the ages. Then one would need to get one's hands on a decent quantity of authentic paper from the period in question: no simple matter, as paper was expensive and therefore seldom left to moulder in a corner. Modern paper would easily be detected by any bookseller or collector worth his salt. And even if one did stumble across a cache of untouched three-hundred-year-old sheets, one would then need to navigate the complex minefield of watermarks. Quality paper usually bears a watermark, indicating the manufacturer, destined market, or date. Thanks to the quiet labour of librarians and bibliographers, we know precisely what watermarked papers were used for what books and when. Frankly, anyone foolish enough to fabricate a first edition of *Paradise Lost* on paper bearing a modern Van Gelder watermark would deserve to be caught.

Then there is the issue of condition. If a book is hundreds of years old, it is seldom pristine. Former owners will have scrawled their names across the title page or the endpapers. There might be a bookplate pasted inside the cover, perhaps belonging to a figure of historical interest, adding a desirable association to the copy. Corners will be dog-eared; paper will have browned; bookworms will have burrowed and twisted their way through the volume. Pages may bear stains from food, drink, squashed flies, pressed flowers, or, if the book was worth reading late into the evening, dribbles of candle wax. The binding will have come loose and the gutters will be packed with years of dust. None of those details is easy to fake.

At a very early stage in his career, certainly by 1887, it must have occurred to Thomas James Wise that his Shelley Society facsimiles could pass as genuine and be put to nefarious ends. All the books he reproduced were originally printed in the previous seventy or eighty years, so the issue of sourcing authentic equipment was no issue at all. The care and effort he had put into securing identical fonts of type meant that his facsimiles would fool all but the most discerning of judges. In his quest for authenticity, he had also committed the cardinal sin of not using paper with a dated watermark. When a facsimile of Shakespeare's first folio was issued in 1807, it was responsibly printed on modern paper with a watermark dated to 1806 to ensure it could not be confused with the genuine book. Wise's facsimiles contained no such security features. All one needed to do was slice the introduction from the front and one would have a passable replica of a first edition by Shelley or Browning.

Whether or not this was Wise's original intention is impossible to prove. But certainly, copies of his facsimile edition of Browning's *Pauline* could be found in antiquarian bookshops, 'faked up' and touted as the real deal. 'I once saw one of Mr Wise's reprints which had been doctored in a masterly manner,' wrote the collector John Herbert Slater in 1894. The title page and preface had been removed and the main text rebound in a 'very expensive' covering of levant morocco: a buttery goatskin leather esteemed by bookbinders for the way it showed off decorative tooling. Slater was particularly impressed by what had been done to the paper, which he thought must have been rotted 'to make it porous' before 'slightly smoking the leaves to give them that mellow appearance which is naturally produced by age'. The effect was highly convincing. And since there were very few authentic first editions at hand for ready comparison with this 'artistically treated reprint', Slater thought it likely that this volume had since 'taken up comfortable quarters' in some unsuspecting gentleman's library.

Such 'faking up' of facsimile reprints was more commonplace than many collectors liked to admit. In the early part of the nineteenth century, printers such as Joseph Smeeton of St Martin's Lane made good business from type facsimiles of old books, oftentimes printed on old paper. While his intention was not necessarily to deceive, Smeeton habitually placed his imprint in tiny letters at the very bottom of the page, so that it might be easily trimmed off by buyers. Nowadays it is difficult to find a Smeeton reprint with the imprint still intact.

Wise himself observed something similar occurring with his Shelley Society volumes, with unidentified troublemakers slicing away his prefatory material until only the facsimile pages remained. In a characteristically boastful mood, he laughed at how 'doctored' copies had fooled 'two of the foremost and most widely experienced antiquarian booksellers in London, each of whom was misled by the apparently genuine appearance of the books'. Yet he must have known that a true connoisseur, someone whose talents matched his own, would always be able to tell the difference when comparing the real edition side by side with the fake. Even if the typography was perfect down to the last tiny detail, the paper stock and watermarks would never quite match.

Wise had agonised about precisely this issue when producing his facsimiles: his edition of *Pauline* was perfect, he wrote, in 'all respects save the paper, which it has been found absolutely impossible to match exactly'. For all his youthful arrogance, he grew convinced that any attempt to pass off these early facsimiles as the genuine article would be folly. Everyone involved in the Shelley and Browning societies knew that he had been responsible for these exact reprints. If caught, anybody else could claim they had been deceived by the person who sold them the pamphlets. But as their originator, Wise would have no such excuse.

At the same time, he must have spotted the enormous opportunity presented by literary forgery. Some thirty-five years earlier, in 1852, the publishers John Murray and Edward Moxon had fallen prey to a man styling himself as the bastard son of Lord Byron. The mysterious 'Major Byron' had sold letters purportedly written by his father and by Shelley to the bookseller William White, who in turn sold them on to the publishers. Large sums of money exchanged hands. Only after Moxon excitedly hurried out an edition of the Shelley letters did he and Murray realise the collection was entirely bogus, forcing the unfortunate publisher to gather in and pulp copies of the print edition. As Dr Furnivall would later recall, chuckling with his friends, 'Murray was slower, and, by the discovery of the forgery, was saved the exposure and annoyance that Moxon incurred in publishing, and then having to suppress, his book.'

Wise was known to have been actively studying the case. When a provincial collector wrote to the Shelley Society asking for information regarding the forged letters and whether the originals had been destroyed, the query was forwarded to Wise, who responded with news that they were indeed extant and could be consulted in the manuscript department of the British Museum. Over the past few years, he had built up a theory concerning the identity of the forger. His name, Wise suspected, was George de Gibler, though that may have been yet another alias. The forger's approach had been simple: copying phrases and subjects from genuine letters, rearranging them, and augmenting them with his own flourishes. He was never caught.

In that case, the forger got away with his deceptions for a while because the letters were inventions, not straightforward copies which could be quickly and conveniently compared to an original. History is littered with such examples of literary fabrication. And no English author has been more fabricated than Shakespeare. By the middle of the eighteenth century, attention had begun to shift from Shakespeare's art to his life. With anyone who knew him long since dead, the conditions were perfect for a treasure hunt. Rival adventurers combed through the archives and attics of Stratford-upon-Avon and London for some trace of the great man. Their first find was Shakespeare's last will and testament, recovered in 1737, followed in 1753 by a signed mortgage deed. In the spring of 1757 a handwritten Catholic 'testament of faith' was reportedly sifted from the rafters of Shakespeare's birthplace on Henley Street in Stratford, seemingly signed by Shakespeare's father. Doubtless more treasures lay waiting to be discovered.

When a teenage William Henry Ireland joined his father, Samuel, on a pilgrimage to Stratford in 1792, both had hoped to join the search and unearth papers that could shed light on the national poet. This father-and-son duo chased leads all over town, to no avail. Despondent and on the verge of heading home, they got talking with one of the locals at the inn where they were staying. If they wanted papers relating to Shakespeare, he informed them, they ought to investigate Clopton House, kept by a farmer called Mr Williams. The following morning, they set out and, finding Mr Williams at home, asked him if he knew of any papers. 'By God,' he replied, 'I wish you had arrived a little sooner! Why, it isn't a fortnight since I destroyed several baskets-full of letters and papers.' He was sure he had seen Shakespeare's name written on some of them. In horror, Samuel called in the farmer's wife, who confirmed her husband's account: 'I told you not to burn the papers,' she chided, 'they might be of consequence.' The intrepid hunters returned home empty-handed.

William Henry did not forget his father's disappointment. Two years later, he unexpectedly announced that he had met an unnamed descendant of one of Shakespeare's theatrical colleagues, who claimed to possess a trunk filled with authentic Shakespearian documents. All through the Christmas of 1794 and the early months of the new year, Ireland brought to light a series of relics, including letters, legal documents, poems, and, most precious of all, manuscripts of the plays in Shakespeare's own hand. The first play to turn up was *King Lear*. Much to the delight of the literary establishment, the manuscript confirmed the widely held belief that many of the supposed faults in the play were interpolations by actors, and did not originate from the author. There followed a love letter from a youthful Shakespeare to his bride-to-be, 'Anna Hatherrewaye', enclosing a silk-entwined lock of his hair; a 'profession of faith' proving beyond doubt that he adhered to the reformed Protestant religion; a lively correspondence with his patron, the Earl of Southampton; letters from Queen Elizabeth herself; and, most thrilling of all, two unpublished plays in the hand of the master, *Henry II* and *Vortigern and Rowena*.

It was the find of the century. London literary society could speak of little else. To be invited to view the documents at 8 Norfolk Street, off the Strand, was considered a great honour. 'I beheld the papers with the tremor of purest delight, touched the invaluable relics with reverential respect', recalled the playwright James Boden, 'and deemed even existence dearer, as it gave me so refined a satisfaction.' So overcome was James Boswell that he kissed the manuscripts before falling to his knees and declaring, 'How happy am I to have lived to the present day of discovery of this glorious treasure. I shall now die in peace.' Demand to view the papers ballooned to such an extent that Samuel Ireland soon had strangers camped outside his door at all hours of the day, prompting him to restrict visits to between the hours of twelve and three on Mondays, Wednesdays, and Fridays. Even the royal princes took an interest, summoning Ireland to exhibit the Shakespeare papers at St James's Palace and Carlton House.

All this was, of course, too good to be true. Young William Henry Ireland was himself responsible for the documents. He had proved himself a cunning forger. His job as a lawyer's dogsbody gave him access to antique vellum; he got round the watermark problem by cutting blank leaves out of old books with a razor. In this respect, the materials used in his forgeries were entirely correct. The problem was the content. Ireland was no literary genius and his efforts at faux Shakespearean verse inevitably stumbled. His rendering of sixteenth-century language and spelling was also wildly misguided, with endless vowels and consonants tumbling out of control. So preposterous was the orthography that one droll bystander composed satirical letters for the literary periodicals, supposedly taken from Ireland's cache of correspondence, inviting 'Missteerree Beenjaammiinnee Joohnnssonn' to lunch 'attt twoo off theee clockee, too eatte sommee muttonne choppes andd somme poottaattoooeesse'.

Despite the accuracy of his materials, and the delirious initial reception, Ireland's sloppiness proved fatal to his overall scheme. The forged letters and manuscripts soon withered under the gaze of experts. Renowned Shakespeare scholar Edmond Malone devoted four hundred pages to demolishing Ireland's claims of authenticity. He demonstrated that the handwriting of the Ireland forgeries bore no resemblance to surviving fragments; that the spelling could not be genuine; that the chain of provenance was spurious in the extreme. Two days after Malone's salvo appeared on bookshelves, Ireland's pseudo-Shakespearean invention *Vortigern* played to an excited crowd at Drury Lane. The play was a flop. According to one member of the audience, 'some ridiculous passages caused a laugh, which infected the house during the remainder of the performance, mixed with groans'.

A generation would pass before London was hit by another hoax on such a scale. This time the perpetrator was one John Payne Collier, an ambitious scholar with an uncanny knack for rooting out previously unknown manuscripts. In the 1830s and 1840s Collier brought to light reams of important documents about Shakespeare's roles in court and the theatre: eyewitness accounts by the quack astrologer Simon Forman of performances of *The Winter's Tale*, *Macbeth*, and *Cymbeline*; tax records; investment receipts; and letters from his patrons and friends. He unearthed the crown jewel in 1852: a copy of Shakespeare's second folio annotated by one 'Thomas Perkins' in the early seventeenth century. Excitingly for Collier, who was working on a new edition of the plays, Perkins had marked corrections and improvements in the margins. Moreover, his annotations appeared to derive from early manuscripts of the plays, perhaps even from copies belonging to Shakespeare himself. Collier ardently publicised his findings as the discovery of a lifetime, even incorporating the corrections into his new edition.

Several years passed before the deception was exposed. Drawing on his considerable knowledge of seventeenth-century handwriting, Collier had annotated the book himself. He had combined his career as a distinguished bibliographer and literary detective with that of a forger. As a result, scholars faced enormous difficulties in fishing out the fabricated papers from the genuine ones he had uncovered. His strategy proved singularly effective, taking genuine books and documents and embellishing them with Shakespearean associations: adding the initials 'W. S.' to authentic but anonymous manuscript poems, or drawing up contracts for Shakespeare's investments in the Globe and Blackfriars, or adding fraudulent annotations to a genuine early folio. Above all else, Collier desired evidence to prove his own scholarly ideas. Having devoted so much of his life to studying and digging up scraps about Shakespeare's life, he knew exactly what documents ought to exist, if his theories about the playwright were true. When he failed to find them in the archives, he forged them.

These sham Shakespearean artefacts get to the heart of why authenticity became such an obsession in the book world. On the face of it there may seem little difference between one copy of a book and another. Books are called 'copies' for a reason. Granting a few minor textual differences for scholars like Collier to obsess over, what matters to the reader are the words and not their vessel. But this is to ignore the visceral pull that books can exert on their readers. In his inaugural address to the Shelley Society, the Rev. Brooke had spoken of the capacity to 'touch the personality' of Shelley through his first editions, intoxicated by the prospect of a near-tangible connection. When Boswell beheld the faux Shakespeare manuscripts, their aura prompted tears of joy. The manuscripts may have been fake, but the emotions were real enough. It was not the words on the page that made Boswell weep; it was the intimacy with genius, the thought that, in another time and at another place, those same pages had rested beneath the fingers of an artist, had staged the dance and flourish of his quill. Some books are more than books; they are relics. To discover that such an object has been cooked up by a modern forger is to risk something more profound and more personal than mere public derision or embarrassment.

The technical difficulties encountered by the literary forgers of yesteryear were twofold. Unless executed masterfully, an imitative forgery would always compare unfavourably to the original. And creative fabrication in the mode of Ireland or Collier needed to pass the most rigorous of scholarly tests. The skills required for imitative forgery were those of a first-rate craftsman; for creative forgery, those of a critic. Once in a generation an expert like Collier might come along, someone who combined both those skills and for whom the step from scholarship into deception was a simple one. More often, though, forgery ended in failure.

Wise discovered his own solutions to these problems in the most unlikely of places. Some five or six years before the Shelley Society first banded together, Harry Buxton Forman, Wise's flinty future mentor, had embarked on a private printing spree of his own. One evening at the home of a mutual friend, Forman introduced himself to an ageing third-rate poet. Richard Hengist Horne was a spirited individual who had spent much of his life in the Australian outback writing verse and prospecting for gold. Taking pity on the man, whose situation was much impoverished since his return to England, Forman helped supervise some of his last unpublished writings through the press. Among those pamphlets was an edition of a poem titled *Galatea Secunda*, originally composed for the Duke of Edinburgh's visit to Melbourne in 1867. It was dull, occasional verse and had remained rightly squirrelled away in a dusty trunk for the past fourteen years. Yet when Forman was asked to print the poem in 1881, he made some creative decisions of his own, instructing the printers to provide a 'Melbourne' imprint with the date '1867'.

It is quite possible that Forman never intended to deceive. The old poet Horne may simply have desired a harmless memento of his Antipodean adventures. Forman was an agreeable sort of fellow and would have likely wished to please this new friend. Whatever his intentions, though, Forman had effectively created a book that had never existed. The text, taken from Horne's manuscript, was genuine enough; no literary fabrication or tampering had taken place, so there were no critical tests to pass. Forman had simply created and antedated a first edition where previously there was none. And although the book was new, there was no original against which it might be compared. Any collector or dealer who encountered the item would have to accept it at face value, as a genuine first edition from 1867, printed for Horne during his time in Melbourne. And after the old poet's death in 1884 there was nobody to say otherwise.

Imagine Forman showing Wise his sham edition of *Galatea* on one of his many visits in 1887. Imagine his reaction when Forman revealed that this cooked-up first edition had been printed for him by Richard Clay and Sons, the very same firm that had printed Wise's recent volumes for the Shelley Society, and that it had done so with no questions asked. Such a book held no inherent literary value but could potentially interest a specialist bibliophile with a hunger for rarities. Now the seed of the idea planted in the printing house began to grow.

So far Wise had not attempted to palm off his facsimiles as genuine editions. He might have been able to fool one or two novices and so earn a quick bit of cash, he reasoned, but the lie would inevitably be exposed by some more experienced collector and traced back to him. The danger was still too great. But what if, rather than producing straightforward copies, he was to conjure new first editions from thin air, the kind of undiscovered gems that he had spent so many years chasing among London's antiquarian dealers? Many Victorian poets had originally published standalone pieces in literary magazines and journals. It was entirely conceivable that they might also privately run off a few separate copies of the poems as keepsakes or gifts for close friends: the kind of slim, ephemeral pamphlet that could so easily slip through the cracks. Given a false date on the title page, might not this kind of fabrication deceive apprentice and veteran collector alike?

Wise and Forman were not the first to perpetrate this sort of ruse in print. In previous centuries, when the English press had operated under strict conditions of censorship, printers often disowned controversial books by setting false names and dates to title pages. It was, for instance, a well-known fact in Wise's lifetime that there were three near-identical editions of Thomas Hobbes's notorious masterwork *Leviathan*, all with a seemingly genuine '1651' imprint. Nobody had yet puzzled out that two of the three were forgeries, covertly produced in later decades after the book had been denounced as heretical. Under these circumstances, fakery was a clever ploy that enabled enterprising booksellers working at the edge of the law to deny their role in producing the book; if discovered with copies, they could claim to be handling real first editions, printed by somebody else many years earlier.

Less cloak-and-dagger, though equally ingenious, were the fabricated copies of the 'graveyard poet' Thomas Gray's *Odes*, originally printed in 1757 on the press run by the antiquarian, author, and dilettante Horace Walpole from the grounds of his gothic villa Strawberry Hill, near Twickenham. Strawberry Hill books were rightly prized by collectors for their beauty and scarcity. Gray's *Odes* was no exception: a gorgeous book with large, neat lettering and ample margins. The rarest copies, and consequently those that commanded the highest price at auction during Wise's lifetime, were printed on a special thick paper. It took many years before collectors realised that the thick paper copies were not in fact the first edition. Close inspection of the watermarks showed that the thick paper *Odes* could not have been printed before 1790. As it turns out, in retirement, Walpole's chief printer had been running off additional backdated copies, selling them to collectors as genuine first editions, and pocketing the proceeds.

Perhaps it started out as a waggish ruse, perhaps an intellectual game, perhaps yet another money-making ploy. Who can truly say why someone takes the leap from minor indiscretion to wholesale fraud? When it comes to Wise, only one thing is certain. Like young William Henry Ireland before him, Wise sought not to discredit the literary establishment, but rather to gain a seat at the table. Through his book-hunting adventures Wise had learned to enjoy the thrill of one-upmanship, of showing his fellow collectors that he could root out rare books where they could not, grubbing for rarities as a pig sniffs out truffles. He had cultivated a certain degree of renown for his skill in doing so.

One unforeseen consequence of his facsimile reprints for the Shelley and Browning societies had been to increase interest in genuine first editions of those poets and their contemporaries. Interest led to demand and demand meant there were fewer bargains to be found. It was becoming more and more difficult for Wise to sustain his reputation as a book-hunter on his meagre salary. Manufacturing new 'rarities' would be cheaper than buying them. And each new discovery would effectively demonstrate his tenacity in the field. Any money he made from selling copies to unwary neophytes could be reinvested in genuine treasures.

Such a scheme would circumvent the issues that had plagued both imitative and creative forgers in the past, but it raised complications of its own. Printing the booklets was only half the problem, as Wise, in the 1880s, knew all too well. Collectors and dealers would be suspicious of purported first editions that had materialised from nowhere. If all the books could be traced back to Wise himself, he would be in no position to deny his involvement. He needed the books to be accepted as genuine before he started to unload them onto the public. Even if only a few copies were printed, a private run of pamphlets commissioned by an author would leave some footprint in the sand. A gift would bear an inscription. Copies would have been found among their possessions or donated to the major libraries.

Wise was sensible enough not to bother faking an inscription in an author's hand, which would convince only until the point of comparison with a genuine signature. Yet he knew that provenance could be manufactured in other ways. Not for Shelley, perhaps, for Sir Percy had already marked Wise out as a troublemaker. But other poets and their descendants were still very much alive and, if Wise was convincing enough, might be hoodwinked into accepting one of his faux editions as the real thing.

First on Wise's hit list was Algernon Charles Swinburne. In his heyday, Swinburne had acquired a reputation for degeneracy. His poems encompassed a range of topics from atheism to cannibalism and sadomasochism, including unnervingly enthusiastic accounts of young boys being flogged by their schoolmasters. 'He was restless beyond words,' observed Georgiana Burne-Jones, 'scarcely standing still at all and almost dancing as he walked, while even in sitting he moved continually, seeming to keep time, by a swift movement of the hands at the wrists, and sometimes of the feet also, with some inner rhythm of excitement.'

London had presented too much excitement, too many temptations. By 1879, at the age of forty-two, Swinburne's health was in tatters: his body a wreck and his mind little better. The poet owed his life to an old friend, Theodore Watts-Dunton, who dragged him from his city dens out to the calm suburb of Putney. In a smart townhouse called The Pines, located on the main road from the river to the heath, Swinburne settled into a more docile existence, collecting books and corresponding on literary affairs. 'Theodore treated Swinburne exactly like a tutor encouraging and patronizing a small boy', recalled Bernard Shaw, though also 'a little like the proprietor of a pet animal coaxing it to exhibit its tricks.' Over time the poet's wild auburn mane thinned and faded to grey; but visitors often observed a hint of wildness that remained behind his eyes.

Wise's plan was simple but audacious. Back in September 1866, at the height of his notoriety, Swinburne had rushed off a poem entitled *Cleopatra* for the pages of the *Cornhill Magazine*, to accompany an engraving by his friend Frederick Sandys. Wise, with his contacts at Clay and Sons, designed and crafted a standalone pamphlet edition of the poem with the name of Swinburne's old publisher John Camden Hotten and a false '1866' date on the title page. Everything about this little booklet seemed authentic, from the arrangement of the letters to the feel of the page. Under the cover of studying Swinburne's impressive collection of original Shelley editions, he began asking mutual friends to introduce him to the poet. If everything went according to plan, he would be able to thank Swinburne for access to his library by giving him a copy of the *Cleopatra* pamphlet in the hope that he would accept it as a genuine first edition. Its presence among Swinburne's own books would surely bestow on it an aura of authenticity, Wise thought, much as paintings found in an artist's studio are assumed to be by the master.

When, early in spring, Mathilde Blind invited Wise to join her and Swinburne for tea in Putney, it was, in his own words, a 'red-letter day'. On his arrival at The Pines, Wise was greeted at the door by Watts-Dunton, a serious-looking man with a heavily dyed walrus moustache, who shepherded him up the stairs, past some large drawings and paintings by Rossetti and Ford Madox Brown, to a well-proportioned, book-lined study. The window overlooked the garden where, nestled among the verdure, gleamed a pale marble statue of Venus, coyly pulling a veil over her shoulder.

If Wise was nervous, he did not let it show. 'Never before and never since have I found anticipation and realization so entirely at variance,' he recalled of the visit. Shameless gossip that he was, Dr Furnivall had been feeding Wise with scandalous tales of Swinburne's previous doings. 'I had looked to encounter a small, unkempt, red-haired man, leaping rather than walking across the room in a state of uncontrolled excitement, and when conversing raising his voice to a scream.' Instead, he found 'a quiet, well-groomed gentleman, slightly below middle height. His hair was grey with just a ruddy trace in it, and his manner of address unassuming and polite.' After half an hour of pleasant, bookish conversation, Watts-Dunton nudged open the study door and ushered Wise away.

Clearly the old poet warmed to his young visitor, for he was invited to call again the following weekend, at three o'clock on Sunday afternoon, to view the collection of early seventeenth-century plays. Habitually punctual, Wise planned his journey to arrive in good time. But the train was delayed and, by the time he had jogged up the hill from Putney Bridge station, red-faced and puffing, it was a quarter-past-three. Watts-Dunton opened the door, clearly agitated. 'Swinburne has been expecting you for the last half-hour', he chided, 'and is quite excited by your non-arrival.' Wise followed him upstairs, to find the poet pacing up and down his study, an extensive collection of quartos arranged in neat rows along the central table.

Some of the old Swinburne had worked its way loose. He was fluttering about the room, pausing every few steps to pluck additional books from shelves and place them carefully in line. As soon as Wise stepped into the room, he was dragged over to the window seat to examine some old quarto playbooks. Two minutes later Swinburne was up again, grabbing one volume and then another to put into Wise's hands. 'Then, before the story was half told,' recalled Wise, 'a third was thrust upon me, and commencement was made by its owner of a relation of its beauty. And so we went on, until my lap was full.'

In truth, Wise did not much care for these old plays and pamphlets. When later asked, he could not remember any of their titles. His host was eager to show off his beautiful Neapolitan copy of Boccaccio's *Decameron* from 1470 and a unique, but alas imperfect, book printed in late-medieval black letter. In his recollections, Wise mentioned neither. He wanted to hear tales of more recent books, rarities from

Swinburne's own lifetime, and he was drawn to the loosely tied parcels of papers that he saw bundled into the corners of the room and along the lower shelves. Squinting from a distance, he thought he glimpsed the poet's scratchy handwriting, and the tell-tale crossings-out and interlineations of working manuscripts.

At first Swinburne was bemused by this young man's enthusiasm for modern first editions. His own interests were exclusively antiquarian. Consequently, when Wise showed him the standalone edition of *Cleopatra*, with the name of Swinburne's former publisher in the imprint, he was unimpressed. 'I did not know that Hotten had republished or reprinted my stanzas,' he told Wise. 'The verses were never intended for reproduction or preservation but simply scribbled off as fast as might be to oblige a friend whose work I admired.' When Wise claimed to have spent the exorbitant sum of seven guineas on the pamphlet, perplexity veered into dismay. 'Heaven and Earth! It would have been dear at as many shillings and not cheap at as many pence,' he exclaimed. 'If I were not a bit of bibliomaniac myself, I should be shocked to think of your wasting good money on such a trumpery ephemeral.'

After his second visit to The Pines, though, Wise insisted that Swinburne accept this seemingly unique copy of *Cleopatra* as a token of gratitude. Unbeknownst to the poet, Wise had plenty of copies tucked away in his own library, so could spare the gift. 'I am almost equally distressed and gratified by the extravagance of your kindness in sending me the little *Cleopatra*,' the poet responded by the next post. 'I do not like to deprive you of what you thought worth—as you mentioned in your previous letter—a somewhat considerable price; considering that the most ardent bibliomaniac, if not a most outrageous egoist, draws the line at his own works. On the other hand, I cannot but value very highly such an evidence of good will, and such an example of generosity ... I am quite certain, quite positive, that I never set eyes on the booklet before nor heard of its existence.' Though a little frantic, Swinburne had no doubts about its authenticity. 'It is to me a fresh proof that the moral character of the worthy Mr Hotten was—I was about, very inaccurately, to say—ambiguous,' he told

Wise. His old publisher must have truly been a rogue to issue such an edition without Swinburne's express permission.

And so the trap was sprung. Rather cleverly, in addition to their personal meetings, Wise conducted much of this business with Swinburne by correspondence, meaning that he had the poet's letters as proof. If Swinburne himself accepted the *Cleopatra* pamphlet as a genuine though unauthorised first edition, who could say otherwise? Once collectors got wind that Swinburne owned a copy, Wise would quietly begin to offload the remainder of his stash. It had almost been too easy.

4
Birrell and Garnett

POLLARD left Oxford in the summer of 1924 with a third-class degree and a plan. Soon after that elder statesman of the book world, Mr Wise, stopped by his college digs to offer words of advice, Pollard had begun offloading some of his collection through Francis Birrell and David 'Bunny' Garnett, booksellers at 19 Taviton Street in Bloomsbury. Only choice bundles of books at first, but soon whole collections worth hundreds of pounds, including his precious annotated copy of Crabbe's *Inebriety*. When Garnett—one of the shop's original partners—decided to part with his stake in the business, Pollard snapped it up. He, the dishevelled communist, had found his calling. He was to become a bookseller.

Under the stewardship of Birrell and Garnett, the old shop on Taviton Street had become something of a Bloomsbury institution. It occupied the ground floor of a communal house frequented by all the usual suspects: Virginia and Leonard Woolf were friends and regular customers; the artist Duncan Grant often stopped by for conversation; E. M. Forster bought his books there. The interior was kept tidy by their 'enormous cockney housekeeper', a redoubtable older woman called Mrs Speechley, who lodged with her ailing husband in the basement. The shop floor had been cobbled together quickly by Birrell, who moved in with a jumble of old leather armchairs, and a friendly neighbourhood carpenter who 'put up cheap deal shelves'. Their initial stock was limited, mostly lifted from their respective fathers' libraries plus 'two or three shelves' of assorted eighteenth-century books scavenged from Hodgson's. It took a few months of frantic buying before the shelves began to fill, clinging to the walls, in the recollection of Frances Partridge, 'like lichen on a rock face'.

Birrell and Garnett had enviable artistic connections but were fairly useless as booksellers. Their real aim, according to Garnett, was to make their shop a 'meeting-place for people interested in the arts' rather than a place to sell books. Everybody agreed that Birrell was charming and could woo customers into returning time and again. But he loathed the everyday business of salesmanship and would instead spend most of his time curled up in an old Victorian armchair by the main window, smoking his pipe and skimming through new purchases. 'Frankie's hands were always damp,' complained Garnett; 'they exuded sweat and our stock was always getting covered with his fingerprints.' It was entirely normal for a customer to return or exchange a supposedly new volume that had been spoiled by tobacco ash and Birrell's smudges.

Though he took the business more seriously than his partner, truthfully Garnett was little better. At auction rooms and provincial sales he seldom won any of the volumes he wanted. And what books he did win were mostly cheap filler. Even when he got his hands on a highly rated item, he was often sadly unaware of its real value. On one of his more successful stock-buying jaunts at Hodgson's, he managed to scoop up an 1818 first edition of Shelley's *Revolt of Islam* for a mere two pounds. Pleased with his bargain, Garnett catalogued the book at four pounds and put it on display in the shop window. A few days later a young American called Peck came in to buy the book. After an hour he returned to the shop to inform Garnett that he had found an inscription in Shelley's handwriting on the flyleaf. Peck was very gentlemanly and offered the book back to Garnett, not wishing to deprive him of its true value. How the bookseller must have kicked himself. But he knew the only gracious response: 'I refused to take the book back and congratulated Mr Peck on his discovery.'

Pollard's arrival provided a much-needed dose of bibliographical and commercial nous. Soon thereafter the shop moved from

Bloomsbury to more bustling environs in Soho. The revamped premises on Gerrard Street were conveniently wedged between the post office and a swanky French restaurant, the Boulogne. At the front of the shop, new books were sold by Birrell, with some assistance from another partner, Ralph Wright. The large street-facing window featured an inviting display of recent titles. 'It was a lovely shop,' recalled one customer, 'stocked with enticing items.' Although Garnett had sold his share in the business, he could still be spotted round and about. He was one of the owners of the Nonesuch Press, a small operation committed to producing exquisitely designed editions of quality texts. Before his departure from the firm, Garnett had arranged for Nonesuch to share the new premises at a discounted rate. Its little hand press was set up in the basement.

The shop's second-hand selection and Pollard's poky office were through another door, towards the rear of the building. His desk, much too large for the room, was covered by a dense blanket of books and papers. Prize volumes and reference works were neatly shelved, but his personal copies and notes were variously piled up and sprawled across the floor. To a visitor or one-off customer peeking round the door, it looked like chaos. And yet, true to form, Pollard knew where every scrap of notepaper could be found. He had a system, albeit the sort of deeply erratic system that nobody other than he could have hoped to fathom.

In those early days on Gerrard Street, Pollard settled into an agreeable routine. Unless there was an important sale at Hodgson's, he would rise late and take a good breakfast of eggs and strong coffee before walking over to the British Museum. He would work in the reading room through till lunch, which he would usually take at Chez Victor on Wardour Street, a fashionable spot for Soho bohemians to eat French food and quaff French wine. After lunch he would shutter himself in his office, light his pipe, and filter through the business correspondence. What remained of the afternoon and evening were Pollard's to use as he saw fit. He often worked late into the night collating and cataloguing purchases for the bookshop, straining his eyes under the dim glow of a gas lamp.

As in Oxford, Pollard continued to balance everyday life as a bookseller with his political activism. He finally married Kay Beauchamp in a small ceremony at St Pancras parish church on 30 July 1924. The young couple made their home at 22 Adelaide Road in Camden Town, a large house which they shared with half a dozen friends from the local branch of the Communist Party, in which they had now become active. Kay was a first-class agitator: resolute, brave, outspoken. She quickly ascended the ranks to become secretary of the St Pancras branch, which was the largest local branch in London, and thereafter assumed the role of delegate to the local trade council.

Although the party was theoretically committed to gender equality and female liberation, women were funnelled into time-consuming administrative roles that left little time for the sharing of new ideas on women's issues. 'Those of us who were active in that way, I suppose, didn't feel any need for any special women's activity, except as a means of winning other women and you hadn't got time to do much of that because you were so busy on other things.' Kay had neither the time nor the inclination to take the traditional roles of wife or homemaker, nor did Graham wish her to. She was overworked as it was. In 1927, anxious friends forced Kay to set aside her role in the St Pancras organisation, albeit temporarily, to allow her precious time to recover from exhaustion.

Pollard was less fanatical in politics than his wife, but still played his part. As a professional bookseller and shopkeeper, he was eligible to join the National Amalgamated Union of Shop Assistants, Warehousemen and Clerks, and, despite his youth, was soon elected chair of the local branch. His eye for typography alongside his previous experience as an editor of the *New Oxford* came in useful when he was asked to edit the new trade union magazine, the *Distributive Worker*, from 1927. It is a curious fact that so many communists of this era were connected to the typographic arts. Or perhaps it is not so curious, for what other field so strongly combines beauty with utility, or had a wider impact on the people? In the Nonesuch basement on Gerrard Street, the printer Francis Meynell was a notable party activist and designer and editor of its weekly paper *The Communist*. Though not a registered member, the famed typographer Stanley Morison was another keen supporter and would soon become a dear friend and customer of Pollard's.

In his influential role as adviser to the British Monotype Corporation, Morison supervised the development of typefaces such as Gill Sans (designed by Eric Gill) and, for the overdue revamp of *The Times*, Times New Roman. So trusting was Morison in Pollard's keen typographical eye that, when the shop was struggling for money in 1926, he arranged a lucrative contract for the junior bookseller: £600 a year for a part-time role as 'adviser on taste, style, culture and the more intellectual sphere of publicity' for the Langstone Monotype Company, which was, as Pollard explained to his father, 'a very big and prosperous maker of the best kind of machine for setting up books—as opposed to rapid newspaper work'.

The addition of advisory typographical work to his bookselling roster left Pollard with little time for party activities. Perhaps the busiest weeks of his political life arrived in the spring of 1926. Over the past decade coal miners' wages had been slashed by more than a third. Coupled with longer hours and more hazardous working conditions, the prospect of further wage reduction was enough to force the General Council of the Trades Union Congress to call a general strike in support of the miners. With the better part of two million workers on the streets, it appeared to some in government that revolution was in the air. 'The general strike is a challenge to the parliament and is the road to anarchy,' argued the prime minister, the true-blue Conservative Stanley Baldwin. 'It is a revolutionary move which can only succeed by destroying the government and subverting the rights and liberties of the people,' wrote Thomas Marlowe, editor of the *Daily Mail*. In solidarity with their fellow workers, the newspaper's printers flatly refused to set his column in type.

Kay was in the thick of it. Within twenty-four hours of the strike being called on 3 May, she had assembled a meeting of fifty or so women, including the wives and mothers and daughters and cousins of strikers and those on the strike committee. Under normal circumstances such a gathering would have seemed impossible. But these were far from normal times. Spurred on by Kay's inspiring leadership, they opened soup kitchens to feed hungry strikers and their families, negotiating with local co-operatives for cheap food and seeking out empty halls to set up crisis centres. Pollard, too, could be found on the front lines. His store assistant, Frances Partridge, remembered how in the Soho bookshop 'knots of customers gathered to argue and prognosticate, and no work was done'. The air was 'dense with emergency' and Pollard was 'restless with excitement, and kept hurrying out to mysterious trysts, and returning to assure us that we were all in for serious trouble. There might well be bloodshed. "Your day is over," he said with relish, standing defiantly in front of the gas fire, hands in the pockets of his pink Oxford bags.'

In the end, the strike came to nothing. After nine days, the trade unionists called the miners off, it having become clear the government would not budge. For the workers and their supporters, the whole affair had been a massive disappointment. But the widespread fear that strike action was being spurred on by foreign subversives underscores the fact that the day-to-day business of local socialist activism was entwined with looming affairs of state.

Communism was seen to jeopardise the British way of life, its institutions, its ruling class. The very survival of the empire was thought to be imperilled by foreign revolutionaries. But the real danger was closer to home. Trade unionism was on the rise. Large swathes of the British working classes were being schooled in the socialist project. Many in government believed that the general strike had been funded by Soviet gold and that the unions danced to Moscow's tune. Warnings of the 'red menace' spreading from Russia contributed to the general sense of paranoia among the British public. Responding to events, the secret services set about planting moles among homegrown communists to discover evidence of conspiracy. This, in turn, fomented a deep-seated distrust between the political left and the British state, which was believed to be in thrall to a conservative establishment.

By the time of the general strike, the domestic intelligence agency MI5 was a shadow of its former self, a tiny operation with only a dozen active officers and some twenty-five staff. It would need to expand to counter the Bolshevik threat. To this end it began recruiting eager freelancers from the world of private investigation. One of these freelancers was called Maxwell Knight.

Few who met Knight could agree on what made him so compelling. He was an odd-looking man: not handsome, but tall and strong-featured, with a swollen nose, muscular jaw, and large, penetrating, pale eyes; his dark hair was parted precisely down the centre of his scalp; he was always impeccably dressed in sharp, double breasted suits, usually with the tip of a tobacco pipe poking out of his breast pocket. Perhaps it was his voice, deep and soft and reassuring. He loved animals and they responded eagerly to his touch. This unspoken way of calming distressed creatures went beyond common understanding and was remarked on by everyone who met him. Most would agree there was something unsettling about the man, an air which made him seem more like a cerebral, spectral figure than a man of flesh and blood.

Having being introduced to Whitehall's intelligence community through his work as a freelancer, by 1930 Knight was running his own operation under the auspices of MI5. His principal task was to recruit and cultivate agents inside the Communist Party headquarters on King Street. It was a role that demanded sensitivity, dedication, and overwhelming force of character. Knight exploited his agents' vanities and desires, their strengths and their weaknesses. 'The officer running an agent should set himself the task of getting to know his agent thoroughly,' he mused, including 'the agent's home surroundings, family, hobbies, personal likes and dislikes.' This sort of knowledge could come in very useful. He held to the mantra that 'one good agent, carefully trained and well placed, is worth half-a-dozen indifferent agents'. Planting assets in King Street was a long-term strategy that required a good deal of up-front investment. But the intelligence results were usually worth the cost in time and energy.

Unusually for his day, Knight believed in recruiting female operatives. 'It is frequently alleged that women are less discreet than men: that they are ruled by their emotions, and not by their brains: that they rely on intuition rather than on reason,' he briefed his superiors. 'My own experience has been very much to the contrary.' Moreover, a female secretary's near-unfettered access to classified memoranda, minutes, address books, and diaries positioned her ideally to report on an organisation's official activities, while her proximity to the gossip mill ensured she would hear about more secretive goings-on. Perhaps the two most successful agents from 'M-Section', as Knight's unit soon became known, were both secretaries and typists: Mona Maund, who used her position to gather information on internal party operations, feeding secrets back to her handler; and Olga Gray, who spent a full seven years among the communists, balancing the demands of her day job in the organisation with her responsibilities as an MI5 asset.

Knight also focused on communications, recruiting two agents from deep inside the offices of the Communist Party's new daily newspaper, the *Daily Worker*, who filed reports on editorial meetings and potentially damaging stories in the pipeline. The first informant was an eccentric barrister called Vivian Hancock-Nunn, who feigned left-wing views and offered the newspaper *pro bono* legal advice while secretly reporting all the party's propaganda activities back to M-Section. The second agent was someone high up in the newspaper's editorial committee, with influence over editorial policy and access to information on the authorship of anonymous articles. In official reports to MI5, that agent went by the codename 'M/1'. But his true name was Graham Pollard.

Pollard was likely introduced to Maxwell Knight during the year he spent at home with his parents in Barnes between school and university. Having worked briefly and unsuccessfully for the Ministry of Shipping after the war, in 1921 Knight landed a dead-end post as games master for Pollard's former prep school on the Upper Richmond Road, a few hundred metres from Swinburne's old house at

The Pines. At this point in his life Knight was, the family agreed, a terrible disappointment: an oddball who kept exotic animals in his small Putney flat and spent his nights in sweaty Soho jazz clubs. At twenty-one years old, he had had no real education and less discipline. Perhaps the teenage idler Pollard, visiting his former teachers, found in Knight a kindred outsider.

There is much about Pollard's undercover exploits for MI5 that cannot be known. Pollard was not one to break his word, and the secrets of his work went with him to the grave. And yet his personal papers and declassified filings do grant us a small window into that shadowy time in his life. His friends all agreed that something shifted after the failure of the general strike. Most assumed that Pollard withdrew from front-line party activism because of the extra typographical consultancy work he had taken on, in addition to his own research and managing the bookshop. But there were a few colleagues who suspected that, whereas Kay was becoming increasingly radical, Pollard had grown disillusioned with the revolutionary left. While the party purged alleged splitters and class-traitors, Pollard remained true to his core beliefs. And, as the years passed, he became increasingly isolated in his own home.

Perhaps the key event was the launch of the *Daily Worker* on 1 January 1930. Comintern—a Soviet organisation that pushed for worldwide communism—had been calling for a daily paper for years and eagerly funded the new venture. Unlike the weekly *Communist*, which the Nonesuch printer Francis Meynell feared had become a 'highbrow socialist magazine' aimed at 'middle class intellectuals', the *Daily Worker* was announced to the world as a 'new weapon in the class struggle, a new paper to deliver smashing blows at the enemies of the working class, a new means to mobilise its forces for battle'. It was a rallying cry for war and, as usual, Kay could be found at the vanguard. She had been present at the meeting on Tabernacle Street in Shoreditch which established the paper, and was named as one of its eight founding editors. When Kay abandoned Pollard for an extended tour of the Soviet Union later in the year, leaving him in London, his last emotional connection to the party was severed. He would not see her again for a long time. They never reconciled.

Here, it seems, is where Knight stepped in, renewing contact with the boy he had had once known in Putney. Come the autumn of 1930, nobody was in a better position than Pollard to leak information on the communist propaganda machine. With his wife out of the country, he was free to move about town at odd hours of the day without attracting suspicion, hurrying to those 'mysterious trysts' mentioned by the bookshop employees. Knight preferred not to work out of Whitehall, instead meeting his agents in an anonymous modern flat in Pimlico. It was vital that they should remain above suspicion. It was equally important that they could have a secure location to discuss confidential matters away from prying eyes.

Every agent had his or her own individual preferences about when and where to meet a handler. It may be that Pollard would traipse across to the M-Section safe house in Pimlico, where he could brief Knight on developments at the *Daily Worker* offices. Perhaps the pair would secretly swap information in Regent's Park or in a nearby underground station, as Knight often did with his other agents. However, the proximity of the bookshop on Gerrard Street to Knight's regular Soho jazz haunts would have made it a particularly convenient meeting spot for both men. Frances Partridge often recalled Pollard burning the midnight oil in his little book-lined office, long after everybody else had disappeared home. It would have been easy enough for Knight to slip by late in the evening, for the two men to light up their pipes and discuss the goings-on over at Communist Party headquarters.

Knowingly or not, working undercover for MI5 changed Pollard. As a bibliographer, he was prodigiously meticulous and blessed with a near-photographic memory of all the books that had passed under his gaze. His espionage drew on those forensic skills and applied them in new and undoubtedly exciting ways, but this line of work also took a psychological toll. Leading the double life of bookseller and spy equipped him with a newfound sense of scepticism and suspicion. In his dealings with the communists, even with his wife, Pollard was forced to wear a mask, to lie, to pretend. Distrust breeds distrust. If he was acting a role, playing a part, who else might not be what they claimed to be?

5
Nothing Surreptitious

In the summer of 1888, Wise renewed contact with Robert Browning. The elderly poet had spent the past year preparing his collected works for the press and was now busy planning three months in Venice with his family. But he took the time to respond to a query from that enthusiastic young collector who had previously dropped by with Dr Furnivall.

Wise claimed in his letter to have made a chance discovery at the recent estate sale of the publisher Edward Moxon. Although Moxon had died thirty years earlier, and most of his old stock had been sold after the family business was taken over in 1873, there had recently been a final clearing out of the warehouse. At the height of his powers, Moxon's stable of big-name authors included Wordsworth, Shelley, Tennyson, and Browning, so there were plenty of treasures to be had. The usual crowd of established booksellers had snapped up all the prize items, Wise explained ruefully. But he had managed to outbid them on a single lot of uncatalogued sundry papers, towards the end of the auction.

Trawling through the jumble on his return home, Wise happened upon several copies of a twenty-eight-page pamphlet by Browning's late and deeply beloved wife, the poet Elizabeth Barrett Browning. It was an edition of *The Runaway Slave*, a poem she had written in 1846 for an American abolitionist publication entitled *Liberty Bell*, but which had never, to the best of Wise's knowledge, been printed separately in England. The date on the title page was '1849'. All the copies were in mint condition.

Unfortunately Browning knew nothing more of an English edition than Wise did. His initial instinct was suspicion. 'I never heard of a separate publication, and am pretty certain such a circumstance never happened. I fear that this must be a fabricated affair,' he informed Wise, somewhat coolly. Most men would be deterred by such a letter. Not Wise. Following a now familiar pattern of bravado, he sent the booklet over in the next post.

Browning's doubts were overwhelmed by the evidence of his own eyes. The little booklet appeared to be a perfectly genuine but hitherto unknown edition published by Moxon in 1849. Everything from the lettering to the ruled margins looked convincing. There was even a short advertisement explaining that the verses had been reprinted 'for the use of a few "friends of freedom" and of the writer on this side of the Atlantic'. The advertisement was signed from Florence, where the Brownings had been staying at the time. The old poet was completely taken aback. On 3 August, he wrote to thank Wise for bringing the pamphlet to his attention.

> Dear Mr Wise,
>
> I daresay the fact has been that, on the publication of the poem in America, the American friends (in London) who had been instrumental in obtaining it, wrote to the authoress (in Florence) for leave to reprint it in England, and that she of course gave her consent—probably wrote the little advertisement. The respectability of the publisher and printer is a guarantee that nothing surreptitious has been done. You may observe that no price is affixed, and no advertisements are to be found on the cover—the pamphlet was clearly a private issue for friends. The appearance of the pamphlet convinces me that things were as I say.
>
> I possess a copy of the Liberty Bell, and when I disinter it from the chaos of my books I will refer to any notice that may be there in reference to your acquisition—which I return with many thanks.
>
> Yours very sincerely,
> Robert Browning.

Unfortunately for Browning, his first instincts had been correct. *The Runaway Slave* was indeed a 'fabricated affair' and Wise was the man responsible, though the story he spun was at least partially true. He and Harry Buxton Forman had indeed purchased several uncatalogued runs of 'remainders', unsold copies of old books which had been left to gather dust in some warehouse or shop corner. Perhaps they bought them at the Moxon sale, perhaps at one of the many other remainder sales held that year at Hodgson's auction room on Chancery Lane. Among the authentic volumes unearthed by these means were bundles of Wordsworth's 1845 poem on the Kendal and Windermere railway and of the Brownings' *Two Poems* of 1854. Both were genuine rarities and would be discovery enough for any ordinary collector, snatched from beneath the noses of their rivals. But Wise was no ordinary collector. Where others would see only a happy triumph, he sniffed further opportunity.

Nobody knew what books the two men might have found at auction. Their lots were catalogued only as 'miscellaneous papers' and could have contained any and all manner of titles, some of which might never have seen light of day. It was a perfect cover story. Working with Forman, whom he had cajoled into his scheme, Wise would concoct backdated first editions of established poems by authors from Moxon's lists. Together they would pick texts which had been printed in newspapers or magazines, but never separately. And then Wise would claim to have discovered unsold copies among the sundry papers they had bought in the Moxon sale. The most ingenious element of the plan was that it would also explain how they came to own multiple copies of the books, and all in mint 'uncut' condition: because they had never left the publisher's warehouse.

With Forman's help, Wise secretly cooked up *The Runaway Slave* in the following weeks, basing the design of the book closely on the genuine *Two Poems* remainder they had found, which Wise showed the printers at Clay and Sons as a template, telling them the job was another facsimile of sorts. Surely this fastidious desire for accuracy contributed to Browning's acceptance of the fake. He says as much in his letter: 'The appearance of the pamphlet convinces me that things were as I say.' Few were better placed than Wise and Forman to understand that appearances could mask all manner of deceptions.

Drunk on the thrill of duping Browning and Swinburne, Wise began to pick up the pace. His model of creative forgery was a proven success, identifying gaps where books ought to exist and filling those gaps with books of his own devising. Over the next year, he and Forman would go on to manufacture more than a dozen antedated first editions of minor works, many of which Wise foisted on unsuspecting collectors. Here was a sequence of sonnets by George Eliot, originally published in 1874 in *The Legend of Jubal* but now available under the title *Brother and Sister*, with the much earlier date of '1869'; here an extract from Shelley's *A Proposal for Putting Reform to the Vote*, not printed until 1817, but here with an '1811' date; here a separate edition of Ruskin's short story *Leoni*, dated '1868', but previously included only in an anthology; here a newly unearthed separate edition of Swinburne's *Dead Love* verses, in bright red wrappers and with an '1864' date on the title page. Each of these oddities was dreamed up by Wise and Forman, printed by Clay and Sons, and passed off as an authentic discovery.

It is one of the great ironies of bibliography that the forged edition of *Dead Love* was itself counterfeited in the early twentieth century by the bookseller Walter T. Spencer, who, like everyone else, assumed it to be the genuine article. Confronted with a copy in 1916 by his friend Richard Jennings, who had just purchased it for eight guineas, Wise was furious to notice the typography of the title page was slightly misaligned, as were some of the lines of verse inside. It was carelessly done, not a mistake he would have made. That 'so acute and experienced an expert' as Jennings could be taken in by the pamphlet was 'sufficient evidence of its extremely dangerous character', Wise noted. 'The whole thing proves once more that, easy as it appears to be to fabricate reprints of rare books, it is in actual practice absolutely impossible to do so in such a manner that detection cannot follow the result.' The sheer audacity of that statement went unnoticed.

Although Wise was evidently well aware of the technical difficulties of replicating genuine first editions, that did not prevent him attempting the impossible. Encouraged by his successes over the past year, on 4 December 1889, under the cloak of anonymity, he consigned for auction a copy of the forged *Brother and Sister* alongside another, seemingly genuine Eliot pamphlet from 1869 entitled *Agatha*. Only twenty copies of *Agatha* were ever printed in London, simply to secure the English copyright on a poem that was first published in America. So it was an immensely important, desirable, and valuable book. Wise was hoping that none of those twenty copies would be made available for comparison with his new fake, which imitated the typography and paper of the original as best it could. He needn't have worried. The book duly soared out of the saleroom.

Meanwhile, Wise had been pestering Swinburne about the 1868 first edition of his poem *Siena* and precisely how the paper edges had originally been cut: a technical detail about which Swinburne, clearly in a tetchy mood, professed to know nothing and 'care, I may add, considerably less than nothing'. Just six copies of *Siena* were known to exist, like *Agatha* having been printed to secure copyright but not for public sale. Wise did not own any of those copies and so he decided to counterfeit them. His imitation of the book may have fooled the casual observer, as his Shelley Society reprints continued to do on occasion. But, unlike the meticulous forgery of *Agatha*, it did not pass more careful scrutiny.

In the September 1892 issue of the *Bookman* magazine appeared a note warning readers of a 'skilfully fabricated' edition of *Siena*, now in circulation. Two years later, John Herbert Slater's voluminous catalogue of *Early Editions of Some Popular Modern Authors* categorically denounced the edition as a 'pirated reprint' which, 'having been very carefully executed', is 'almost impossible to detect ... from the original. It is in every respect but one a masterly production, the only apparent defect being in the description of the paper, which it was probably found impossible to match exactly. There is no doubt that many of these forged copies are on the market.' On the other side of the Atlantic, this warning would later be echoed by the accomplished Harvard rare books librarian, Flora Livingston, who labelled *Siena* a 'torment to collectors' because of reprints 'so nearly like the originals that many have been uncertain which was the genuine first edition'.

This news must have come as a blow to the confident young forger. Wise was no great believer in luck. Even so, it had been a stroke of good fortune that nobody had managed to trace the *Siena* forgery back to him. He had covered his tracks well but would not be tempted to make the same mistake again.

Inventing first editions where previously none had existed proved an immensely successful formula. The money came in useful and Wise's reputation as a book-hunter continued to climb. From time to time, however, Forman would encourage him to break the mould and experiment. The resultant forgeries followed an altogether different and perhaps subtler pattern—and for that reason were likely instigated by Forman. One such example was inspired by the very common first edition of Tennyson's haunting narrative poem *Enoch Arden*, published by Moxon in 1864. Copies could be picked up for a mere shilling apiece at second-hand bookstalls. Tennyson's original title for the poem had been *Idylls of the Hearth*, under which it had been advertised in all the newspapers. But, at the final stages of correcting the proofs, Tennyson experienced a change of heart, switching the title to *Enoch Arden*, after the poem's protagonist. Copies of the proof sheets with the original title and Tennyson's handwritten corrections were known to have been purchased by wealthy collectors for hundreds of dollars. This got the forgers thinking. What if several more copies had been run off before Tennyson stopped the press at the last minute to change the title? What if those copies had been squirrelled away in Moxon's warehouse until it was finally cleared out in 1888 and they were bundled up with other random papers for sale?

To bring this chimera to life, Wise and Forman gathered up fifteen or so good second-hand copies of *Enoch Arden*, which were easy enough to find and cheap. Wise then paid the foreman at Clay and Sons to print a new title page for the book, identical in every respect except the title, which was replaced with *Idylls of the Hearth*. In their quest for accuracy, the new title was printed on a blank page cut from the back of the original, which meant the paper was a perfect match. Next the books went under the knife. The *Enoch Arden* title page was carefully sliced out with a razor, leaving a minute stub to which the new leaf was pasted.

So beautifully precise was this job that the forgers must have had an accomplice. Only one London firm was capable of working this kind of magic with books: Riviere and Son of Heddon Street, a family firm whose skill in bookbinding and paper restoration verged on the miraculous. To disguise their handiwork, Riviere tightly bound the little booklets in expensive dyed morocco. The snug binding made the books difficult to read but, more importantly, ensured the stub remained hidden from view.

Once the books were out of surgery, Forman made a note in pencil on the flyleaf of his personal copy, dated 15 October 1888, which verified the spurious remainder story: 'This book was entirely unknown under the title *Idylls of the Hearth* until a short time ago, when five copies turned up in a sale room with other effects of Moxon,' he explained. Of the 'five copies', one was 'now in Mr Wise's possession' and another had Tennyson's handwritten corrections to the title page. This story was designed to highlight the book-hunting prowess of Wise and Forman, but was of course entirely bogus. The reference to Tennyson's handwritten notes effectively but falsely linked these spurious copies to the authentic proof sheets. Auction records show at least seven copies eventually doing the rounds. Nonetheless the backstory of a remainder turning up in the Moxon sale was entirely convincing to the forgers' fellow bibliomaniacs, whose desire to get their hands on a Tennyson rarity overwhelmed any scepticism concerning provenance. Many years later, in 1923, the eminent antiquarian bookseller Maggs Bros. of Conduit Street was still advertising the 'excessively rare trial issue' of *Idylls of the Hearth* for more than thirty pounds.

Another ingenious scheme involved overprinting sheets from genuine old books. There was, for instance, the unauthorised piracy of

Tennyson's minor poems, issued in 1870 by the rogue publisher Richard Herne Shepherd. Forman had bought the remaindered copies of this undistinguished piracy in bulk and, with a little encouragement from Wise, decided to work some mischief with them. He unstitched his copies and carefully removed the first sheet of each. He then took the original sheets and gave them to his preferred printer—William Bowden, not Wise's preferred Clay's—who fed them back into the press. Over the front page, which originally read simply 'POEMS' halfway down the page, Bowden set a new title from a fresh setting of type, closely matching the details of the original: 'The New Timon and the Poets: By Alfred Tennyson, D.C.L. With Other Omitted POEMS', the last word being from the original printing. To this he added a false imprint trumpeting the extreme scarcity of the book—'PRIVATELY PRINTED, 1876'—before having the volume stitched back together.

Wise later remarked disingenuously that this fanciful book possessed 'far more interest and importance' than any other Tennyson piracy, and that the edition 'must have been a small one, for the pamphlet is now by no means easy to find'. In this case, he and his friend had manufactured a forgery from completely authentic materials, taking a genuine book and adding a unique detail of their own invention, though a trained eye can distinguish the slender font of the original 'POEMS' from the later additions without much trouble. Once one knows what one is looking for, the variance becomes almost impossible to miss.

With the 'remainder' cover story in place, these fake books needed to be laundered of any association with the forgers. This was not such a problem for Forman, who had no desire actually to *sell* any of the books. Such a thing was unthinkable. While he might give copies to friends or season a bundle of 'swaps' with one or two concoctions, the exchange of cash left him cold. Quiet transactions and anonymous lots at auction were all well and good in the short term but would prompt questions before too long. It was essential that Wise got the books onto the market without drawing attention to himself.

In matters bibliographical, the British Museum was the unquestioned authority in the land. Copyright legislation required copies of all books published in England be deposited with the museum, to be consulted under the magnificent domed ceiling of its reading room. The absence of a book from the museum catalogues was therefore an immediate red flag to collectors. If the law stipulated that copies of every new book should immediately be deposited there, why were all these old pamphlets and volumes of poetry missing from the catalogues?

For Wise, the solution to this problem was simple enough: donate or sell a few of the books to the libraries and hope nobody noticed. In charge of the British Museum library was Edward Maunde Thompson, a reputed palaeographer who had trained in the manuscript department under the eye of Sir Frederic Madden. He had worked behind the scenes for years, compiling catalogue after catalogue of the museum's classical and medieval manuscripts, but was no expert on modern first editions. Nor did he and his subordinates much care for them; they were scholars not dilettantes. And so, for the most part, the museum's cataloguers relied on the provenance notes supplied by Wise himself.

Trusting Wise would prove an incalculable blunder. With the fabricated copy of *Siena* he donated to the British Museum, the forger included a note clarifying the book's status, contrary to the rumours that it was a 'masterly' piracy. 'This is a copy of the first published edition which has hitherto been generally accepted as the original semi-private pamphlet,' he explained. Swinburne himself had told him that the publisher, after the initial private run of six, 'caused it to be reprinted as precisely as possible, and sold the books readily at five or ten shillings apiece'. Why would Thompson or his fellow librarians challenge such a confident and seemingly authoritative account? Wise spun a similar yarn for the spurious George Eliot pamphlet. Once the initial run of *Agatha* sold out, Eliot had ordered a second batch of fifty copies, he claimed, only 'the types had already been distributed, and were set up afresh for the second printing', hence the minor differences. All these details were dutifully incorporated into the catalogue.

Not all the books could be seen to come from Wise, of course. But the solution to that problem was easy enough. Wise could be a very persuasive man when he needed to be, and his colleagues were not immune to the force of his personality. In his day job at the Rubeck company, Wise had grown close to several other young traders, in particular a man named Schlengemann and another named Otto Rubeck, the son of their employer. Both were impressionable men and Wise was only too happy to manipulate them into doing what he wanted.

On 16 August 1888, Schlengemann approached the British Museum with a copy of *The Runaway Slave*, less than a fortnight after Browning had accepted it as genuine. It sold for five guineas. He approached the museum again in October with another rarity, the fabricated edition of George Eliot's *Brother and Sister*, which the museum gladly purchased for three guineas. On 12 April 1890, Wise himself donated a trio of Swinburne fakes, including *Dead Love*. And, the following month, the museum bought from Otto Rubeck copies of both *Idylls of the Hearth* and the forged *Cleopatra* pamphlet for five guineas apiece. Later that year, the same gentleman sold two Ruskin fakes to the British Museum at two guineas each. He was also hitting the private market, flogging counterfeit Tennysons, Swinburnes, and Rossettis to any bookseller or collector who would buy them, purportedly genuine but all from the studio of Thomas James Wise with help from Harry Buxton Forman and Clay and Sons. Rubeck thought he was Wise's friend. In truth, he was his stooge.

Wise had one more trick up his sleeve—perhaps the most audacious of them all. The best way to get a forgery authenticated is to ensure it is included in the standard reference books. In the spring of 1889 it came to Wise's attention that a new catalogue of the writings of famed art critic John Ruskin was being compiled by James P. Smart of the Ruskin Society of London. Despite Smart having already completed much of the primary research, Wise somehow managed to wheedle his way into the project. Working through Smart's notes, he identified gaps in Ruskin's output and plugged them with his own forgeries. Under Wise's seemingly expert guidance, Smart included in his bibliography previously unnoticed editions of Ruskin's letters on the National Gallery, dated '1852', his *Catalogue of the Turner Sketches*, dated '1857', his essay on Samuel Prout, dated '1870', and his lectures on *The Queen's Gardens* and *The Future of England*, dated '1864' and '1866' respectively. As usual, the texts were all genuine. But the books themselves were fake.

Most audacious of all was the edition of Ruskin's short story *Leoni*, originally published in an 1837 literary annual alongside dozens of miscellaneous stories and poems, but separately reprinted by Wise in the spring of 1890 with a false '1868' date. According to his agreement with Smart, one of Wise's duties was to hunt down lost or previously unknown editions. In recent years Ruskin had become something of a recluse, hiding away from London society at his home in a remote corner of the Lake District. Without access to the great man, Wise's investigations brought him into contact with Ruskin's old manservant, Frederick Crawley, and his former assistant, George Allen. He saw in these unsuspecting associates of Ruskin's his chance to weave a backstory for *Leoni*, even convincing Allen to inscribe the book on his former master's behalf: 'George Allen with friendly regards to T. J. Wise'.

Early in 1891, Wise showed a copy of this book to his associate William G. Kingsland, who acted as the London correspondent for the American bibliographical magazine *Poet Lore*. The next issue of the magazine contained a breathless note from Kingsland, excitedly informing readers about 'two or three pamphlet-works of Mr Ruskin's which appear to be extremely scarce', of which the most exquisite was the newly discovered *Leoni*. 'It has evidently been privately printed by some friend of the author's,' asserted Kingsland, having been fed the story directly by Wise. All this was, of course, highly persuasive nonsense.

And yet, when the fifth volume of the Ruskin bibliography appeared in May 1890, it duly contained a full description of the book, confidently asserting on no evidence whatsoever that copies of this separate edition were 'reserved for private distribution only'. The supplementary volume of illustrations included a line engraving of Wise's personal copy of the spurious *Leoni*, with a short note describing it as the 'First and only Edition'. Clearly visible at the top of the flyleaf was the inscription from George Allen. Dealers previously had only had Wise's informal assurance that all these newly unearthed books by Ruskin were genuine. The bibliography made it official.

Although Wise's original motivations had been financial, selling illicit offprints to feed his expensive book habit, money was no longer in short supply. He was now in his early thirties. From his position as a lowly office clerk at the Rubeck trading company, he had risen through the ranks to become a fully fledged broker of essential oils and other exotic goods. With the increased salary came a corresponding shift in his motives. Once a handy means of earning some additional cash, book-hunting had become a game for Wise. He quickened at the sensation of beating his opponents in the field. Creating the forgeries had given him an advantage in this game, an additional means of demonstrating his taste and judgement. Each new 'discovery' reannounced his pre-eminence among bibliophiles, winning him acceptance and even admiration from the rarefied heights of the literary establishment. Privately, Wise must also have found immense satisfaction in the knowledge that he could dupe his rivals into paying good money for books which he knew to be worthless fabrications. The thrill of the hunt was augmented by the thrill of taking money from their pockets.

Forman may have begun as an equal partner in the trickery; he was very quickly browbeaten into becoming an unwilling participant. As the committee of the Shelley Society knew only too well, arrogance and ego made Wise a difficult man to control. Lying came as easily to him as putting one foot in front of the other; it was simply his means of getting where he wanted to go. It came far less naturally to Forman, who was by some yards the more punctilious of the pair, the more distinguished bibliographer, and the one with most to lose. Though he had few scruples about hoodwinking his fellow collectors, Forman had always been uncomfortable with selling fake books for profit. For all his trades, adding one or two fakes to sweeten the deal, money would never pass through his hands. Such a thing seemed ungentlemanly. He was more inclined to see the forgeries as an elaborate intellectual exercise, whereas Wise's mindset was firmly that of a commodities broker. He counted his wins and losses not merely by the books on his shelves, but by the sums in his bank account.

Wise was not so clever as he thought, though, as Forman often needed to remind him. There had been the near scrape with the forged first edition of *Siena*, identified as a fake in 1892 and henceforth rebranded by Wise as a surreptitious *second* edition. And its companion piece, the counterfeit first of George Eliot's *Agatha*, was a slapdash production until Forman took his pencil to the proofs: 'The enclosed proof shows how I fancy the new title page would look decent if properly done,' he wrote to Wise. 'I send you the book again because the imprint on verso should be given with all attainable exactitude.' Even once Wise had become used to the formula of creative forgery, Forman was still having to point out potentially catastrophic blunders. As a single pertinent example, early in 1890 Wise was devising an '1857' edition of Rossetti's poem *Sister Helen* but planned on using the much-revised text of 1881 rather than the original 1870 printing. Had Forman not intervened, the ruse would have been discovered within the week.

Occasionally, Forman was not consulted until it was too late. In 1893 Wise was working on a perfectly legitimate facsimile reprint of *Alaric at Rome*, a scarce poem written by Matthew Arnold while still a schoolboy in 1840. For once, Wise followed best practice for printing facsimiles and used watermarked paper with the date '1889', to ensure against con artists who wished to doctor the book and pass it off as genuine. Towards the end of the print run, though, he demanded several additional copies from Clay and Sons, to be printed on unwatermarked paper, just like the original. These he then passed off as genuine.

It was one of the stupidest errors Wise ever made. Unwatermarked copies might easily be compared and found identical to the watermarked facsimile, which bore Wise's name on the title page. Had he told Forman about his plan, doubtless he would have been dissuaded. All the pieces of the puzzle were lying in open sight, waiting for someone to come along and put them together, someone whose bibliographical acumen was matched by their scepticism. Decades would pass before they finally did.

6

The Biblio Boys

POLLARD arrived a little after six o'clock. The London bookselling firm of Elkin Mathews was, he knew, a place of unyielding routine. It was the kind of establishment where one might mark the passage of time as easily by the movement of people as by the ticking of the clock. Despite the absence of any considerable trade before noon, the shop doors on the corner of Conduit Street and Bond Street would open at precisely nine o'clock each and every morning. A single hour was granted to staff and partners for lunch, not a second more, and there was a quiet expectation that it ought to take the form of sandwiches eaten at one's desk while skimming through sales catalogues or pricing new stock. It was, in short, an unlikely place for an adventure to begin.

When the bells chimed six, the partners would religiously down their pens and shut their books for the day. Any straggling customers would be enjoined to leave off browsing the shelves and either discreetly ushered towards the door or invited to join the partners and their friends upstairs for a glass of dry sherry and an hour or two of book-chat. The steady rhythms of the shop gave comfort to the people who worked there. And their comfort in turn rubbed off on the customers, for whom the shop was an oasis of calm in the hubbub of Mayfair.

This daily ritual was inaugurated in 1928 when the firm moved from its poky old location around the corner on Cork Street. Their new premises sprawled across five floors of a grand Georgian terrace, embellished with tall classical windows and beautiful cornicing. At the front, the shop was distinguished by elaborate gothic tracery which extended through into the store itself, clambering across the bookcases in a pattern of untamed vines and flowers. Elsewhere this archaic flourish might have jarred against the building's clean architectural lines, but here it added a whisper of magic.

The ground floor was the envy of London booksellers, shelves neatly packed with complete sets of the most desirable authors, all 'beautifully clothed' in glittering morocco bindings in shades of ruby and emerald. Downstairs in the basement and upstairs on the first floor were kept the scruffier books and pamphlets, ranging from orphaned antique quartos to the later works of Browning and Tennyson, while the upper floors were given over to the partners' offices, where the common business of cataloguing and corresponding went on in hushed dignity.

The personnel at Elkin Mathews were a curious bunch. For several years, the business had been owned and fronted by A. W. Evans, a self-taught scholar whose literary judgement and book-hunting tenacity were legendary among his brethren in the trade. At the flanks were two junior partners: a pair adjacent to our story, but worthy of stories all of their own. Percy Muir was studious, industrious, neat, precise, and, despite his youth, balding at the temples. Eddie Gathorne-Hardy was raffish and willowy, with floppy hair that drooped over one eye, little round spectacles kept perched on his nose by the constant intervention of his index finger, and such a surfeit of good taste that, as Muir enviously recalled, it 'oozed from him almost as effortlessly it seemed as sweat oozes from the pores'.

These two young booksellers would be the secret weapon at Elkin Mathews. Between them, they developed a knack for unearthing beautiful copies of significant books and, perhaps more importantly, for pricing them at such a level that, 'albeit with groans and maledictions', customers kept returning for more. Back when the new shop opened in 1928, Evans had circulated a pamphlet with testimonials from the most distinguished bookmen in the land. The soon-to-be Nobel laureate John Galsworthy expressed delight at the relocation to larger grounds, as did the American collector A. Edward Newton, whose recent publications included the playful handbook *This Book-Collecting Game*. The final endorsement in the pamphlet spoke eagerly of the 'more suitable premises in Conduit Street' and singled out Evans and his protégés for special praise: 'I do not know of anyone among my many friends in the bookselling world who is possessed of larger knowledge in his own particular field of operations, or who is more ready to place that knowledge at the disposal of his customers.' Those words carried undeniable weight, for they had been contributed by none other than that grandest of collectors, greatest of connoisseurs, Mr Thomas James Wise.

In the early days, Wise and the older generation of book-hunters were a common sight around Evans's table, sipping sherry and spouting tired anecdotes about Browning and the golden days when Tennyson firsts could still be scavenged from the barrows of Farringdon. After Muir and Gathorne-Hardy joined the firm, though, a younger crowd began to congregate each evening at Elkin Mathews: a combination of Bloomsbury hangers-on, literary enthusiasts, bibliographical wunderkinds, and bohemian tipplers in search of a drink.

Often the groups overlapped. When Evans retired for the evening, leaving the shop in the hands of the junior partners, the gatherings inevitably grew merry. Muir described one such occasion when Evans left early, 'leaving a large party in charge of Eddie who, when it came time to go, discovered that he hadn't brought his key to the shop door and we were all locked in. Brandishing his monocle for all it was worth from the first-floor window, he persuaded a policeman—heaven knows how—to procure a ladder—from heaven knows where—down which we all clambered to the street.'

It is difficult to imagine Wise scrambling out of an upper floor window. Indeed, by the time Muir and Gathorne-Hardy joined the business, the elder statesman of book-hunting was rarely sighted at the sherry parties. Outside browsing hours, Muir recalled seeing him only once during all his years at the firm. It had been a memorable occasion. 'He was one of the few really unpleasant people that Evans tolerated,' Muir later wrote. The young bibliophiles who gathered at Elkin Mathews were notable not solely for their expertise and love of gossip, but also for their wit and irreverence, neither of which were qualities that this titan of bibliography appreciated. He demanded deference from his audience, humility in the face of his superior book lore.

Gathorne-Hardy and a few others took the opportunity to quiz Wise about some of his pronouncements, at one point sniggering among themselves at the demonstrable errors that had slipped into his many catalogues and literary editions. Wise was having none of it. 'In his ugly cockney voice he laid down the law about everything,' Muir remembered, 'from bibliography to dentures,' on this second topic growing so animated that he finally removed and brandished his own set of false teeth to illustrate a point. The junior booksellers averted their eyes at this 'ghastly dental display'. It proved precisely what they had long thought about Wise: the pompous old dinosaur did not know when to keep his mouth shut.

They called themselves the Biblio Boys, a name that reflected youthful bravado in a profession still dominated by gruff whitebeards. For the past year, since the start of 1931, they had been gathering once a month in a dingy Soho bistro where, over dinner and drinks, late into the night, they would joust back and forth in 'informal, convivial, disrespectful' debate. More frequently they could be found bonding over a glass of sherry at Elkin Mathews. By the time Pollard arrived on this particular evening in January 1932, the core group was already gathered around Evans's table. Removing his coat and gloves, he gave a little wave to Gathorne-Hardy, with whom he had several friends in common from their Oxford days, before making his way over to another fresh-faced but unusually well-dressed bookseller lurking by the decanter. Enter John Carter.

On the face of it, Carter was everything that Pollard was not: tall, patrician, sophisticated, and deeply handsome. He had been rewarded for his diligence at Cambridge with a double-first in the classics tripos, against which Pollard's third in history looked rather feeble. Whereas Pollard had always struggled at school, Carter had distinguished himself both in the classroom and on the playing field, first taking a scholarship at Eton before moving effortlessly to King's College, Cambridge in October 1924, a few months after Pollard abandoned the academic world for the bohemian life of a Soho bookseller. 'His style was already all of a piece,' remembered one schoolmate. 'As he came out of a Wall Game on a wet St Andrew's day, with mud apparently his only covering, the essential underlying elegance was unmistakably the same as it was at the start of a school field match when his white shorts were still immaculate. That exquisite calligraphy, which made his post-cards things that you could not throw away, already had the same style as the knife-edge of his trouser-crease.'

Although the university towns were both fertile book-hunting territory, Carter's adventures at Cambridge had been somewhat different from Pollard's at Oxford. For one thing, he chose to isolate himself from the distractions of politics and London auction houses, instead prowling the shelves at Gustave David's bookshop around the corner from King's and absorbing the wisdom of his tutor A. E. Housman, whose sage advice on deciphering bibliographical puzzles he would never forget: 'Knowledge is good, method is good, but one thing beyond all others is necessary; and that is to have a head, not a pumpkin, on your shoulders and brains, not pudding, in your head.' Judged by those standards, Carter was a model student. His vacation work cataloguing medieval books at Jesus College and the small but growing collection of exquisite tomes displayed in his college digs were ample testimony that his head was filled with brains, not pudding.

Bookselling was not an obvious vocation for this debonair young graduate of Eton and King's. His experience was all in buying books, not selling them. At first, he seems to have contemplated librarianship. A chance conversation with the Bodleian librarian, Arthur Cowley, soon disabused him of that notion. The money might seem acceptable for a young man fresh out of university, Cowley explained, 'but what do you suppose you would be getting when you are forty, and irretrievably addicted to wine, women and song?' The older man gave an embittered little snort. 'Go away, my dear boy, and think again.'

Next Carter turned to Cambridge University Press, explaining to them where his interests lay. Again there were no suitable openings. But in the weeks after taking his degree, Carter got lucky. His contact at the university press passed on news that the American publisher and bookseller Charles Scribner's Sons was looking for an assistant to handle the rare books division of their London business. Before the end of summer, Carter had secured the position.

Though it took Carter a few months to settle into his new role, it was to prove a perfect match. Mostly the job seemed to involve buying interesting books with his employer's money and shipping them over to New York, where they could be sold with a colossal mark-up to wealthy American clients. Carter gladly spent his days marching from shop to shop. The labyrinthine basement at Elkin Mathews was a favourite haunt, as, of course, was Pollard's office round the back of Birrell and Garnett in Soho.

What started as a loose working acquaintance soon hardened into friendship. Carter would find himself dropping by Birrell and Garnett in the mornings, even when there was nothing enticing in the catalogue. And whenever a book of real interest came into stock, Carter would be the first person on whom Pollard would call. They made a curious duo: the one handsome and meticulously clad in sharp worsted; the other scruffy to the point of shambolic, corduroy trousers wearing out at the knees and fraying at the turn-ups.

For all that their temperaments and looks may have differed, this pair of young booksellers shared an enthusiasm—though not for the simple joys of book-hunting, which in their eyes boiled down to trawling miles of shelving simply to tick items from a wish list. They were altogether more enthralled by puzzles: by a change of font halfway through a book; by an unexplained variation in paper size between two copies; by an impossible date or inscription that did not make sense. They pursued these sorts of conundrums the way that some people attempted the weekend crossword. Not all booksellers were interested in such mysteries. There was always the danger that too many questions would lead to inconvenient answers, that in the process of investigation a presumed first edition might be demoted to a second printing; or that a seemingly pristine copy might reveal subtle traces of damage and repair; or that an author's signature on the flyleaf might be identified as some mischief-maker's forgery. Better to leave such matters alone and assume the best. Neither Carter nor Pollard took that attitude. They were hungry for knowledge. And gaining knowledge meant asking difficult questions.

One year into his job at Scribner, in January 1929, Carter was seconded to the New York office to learn the ropes. To his American employers, he was the quintessence of the refined young Englishman, with his combination of intellectual flair, astringent wit, and restrained Savile Row tailoring. The love affair was mutual. 'I enjoy this perfectly bloody town hugely,' Carter wrote to Pollard from the company offices on Fifth Avenue. The city enchanted him: the galleries and museums, the cocktail parties, the restaurants, the hotels, the bars. He developed a taste for the dry martini, a drink which he found to be 'extensively travestied' back in England but which had reached the height of perfection here. 'A dry martini should be very dry, very strong and very cold,' he would tell friends on his return to London. 'No olive, no onion, no nonsense. Just the best drink of its kind in the world.' His taste in drinks mirrored his own sense of self. No nonsense. Just the best of his kind.

And then there were the books. In Cambridge and in London, bookselling was a modest profession. Granted it occasionally brought one into contact with extreme wealth, and very large sums of money would often exchange hands. But the business was generally conducted with a respectable sense of decorum. Not so in New York, where showmanship and bluster ruled the day. Seemingly within minutes of stepping off the boat, Carter was whisked to the Anderson Galleries on Park Avenue, where the library of the composer Jerome Kern was being auctioned over the course of ten sessions.

Kern was known as an avid collector, so the trade was expecting a blockbuster event. For the past week, the room had been abuzz with excited buyers inspecting lots. Yet neither Carter nor his employers could have anticipated the ensuing scenes of frenzied bidding and counterbidding, with prices quickly soaring to the stratosphere. The young Englishman watched in awe. Unlike the London auction houses, where quiet men traded stock during working hours, here he found a glamorous and 'fashionable crowd' enraptured by the mesmerising patter of the auctioneer. Like most American auctions, it was held in the evening and people came along as though to the theatre or concert hall. Each lot was 'reverently displayed on a dais' and illuminated by a lone spotlight; 'in short, an atmosphere eminently conducive to the painless extraction of that extra bid'. The technique, Carter would reflect, 'proved very effective'.

'The result of the first part of the Kern sale leaves a sadly bewildered and disorganized rare book world scratching its head and wondering what it all means,' reported the *New York Times*. The star items were, of course, the manuscripts. Between them, two important Alexander Pope holographs raised $25,000. A set of manuscripts in the hand of Charles Lamb went for an eye-watering $48,000. All yet unwatered eyes were on the first edition of Shelley's poem *Queen Mab*, the margins of which were jam-packed with the author's personal notes and revisions, and which the auction catalogue loudly described as 'WITHOUT DOUBT THE MOST VALUABLE AND DESIRABLE SHELLEY VOLUME WHICH HAS EVER OCCURRED FOR SALE BY AUCTION'. After a round of ecstatic bidding, this extraordinary book reached a hammer price of $68,000. Back in England, the volume would have been very familiar to Thomas James Wise. Before it came to New York, it had belonged to his partner Harry Buxton Forman, from whom Wise had attempted to wrestle it on several occasions, though always without success.

On closer inspection, many of the volumes at the sale would have been familiar to Wise, for he himself had made them. More than half a dozen of his forgeries were scattered through the catalogue, with item descriptions that would surely have prompted a wolfish smile from their originator. Elizabeth Barrett Browning's *The Runaway Slave*, which Wise had so callously foisted on Robert Browning, was touted as the 'FIRST SEPARATE EDITION, of which only a very limited number of copies were issued'. A fake Robert Louis Stevenson pamphlet,

The Story of a Lie, was given an elaborate backstory about being the original sheets of an edition prepared in 1882, but which had been 'withdrawn before publication' owing to a 'misunderstanding' with the author. It made $275. The fabricated edition of Swinburne's poem *Dead Love* was catalogued, without a hint of irony, as the 'GENUINE FIRST EDITION, NOT THE FRAUDULENT REPRINT. AN EXCEPTIONALLY FINE COPY.' In most cases these errors and incongruities could be traced back to the forger himself.

Carter could hardly have been expected to spot the dubia among the authentic lots. In truth, he had been overawed by the whole experience. When the receipts were tallied on the Friday, the Kern auction had become the most profitable book event in history, totalling more than $1.7 million in sales. Nine months later the Wall Street stock market would collapse. Such wild prices for books would never be seen again.

On his return to London in springtime, Carter became one of very few dealers with expertise in how things worked on both sides of the Atlantic. He had been sent home with the mission of reinvigorating his firm's catalogues. Like most antiquarian booksellers, the Scribner lists were filled with the same tired subjects: poetry and history and geography and botany and so on. Carter's task was to overhaul the business by pioneering exciting new paths in book collecting, much like Wise had pioneered the collecting of modern firsts some forty years earlier.

Following the dire economic slump of 1929, it had become crucial to expand the appeal of book collecting beyond a narrow elite, who could no longer be relied on to splurge their wealth on first editions. Carter's initial thought was that philosophy was due an uptick soon. Naturally, he consulted Pollard. 'You asked me for some new ideas,' wrote his friend, drawing attention to a Descartes first edition that had just come into the shop. 'Although *cogito ergo sum* is an obvious lie about most of your American customers, I believe the idea is sufficiently well known to attract them.' Collecting classic works of philosophy would have been a sound investment but was hardly the radical proposition expected by the higher-ups at Scribner. Where was the mass appeal? Carter went back to the drawing board.

He pondered the question. What did he and his friends like to read in their spare time? What books were cheap now but would surely become prized for both literary quality and bibliographical scarcity in years to come? The answer was in front of him all along. Ever since coming down from university, Carter had been an enthusiastic collector of detective stories. His rationale was simple enough. The first rule of the rare books trade is that everything is for sale. Any bookseller who also wished to assemble a collection of their own was therefore strongly advised to steer clear of anything that their customers might want. Carter had always been, in his own words, 'a keen reader' of detective fiction: not just Arthur Conan Doyle and Wilkie Collins and Edgar Allan Poe, but also the modern pioneers of the genre: R. Austin Freeman, Henry Wade, and Dorothy L. Sayers. Within three years of moving to London, he had some 350 first editions of modern detective stories packed into his flat. It hardly seemed likely that any of his customers at Scribner would take an interest in this sort of material, so he kept it to himself.

And yet, following weeks of false starts and unproductive leads with the philosophy idea, Carter's doubts about the commercial prospects of modern detective fiction began to fade. 'It is notorious that the detective story is the favourite reading of statesmen, of dons in our older universities, and in fact of all that is most intellectual in the reading public,' he reflected. With their puzzle-box plots and intricate twists, modern detective novels were both wonderfully entertaining and intellectually stimulating. Recalling his own years working in a second-hand bookshop around this time, George Orwell noted that men would 'read either the novels it is possible to respect, or detective stories', and that their consumption of the latter was often voracious. Holmes first editions had seen a tremendous spike in price in recent years, ever since Evans and the Elkin Mathews boys first discerned their value and began rescuing their fragile pages from the outside shelves on Charing Cross Road. Why not the same for more recent books?

Looking around at his fellow Biblio Boys, it must have dawned on Carter that his personal stash of first editions could be worth a fortune. Evans was quite open about his love for stories of investigation and adventure. And, when he wasn't out plundering the London bookstalls, Eddie Gathorne-Hardy could often be found tucked upstairs in his office absorbed in a good 'cosy'. Another of the regulars (incidentally also the vintner who supplied the sherry), Dennis Wheatley, was industriously working away on his own unpublished tales of espionage and derring-do. Indeed, he wouldn't stop talking about them, much to the amusement of Percy Muir, who deemed Wheatley's professional wares 'very much more thrilling' than his writing.

Within a few years their company would be joined by yet another enthusiastic book collector with literary aspirations, a young stockbroker named Ian Fleming, with whom Carter must surely have shared his recipe for the perfect dry martini (even if Fleming would go on to butcher it). Pollard alone seemed to exhibit no interest in the subject of fictional crime, preferring the bibliographical mysteries of his day job to the brain-teasers posed by Sayers or Agatha Christie. Carter could not have known that his friend had more than enough intrigue in his life already, without adding fictional spies and skulduggery to the mix. Nor could he have foreseen how, before the year was out, his beloved detective stories would become not only a source of income but a very practical handbook for an investigation of his own.

Once Pollard had taken a seat next to Carter, put a match to his pipe, and poured himself a drink, the evening began to settle into its usual pattern. The decanter was allowed to drift in a more-or-less clockwise direction around Evans's table, navigating the accumulated maze of loose papers and books and ashtrays, with occasional detours for odd members of the group who were perched on a windowsill or near the shelves. Against the crackle of the fire in the grate and the rich haze of tobacco smoke, the conversation meandered as aimlessly as the sherry.

At one moment the gossip would be all business. Had anybody else noticed that modern firsts were not performing so well in the auction room? What was the general opinion of Dobell's latest catalogue of eighteenth-century poetry? Who did people think would buy the newly discovered Byron manuscript on sale at Sawyer's bookshop on Grafton Street? Was the £18,000 demanded by Quaritch for a copy of Shakespeare's first folio truly the highest price ever asked for a printed book in England? At the next moment the discussion might swerve like a leaf on the breeze and drift into more personal territory. Who had managed to escape London for Christmas? Had Gathorne-Hardy spotted any notable individuals during his late-night perambulations around Soho nightclubs?

In this manner the table talk eddied back and forth until a voice piped up from a quiet corner of the room. Greville Worthington was a businesslike individual whose sharp pencil kept the Elkin Mathews accounts in good working order. More passionate about book-keeping than book-hunting, he was something of an outlier at the parties. But he was fresh back from a trip across the Atlantic and had tidings to share with the group. Over in New York there had been whispers, he reported. Whispers of foul play.

Ears pricked at this news. Nobody had ventured anything firm, he quickly explained. But over the course of a long, wet lunch he had got into an interesting conversation with the gregarious Lexington Avenue bookseller Max Harzof. Normally forthright and brash, a wellspring of trade gossip, Harzof was subdued that day, burdened by a mystery. There was 'something funny' about certain Victorian pamphlets, he hinted: those little 'PRIVATELY PRINTED' booklets of verse by Browning, Tennyson, Swinburne, and so on that could occasionally be spotted in the windows of the fancier dealers. It was difficult to put one's finger on precisely what gave these books their 'vaguely phoney' quality. There was something 'off' about the feel, he said, something about the way in which the pages always appeared to be in a 'beautifully clean state' when by rights they ought to be crumpled and creased. Of course, Harzof chuckled, he was perfectly happy to sell the books at the going market rate, especially because their authenticity was buoyed up by authoritative statements in all the standard reference works. What would be the point of rocking the boat when there was money to be made?

As Worthington began to wind up his story, Pollard reached for an ashtray and knocked the smouldering remnants from his pipe. Drawing a fresh pinch of tobacco from his breast pocket, he secured the attention of the room with a low mumble. 'When I was doing Ruskin for [Freddy] Bateson's *Cambridge Bibliography*,' he said, fiddling with his pipe, 'I did what few people can ever have done; I ploughed through the thirty-nine volumes of Cook and Wedderburn's edition of Ruskin, and I discovered some very striking facts.' During the course of his researches, in a dense block of tiny lettering, on the two hundred and eighty-eighth page of the first volume of the colossal Ruskin edition, Pollard had found a withering assessment of the '1868' stand-alone *Leoni*, the authenticity of which Wise had announced to the world in 1891.

The suspicions of the editors, Edward Tyas Cook and Alexander Wedderburn, had been initially raised by the short preface to this edition, written in something close to Ruskin's style, but in their judgement 'somewhat constrained and artificial', as though 'his pen forgot its more characteristic touch in the discharge of a tiresome exercise'. If the preface was dubious, then it stood to reason that the entire book must also be questionable. Despite a protracted search, the editors had not been able to discover any mention of a *Leoni* separate edition until decades later than the '1868' date on the title page. The printing firm named on the title page, Strangeways and Walden, kept full account books stretching back to 1845, but had no record of printing *Leoni*. Indeed, the only positive evidence for the pamphlet came from Wise and the seemingly authoritative Ruskin bibliography he had compiled years earlier with James P. Smart, which had by now become a standard tool in the trade.

Ruskin's editors raised similar objections about the '1849' edition of *The Scythian Guest*, which appeared with a preface in a style 'certainly not characteristic of Ruskin'. The standalone essay *The National Gallery* was conclusively shown to have been printed from a revised text of 1880, and yet the date in the imprint was '1852', which made no sense whatsoever. Perhaps their most brutal remarks were reserved for the '1864' edition of *The Queen's Gardens*, which the two editors dismantled with iron-clad logic.

> This pamphlet, which figures in dealers' language as 'of the extremest scarcity', is—like the separate issues of *Leoni* and *The National Gallery*—what is known in the trade as a 'fake'. It purports to have been 'printed in aid of the St Andrew's School Fund'; in which case the issue would obviously not have been limited to a few copies; yet until 1893 no copy of it ever came to light. It bears the imprint of a firm which now at any rate is 'not known' by the Post Office. The first copy of it to appear was elaborately described in the *Bookman* for February 1893, with a reduced facsimile of the title-page; the facsimile was also given among the illustrations accompanying the *Bibliography*, edited by T. J. Wise. Several copies of it subsequently appeared in the market, and changed hands at very high prices—copies in remarkably clean condition.

Pollard relayed this swathe of information to his audience before casually lighting his pipe and puffing out a huge billow of pungent smoke. There was a lot to digest. He was right, of course. In the twenty-nine years since the first volumes of this monumental edition of Ruskin were published, nobody had thought to check the small print. Or at least nobody had thought to take it seriously. Why would they need to when they had the Wise bibliography? Could all these Ruskin books seriously be fake?

After a moment of quiet, Gathorne-Hardy leaned forward. 'I've had my suspicions about some others,' he confided, raking his fingertips through his hair. Carter allowed himself a wry smile, looking first at Pollard and then squarely at Worthington. He had suspicions of his own.

During his conversation with Harzof, did the dealer focus on any single book?

Worthington nodded.

What was the title?

That was easy, Worthington explained. It was a book they all knew well, a book that was counted among the most expensive and desirable of all modern first editions, though also a book that none of them had seen in the flesh. Elizabeth Barrett Browning's *Sonnets*.

7
Making a Market

ONE pleasant summer day in 1892, Wise received a visitor at 52 Ashley Road. He had finally left the family home in Holloway two years earlier to move into this handsome redbrick terrace with his bride, a local girl named Selina. A pretty, spirited woman of twenty-two, Selina did not share Wise's passion for matters bibliographical, preferring to spend her days with the handsome young men at the neighbourhood tennis club. Once her husband's guest was settled into the library upstairs, it is not difficult to imagine Selina absenting herself for the afternoon. She had better things to do than sit and listen to book-chat.

The visiting gentleman was an American banker called John Henry Wrenn. He was in town on business but, at the suggestion of a publisher friend, had carved out a few hours with this celebrated young collector. Back home in Chicago, Wrenn was known as an avid collector himself. His tastes fell mostly at the traditional end of the market, with a special interest in books from the seventeenth and eighteenth centuries. But he was also a humble, quiet man who kept an open mind. Being an irrepressible evangelist for modern first editions, Wise was always quick to pounce on such vulnerable company.

Mirroring his initial visit to The Pines all those years ago, when Swinburne had skittishly shown off the treasures of his library, Wise brought out all the most cherished items from his Shelley collection. Cradled like relics, the books were placed before Wrenn one by one for him to nod at in approval. Here was the original manuscript of Shelley's *Hellas*, written in Pisa just a year before the poet's death in

1822. Mary Shelley had conferred the manuscript to her friend, Sir John Bowring, from whom, Wise told his guest, he had recently bought it. Snapping that book shut, Wise ushered his visitor over to the desk, where lay several letters in Shelley's hand, passed down by his sister-in-law, Jane Clairmont. Over here was his copy of the censored drama *Oedipus Tyrannus*, one of only seven that had survived destruction, given by Shelley himself as a gift to Edward Trelawny. And what did Wrenn make of this rare pristine copy of *Adonais*? It had been one his earliest and most expensive purchases, Wise confided to his guest. Back in the early days, other collectors had scoffed at him for paying the record sum of £45 for this little booklet—equal to the average annual wage in England at that time. Wise chuckled. It was worth many times that now.

Long ago Wise had made it his policy to buy 'only fine copies of desirable books' for the Ashley Library, the grandiose title he bestowed on his collection. He told his guest that he ought to do the same. Each book must earn its place on the shelf; there must be a story or an association, an added layer of personal romance. Shelley himself once held those pages in his hands, explained Wise, gesturing to another pamphlet on the desk. Several titles had come from the private collections of Browning and Swinburne, or had been gifts from those poets to their friends, before eventually making their way to Ashley Road. Wise was always on the lookout for superior copies, he explained. If Wrenn wanted first call on any duplicate volumes from his library, he need only mention it. The businessman had been soaking up advice from the moment he entered the room. He assented eagerly to the proposal. Listening to Wise preach the excellences of his collection, Wrenn was increasingly convinced that his own should be built around an equally strong core of modern first editions.

Wise was not alone in dispensing this counsel. In the previous year had appeared John Herbert Slater's handbook for book-hunters, *Round and About the Book-Stalls*, wherein was outlined practical guidance for would-be collectors. One or two scholarly bibliophiles might purchase old books to read them, Slater conceded; but such men were none of his concern. Instead, he suggested approaching book collecting like a treasure hunter or, perhaps more accurately, a commodities speculator. 'At the moment there are books to be purchased for trivial sums which will eventually be worth their weight in gold,' he wrote, 'but to identify them among the mass of worthless literature visible on every hand is a matter of great difficulty.' The aim of the game was to hunt down bargains and hold on to them until their value had peaked. Though of course the true end of book-hunting was not simply to make a quick profit by selling the spoils, he explained: it was to see the flash of envy in the eyes of one's rival collector when they spotted an impossible-to-find volume on one's shelves.

There was a time earlier in the century when black-letter ballads and Shakespeare quartos could be picked up by the dozen for two or three pounds, Slater remarked wistfully. Only the wealthy could afford those books at the current market rate. Nowadays the middle-class book-hunter would need to look closer to home. 'I feel persuaded that any book-hunter who will take the trouble to purchase originals of Scott, Byron, or Shelley, and to keep them free from dirt and damp, will reap a rich harvest before long,' he advised. Only a few years ago, first editions of Tennyson could be picked up at auction for less than a pound apiece. 'These books, too, should be worth five or six times as much as they are now in the near future, and the same remark applies to the works of Browning.' Already prices were on the rise.

These pearls of wisdom came as no shock to Wise, who had been ahead of the curve for a long time: sweeping up modern firsts and advising others to do the same in his regular column for the *Bookman*. Still, the publication in 1894 of Slater's next book, *Early Editions of Some Popular Modern Authors*, caused shockwaves. For while there was a growing interest in the scarcer works of great modern poets, the market was still dominated by the prejudices of earlier generations. Many well-heeled collectors continued to turn up their noses at books of the past hundred years. For the most part, their attentions remained focused on older volumes: on little playbooks by the contemporaries of Shakespeare, or on prized specimens from the workshops of famous printers such as Aldus or Elzevir. If upper-crust bibliophiles had any interest in modern titles, those were usually beautifully illustrated botanical or geographical tomes, not the scrappy, ephemeral productions treasured by Wise and his associates.

In the eyes of more traditional connoisseurs, the appearance of Slater's new guidelines was symptomatic of a fresh madness infecting the market for rare books. The backlash was immediate and extreme. In March the *Fortnightly Review* published a response to Slater, written by the perennially grouchy art critic William Roberts. The opening was characteristic of the whole:

> The craze for first editions is not by any means a recent one, although it may be said to have now reached its extremest form of childishness. Time was when the craze existed in a perfectly rational form, and when the first editions in demand were books of importance and books with both histories and reputations, whilst their collectors were scholars and men of judgment. Now, every little volume of drivelling verse becomes an object of more or less hazardous speculation, and the book market itself a stock exchange in miniature.

Roberts did not begrudge connoisseurs who sought out monuments of 'typographical skill and artistic beauty', great books written by major authors and printed and bound by talented craftsmen. These were beautiful objects which deserved to be preserved and admired. But 'the first (and last) editions of today are neither typographical monuments nor artistic successes, for, apparently, the only two motives that have operated in the making of these books are the getting of the smallest amount of text into the widest size of page, and the skill which can spread over the greatest amount of space the smallest quantity of original thought.' He may even have had Wise himself lined in his sights, calling out those 'too-zealous persons who feed their own vanity by hanging on to the coat-tails of eminent men and claim the title of public benefactors by "resurrecting" from a well-merited obscurity some worthless tract or obsolete and ephemeral magazine article, and trumpeting it about as a masterpiece'.

Wise was easily goaded at the best of times and, within days of the initial salvo, fired off a riposte to be published in the following issue of *Bookman*. If onlookers expected a robust defence of the artistic merit or scholarly value of modern first editions, they would be disappointed. Wise had no such plan in mind. Instead, his piece defended the market for modern firsts simply by quoting the going rates for some rare pamphlets. Old-fashioned collectors could be dismissed by the basic fact that the market for modern firsts was booming. Just look around, Wise told his detractors: a copy of Browning's *Pauline* was now worth £100 or more. First editions of his *Cleon*, *The Statue and the Bust*, and *Gold Hair* were all worth ten or twelve guineas apiece, a handsome price for such slim little things. Of course, Wise conveniently failed to mention that those last three booklets were all modern forgeries of his own making.

He pulled the same trick in his formal review of Slater's handbook, drawing attention to a dozen or so forgeries and fixing on them very high prices. Twenty or thirty years earlier these books had been worthless nothings, Wise remarked. Now they were 'among the most eagerly sought after of the book-hunter's treasures'. The market backed up his statement. In 1891 somebody paid more than £15 at Sotheby's for the counterfeit firsts of Swinburne's *Cleopatra* and *Siena*. In the following spring another cache of fake Swinburne pamphlets, consigned anonymously but probably from Wise's stash, raised a further £10. Fabricated copies of first editions by Dickens, Tennyson, and Ruskin continued to appear in the auction houses, all making good prices. The literary critic William Sharp legitimised several of the Browning forgeries in his 1890 biography of the poet, describing them as 'among the rarest finds for the collector' and as 'literally worth a good deal more than their weight in gold'. Blinded by greed and delusion, neither the auctioneers nor the bibliophiles detected the fakes in their midst.

Collectors like John Henry Wrenn were a symptom of a rapidly changing book world. 'Time was when the mad hatters of rare-bookdom, which included each and all who skulked the bookshops and bookstalls of the world in search of treasure, went their frenzied way in seclusive peace and contentment,' recalled the misty-eyed New York bibliophile Barton Wood Currie. No longer. The rapid growth of the

American economy in the final decades of the nineteenth century had elevated a new class of moneyed industrialists, many of whom decided to use their new world gains to purchase old world culture.

Some collected art. In just four years, the railroad magnate William Henry Vanderbilt managed to acquire more than two hundred top-quality paintings by some of the foremost contemporary European artists: an average of more than a painting per week. His Fifth Avenue mansion was widely acknowledged to be the finest gallery of its kind on the continent. The Pittsburgh industrialist Henry Clay Frick spent his enormous wealth on old masters, gathering up works by Bronzino and Holbein and Bellini. Others spent their money on rare books, a comparatively modest vice. On the west coast, Henry E. Huntington was amassing one of the world's greatest collections of rare books and manuscripts. Meanwhile in New York the financier John Pierpont Morgan was sweeping up rare early books for record sums, and in the process bringing the dusty world of the bookmen 'to the front pages of the metropolitan dailies'. The newly established Grolier Club offered a meeting point in Manhattan for these wealthy bibliophiles. By the dawn of the twentieth century, journalists had good reason to label book collecting the new 'sport of money kings'.

These recent developments were 'disturbing and annoying to many collectors', explained Currie. 'If too many American millionaires were to follow the lead of Huntington and Morgan, the collector of moderate wealth was doomed.' Priced out of the game at home, they would be forced to look abroad. Here American collectors of limited means were already at a severe disadvantage to their British counterparts. Most were forced to work remotely from catalogues. By the time an English bookseller's list had been shipped across the Atlantic, any treasures had already been snapped up by local customers. American collectors were left fighting over the scraps. Only very occasionally would such a collector be able to scoop up poorly described or miscatalogued gems. One of the most prominent American book-hunters of his day, William Harris Arnold, recalled precisely such an episode in his 1898 memoirs. Included in the catalogue of a minor county bookseller had been a 1775 first edition of Samuel Johnson's *A*

Journey to the Western Islands of Scotland, a desirable but common item, Arnold explained. It was priced at ten shillings, which was about usual for an ordinary copy. And yet the book that Arnold received was very special. 'My copy happens to be uncut, and on large paper, and, what is more unusual, is in the original board covers,' he gloated, 'so that it is safe to say I unwittingly obtained for ten shillings a book worth more than ten times as much.'

If a collector lacked the patience to wait for a book to be shipped across the Atlantic, he would turn to local dealers. Having opened London offices, many of the larger booksellers benefited from access to the English market. Long before John Carter joined the firm in 1927, Scribner kept rooms at 168 Regent Street for a small team to acquire rarities for their New York store. Heading up the rare books department was Lemuel W. Bangs, a bewhiskered bon viveur with a fondness for loud waistcoats and vintage champagne. Bangs was not one for getting his hands dirty. He enjoyed the glamour of Mayfair and could be found more often in the Garrick Club than riffling through the book stalls. Rumour has it that on rainy days he would wait outside antiquarian shops in a hackney cab while the staff brought out boxes for his perusal. Sometimes he was on the lookout for specific volumes requested by longstanding clients. More often he would simply buy any books that he thought would turn a profit.

Back in New York, casual hunters perused the shabby bookshops and discount barrows lining 'Book Row', which stretched along six blocks of Fourth Avenue from Union Square. All the serious dealers and collectors could be found at Bangs and Co., an auctioneer on Fifth Avenue (and, despite the name, nothing to do with Scribner's agent in London). Bargains could occasionally be found at auction, though William Harris Arnold warned that it could be a hazardous process for the uninitiated. 'It is more fun to attend the auction yourself, and make your own bids; but unless you are well acquainted with editions and prices, and have had considerable practice in collecting, you had better depend upon an agent or dealer.' He had seen too many collectors lose their inhibitions while bidding, paying extraordinary prices for rather ordinary books.

Instructing an agent to win a lot at any price could still be an equally foolish move, though. 'It seems superfluous to caution the novice against the danger of placing an unlimited bid; yet I have known an old collector to indulge in this recklessness. In justification he may plead that he wants the book as much as anybody else, and is willing to pay as much for it as anybody else. But if two bids of this sort are made by different persons for the same lot it needs no argument to show the danger of the practice.' Arnold remembered 'several such occurrences' in which the bidding had tumbled out of control. The lot would eventually be won only when one of the agents asserted their common sense against the instructions of their employer and ceased their bidding. In such cases the delight of the auctioneer was usually matched by the dismay of the winner, having paid considerably over the odds.

Much safer to rely on expert advice, to find a trustworthy, experienced, and impartial agent to represent one's interests directly in the English market. For such advice, many collectors turned to veterans of the trade such as Alfred James Bowden, a hard-drinking petty gambler who was also, in Arnold's words, 'not only full of old-book knowledge, but quick to scent a bargain'. A select few also looked outside the trade, to figures such as Wise. This prodigious collector was able to get his hands on books that nobody else could, they reasoned; indeed, he regularly managed to sniff out books that nobody else even knew existed. He was independent from the commercial interests that so often soured the relationship between a professional bookseller and his customers. And his reputation for knowledge, taste, and judgement was unsurpassed by anybody in the trade.

From Wise's perspective, the ultracompetitive new American market was perfect. With competition came opportunity. Not only were collectors willing to spend huge sums; they were also more open-minded than their English counterparts, more willing to accept the value that Wise bestowed on modern first editions. Even more important from Wise's perspective was the relative paucity of major public American libraries. There were very few actual first editions available for comparison with his forgeries, and those that existed in private collections were dispersed across the enormous country. America lacked a central bibliographical authority like the British Museum, and it was hardly practical for American collectors to drop by London to check the museum copy every time they wished to make a purchase.

The circumstances in America made it possible for Wise to palm off even his most egregious forgeries. His slapdash counterfeit of Matthew Arnold's *Alaric at Rome*, carelessly printed from the same setting of type as his facsimile edition, was sold via a New York dealer in 1897 as the 1840 original. Under the impression that it was in fact the genuine copy from which Wise designed his facsimile, the buyer, an American lawyer called Frederick Robert Halsey, paid the premium sum of $400. A quick comparison against the original would immediately have debunked this theory. Fortunately for Wise, there was no original to hand. The great collector Charles B. Foote had five of the forgeries in his library when it was sold at Bangs and Co. in 1895. Covering the proceedings of the sale, a journalist for the *New York Times* was taken aback by the 'charmingly exorbitant' prices demanded by these nineteenth-century pamphlets, but never suspected the auctioneers were peddling worthless fabrications. Another grand American collector, the cartoonist George T. Maxwell, owned three, including yet another copy of the supposedly rare edition of *The Runaway Slave* and the counterfeit first of George Eliot's *Agatha*, now being described by Wise as the *second* edition after minor typographical differences between the books were detected.

Even so discerning a book-hunter as William Harris Arnold was fooled into buying eight supposed Tennyson firsts from Wise. He proudly reproduced images of four of the title pages in his 1898 memoir. 'So little known are these rare Tennyson books that until 1896 none of them has ever been mentioned in any bibliography or catalogue,' he declared. 'Through the kind offices of my new, but now dear old, friend, the distinguished collector and bibliographer Thomas J. Wise ... I obtained one Tennyson rarity after another, most of which at the time were unknown to American collectors.' All told, he had paid the best part of a thousand dollars for the books. The naïveté is shocking. He ought to have known better, but honey-tongued Wise was above suspicion.

John Henry Wrenn was altogether slower to take the bait. His earliest dealings with Wise were formal, businesslike, and completely above board. The pair exchanged offprints of articles and enquired after the state of each other's libraries. Mostly Wrenn seemed to want stories of his correspondent's enviable adventures grubbing for rarities in the old country. But in the winter of 1896 he wrote seeking advice on some volumes being advertised by Henry Sotheran and Co., the distinguished bookseller on Piccadilly. With his usual authority, Wise informed Wrenn that neither the Milton nor the Spenser nor the Tennyson volumes were worth buying; they were in 'miserable' condition and too ambitiously priced. However, Wise added, 'If you are collecting Tennyson, I daresay I can help you a bit during the next few months. I am compiling a complete *Bibliography of Tennyson* and am hunting things up all around. Let me know, and anything that crops up in duplicate I'll let you know about.'

How could Wrenn refuse such a generous offer? His first purchase from Wise had been a safe one: a book he had seen before, during his visit to Ashley Road. 'Upon the occasion when I had the pleasure of meeting you here at my home,' Wise wrote, 'you expressed a wish to buy my copy of Goldsmith's *Vicar of Wakefield*,' a first edition sumptuously bound in red morocco. 'I was compelled to refuse you then, as it was my only copy. But I promised you that whenever I succeeded in obtaining a better copy you should have this one.' He had now bought such a copy and would willingly part with the original for £50, which was not a penny more than he paid for it several years earlier: a fair deal indeed. A few months later and Wise was looking to dispose of his first edition of *Paradise Lost*, having replaced it with a superior copy, supposedly the very copy which had belonged to Milton's great successor in the English tradition of epic verse, John Dryden. 'I do not think that £80 is an unfair price for the *Paradise Lost*,' he told Wrenn, 'but I cannot bear at any time to "drive a bargain" and will accept your estimate of £70 for it,' protesting only that he had originally paid £90. In actual fact, he had paid only £55, remarking to Forman at the time that he had snapped it up for a 'very cheap' price. Dishonest behaviour, certainly, but Wise was hardly the first salesman to inflate his costs.

All this while, Wise was setting a trap. Signing off his acceptance of Wrenn's offer on the *Paradise Lost*, he added a few enticing words about 'one of the very rarest of Tennyson's books', the recently found 'privately printed' first edition of *The Promise of May*. 'You will remember that the play caused a lot of opposition when put on the stage in 1882, and the result was that Tennyson held it back from publication, and just had a few copies printed off for private circulation. These are horribly rare, and there has never been an example in the auction room. I'm sure you will congratulate me upon my acquisition.' Unbeknownst to Wrenn, his rival Arnold already had a copy of this fake in his New York collection, courtesy of the forger. Doubtless this offhand reference to such a 'horribly rare' volume was calculated to make Wrenn salivate.

One month later, the Chicago businessman received a different Tennyson title, unsolicited in the post. It was a copy of the cobbled-together 'trial issue' of *Idylls of the Hearth*, the common first edition to which Wise and Forman had added their own false title page. Wise claimed to have seen it in a London bookseller's window. 'As the book was too cheap to pass I bought it,' he told Wrenn. And because a new American import duty of twenty-five percent was due to be levied within the fortnight, he had posted it with all haste, hoping to beat the introduction of the tax. Such anecdotes were typical of Wise's patter, concocting a plausible backstory to draw attention away from the dozen pristine copies he kept locked away at home. 'Pray understand that you are at perfect liberty to return the book if you don't care for it,' he explained, 'as more than one friend here will be glad to have it.' Wrenn had not asked for the book. There was no inkling he desired it. But who has the willpower to turn away such a jewel once it arrives in one's hands? It is far more difficult to return something than it is to decline it in the first place. Wrenn received the fabricated book with thanks, reimbursing Wise for his expenses and asking him to keep a lookout for similar volumes to send his way. Wise was happy to oblige. The trap had been sprung.

With the rapid growth of the American market, the conditions were perfect for Wise to perpetrate his greatest fraud of all. Back when Wrenn first visited the house on Ashley Road, he had been impressed not merely by the quality of the books on show, but by the delightful tales that Wise rattled off about how they had all come into being. And no bibliographical tale was more romantic than that of Elizabeth Barrett Browning's celebrated *Sonnets*. The poet had first met Robert Browning in the spring of 1845. According to all the stories, it had been a turbulent courtship. Elizabeth's father was an ill-tempered prig who scarcely ever let his daughter outside the family home in Marylebone. After a brief initial correspondence, Robert visited her in secret and by autumn the two were smitten. Unfortunately her overbearing father would not countenance a marriage. So, on 12 September the following year, the two quietly met at the local church. There, with Robert's cousin and Elizabeth's maid as their witnesses, the couple were wed. A few days later they eloped to Paris, en route to Pisa via Avignon and Marseilles.

Elizabeth suffered from poor health all her life and died fifteen years later, in 1861. Robert followed her to the grave in the final weeks of 1889, at the respectable age of seventy-seven, whereupon many anecdotes and whispers about their courtship were finally put to paper. For the first time, in 1890, William Sharp's biography opened a window onto the couple's honeymoon months in Pisa and Florence, where, Sharp claimed in characteristically ornate prose, she had composed a sequence of forty-three love sonnets for her husband.

> It is pleasant to think of the shy delight with which the delicate, flower-like, almost ethereal poet-wife, in those memorable Pisan evenings—with the wind blowing soundingly from the hills of Carrara, or quiescent in a deep autumnal calm broken only by the slow wash of Arno along the sea-mossed long-deserted quays—showed her love poems to her husband. With what love and pride he must have read those outpourings

of the most sensitive and beautiful nature he had ever met, vials of lovely thought and lovelier emotion, all stored against the coming of a golden day.

Such intimate, personal verses would not see that 'golden' light of day until the second edition of Barrett Browning's *Poems* appeared in 1850, where they were published under the misleading title *Sonnets from the Portuguese*—a title designed to conceal the private passions which had originally inspired the author by feigning the sonnets were a mere translation from some fictitious Portuguese original.

The romantic legend of the *Sonnets* and their central position in this most famous of literary love affairs continued to blossom after Browning's death, spurred on by Sharp's whimsical storytelling and the adoring members of the Browning Society. But what if the biographer had failed to give a full account of the *Sonnets*? What if, soon after putting these 'vials of lovely thought' to paper, Barrett Browning had been persuaded to print them in a strictly limited, private edition for close friends? What if she had entrusted this task to her bosom companion, Miss Mary Russell Mitford? And what if Mitford had overseen the printing of the book in her home town of Reading? The episode contained all the ingredients for the perfect scam: a famous name, a romantic backstory, a gap in the publication history. All were grist to the forger's mill.

Having consulted Forman on how to breathe life into this fancy, in the spring of 1893 Wise returned to Clay's with instructions for a new book. He had stripped out the text of the *Sonnets* from the collected *Poems* with the intention of printing them as a separate, standalone volume. If the book was to fool anyone, the layout and overall design would need to be perfect. An unassuming octavo of forty-eight pages, the book would of course require an '1847' date on the title page and the location where it was printed, in this case 'READING'. Below the imprint there was to be an explicit notice that the book was 'NOT FOR PUBLICATION', an addition that would help explain why it had evaded the notice of so many collectors for so long. And of course, in a market increasingly saturated with modern rarities, such a note would serve to heighten the book's desirability and value. At the top of the page, the title would read simply 'SONNETS. BY E.B.B.', dropping the charade of translation from the Portuguese. Everything about the book was calculated to suggest intimacy with the poet, a window into the most private corners of her heart.

This fabricated book would need a fabricated history. Despite its proven success, in this instance the 'remainder' ploy would not suffice. After all, if the book had not been intended for publication, how could copies have turned up in the dusty crevices of some publisher's warehouse? And so, with typical gusto, Wise spun an elaborate tale explaining how several pristine copies of the *Sonnets* had come into his hands. Through the lectures of the Browning Society, Wise claimed, he had been introduced to an elderly bachelor named Dr William Cox Bennett, a minor published poet who had once been a close confidante to Miss Mitford. Speaking to Wise in private, Dr Bennett confessed that, many years earlier, a little before Mitford's death, he had received a slim parcel of books from her. He invited Wise to his lodgings in Camberwell to see if it contained anything interesting.

According to his later recollections, Wise had to sit through a meal of 'hot buttered toast and sausages' before finally being presented with Dr Bennett's treasures. Once the landlady had cleared the table of dirty crockery, the 'letters and books were brought out, among them the much-longed-for *Sonnets*'. There were a dozen copies, Wise claimed, one of which contained Barrett Browning's manuscript of an additional sonnet slipped between the covers. Wise bought two of the books on the spot, including the special copy with the additional manuscript, and carried them home rejoicing at the bargain. Shortly thereafter, Bennett relinquished the remaining copies to Wise for £10 apiece, which he sold on to Forman, Gosse, Stopford Brooke, and various other friends from the Shelley and Browning Societies. The whole thing was a cock-and-bull story from beginning to end. Wise did not commit his version of the discovery to paper until after Dr Bennett's death in 1895, at which point there were no witnesses to contradict him.

But Wise did not stop there. Indeed, he could not, for there was nothing in the historical record to confirm that Barrett Browning ever put her *Sonnets* to print in 1847. Sharp mentioned nothing of the sort in his biography. And so Wise took another extraordinary step. He decided to embellish the established record of the Brownings' time in Pisa with a fanciful account of his own. He quietly fed the tale to Edmund Gosse, a literary hanger-on, second-rate poet, slapdash critic, and devout Browning enthusiast, requesting only that Gosse should not divulge his source. When Gosse published his own edition of the *Sonnets* in the following year, he included in the preface a sentimental new version of the episode in Pisa, as conveyed to him by Wise, filling in the gaps with his own imagination.

The new story went something like this. During their honeymoon, it had been the custom of the two poets to write in separate parts of their apartment: Robert downstairs in the dining room; Elizabeth upstairs in a private study of her own. Occasionally Robert would share his work with Elizabeth in the evenings, though she preferred to keep her own writings private, as is sometimes the wont of poets. Then, one morning early in 1847, a little after breakfast, Elizabeth came downstairs to find her husband standing at the window, staring out over the bustling piazza. Sneaking up behind him, Elizabeth 'held him by the shoulder to prevent his turning to look at her' and slipped a folded sheaf of papers into his jacket pocket. 'She told him to read that and to tear it up if he did not like it; and then she fled again to her own room.'

Surprised by this unusual behaviour, Robert sat down and began to read. 'As he read, his emotion and delight may be conceived,' wrote Gosse. Before he had even finished with the papers, he 'rushed upstairs' to tell his wife that these were 'the finest sonnets written in any language since Shakespeare's' and that such 'treasures' could not 'be kept from the world'. Elizabeth protested. They were private verses, written for her husband and her husband alone. But, after much persuasion, Robert finally got his way. A copy of the manuscript was sent to Miss Mitford back in England, granting permission to put the poems into print. Elizabeth 'absolutely declined to accede to Miss Mitford's suggestion that they should appear in one of the fashionable annuals of the day,' explained Gosse. 'Accordingly, a small volume was printed, entitled *Sonnets by E.B.B.*', previously unknown to all but the very closest friends of the poet.

News of this 'small volume' set the literary world ablaze. It was precisely the kind of overly sentimental tale that appealed to disciples of the Brownings. Rumours began to fly that a tiny cache of the books had now been unearthed. Gosse claimed to have seen a copy. In March 1894, the book was enthusiastically announced to the American market by William G. Kingsland, in his monthly column for *Poet Lore* magazine. 'It will be somewhat of a revelation, we imagine, to most lovers of the Brownings to learn that a copy of a privately printed issue of the *Sonnets from the Portuguese* is in existence. Until we were afforded a sight of this tiny volume, we were quite unaware that these exquisite gems had been issued in any other form than the volume in which they were first given to the public.'

Perhaps Kingsland initially harboured doubts about the story, which must have seemed too good to be true, until, like Browning and Swinburne before him, he was overawed by the evidence of his own eyes. Already he was attempting to make sense of the book. Why was it never mentioned by the Brownings in their correspondence? Why had no copies previously found their way onto the market? 'It is not easy to conjecture the reason for this semi-private mode of publication, or indeed to hazard a guess as to whether it was due to the inception of the poet or her friends,' pondered Kingsland. 'One possible explanation may be that although it was thought desirable to mislead for a time the general reading public as to the real origin of the *Sonnets*, yet the author had no desire to withhold the information from her own personal friends, and therefore a few copies were issued in this form.'

If only Browning was still alive to shed some light on these mysteries. In his absence, the natural authority seemed to be Wise himself. For a long time the common assumption among collectors was that the ten or twelve copies he unearthed in Camberwell were the only ones to have survived. Certainly, that is what Wise told the curious bibliophiles who wrote to him asking about the book. In actual fact he had printed at least three dozen of the *Sonnets* and stashed them under lock and key in his home. His strategy for unleashing these copies was quite simple. Drawing on his years of experience on the stock exchange, he would manipulate the supply and demand. As news of his supposed discovery spread through the book world, demand for a copy of the *Sonnets* would grow and grow. But the supply of copies would remain minute, pushing prices skyward. Only once demand had peaked would Wise—slowly, carefully, quietly—release copies from his stockpile.

8

A Book We Don't Much Care For

At the mention of Browning's *Sonnets*, murmurs of disbelief rippled across the room.

Poor old Worthington looked both pleased and a little taken aback by the reaction. He was seldom in the position of breaking fresh book-gossip to the boys at Elkin Mathews and did not quite know how to handle the situation. He and Harzof had only been asking questions, he assured the group, urging them all to calm down despite the slightly panicked look in his own eyes. But some of the concerns raised by their American colleague seemed, even at first glance, disturbing.

Old books usually exhibited signs of their age, scrapes and bruises left by encounters with the world. So why were copies of the 'Reading' *Sonnets* always in such exquisite condition? Why had they invariably been rebound in glamorous shades of morocco leather? Where was Browning's personal copy? Or, indeed, any copy signed by the author or inscribed to one of her friends? Carter alone did not appear shocked by this tumble of puzzles. He leaned back in his chair, drained his thimble of sherry, and cleared his throat. 'Gentlemen,' he said, hushing his friends into silence. The tentative smile had now reached his eyes. 'I can answer some of these questions.'

Six months earlier, Carter had been given a mission by the New York office. One of Scribner's most loyal customers, the affluent widow Mrs Natalie Blair, had come into the shop and asked them to find a copy of the *Sonnets* for her library. Price was not an issue—magical words to any bookseller—and Carter duly received a telegram explaining that he was just the man for the job. Finding this little book would prove a significant challenge. It was notoriously rare and desirable. Just a few years earlier, in 1927, the wealthy Californian collector William Andrews Clark had despaired of ever getting his hands on a copy. Despite the near-limitless financial resources at his disposal as the heir to a vast mining fortune, Clark had to make do with commissioning a local printer to reproduce the *Sonnets* in photo-facsimile, plugging the gap in his bookshelves. Lavishly bound copies of this fastidious reproduction were sent to all his friends in the book world, including that undisputed authority on the Brownings, the man who had originally brought the *Sonnets* to the attention of the world. 'What would Mrs Browning have said, if she had ever dreamed of the magnificent form which would one day be given to her beautiful sonnets?' Wise wrote to Clark, thanking him for the book. What indeed.

So far as Carter was aware, only two copies of the *Sonnets* had gone to market in recent years, both on the other side of the Atlantic. One of the copies had been sold at public auction on Madison Avenue, with a final hammer price of $1,250. The other copy had been sold privately and, rather strangely, by accident. The protagonist in this drama was a major New York bookseller called Edgar Wells, who brokered the sale on behalf of an important but nameless client. Once the transaction had gone through and the book had been picked up by its delighted new owner, the client turned round and denied ever instructing Wells to sell.

It was a deeply fishy business, in which wires seem to have got crossed and then crossed again. Naturally, the client furiously demanded that his bookseller replace the mis-sold book. Wells was promptly dispatched to Europe in search of a comparable copy at more or less the same price. He returned home weeks later, penitent and empty-handed. Not only had he failed to find a copy of the *Sonnets* in similar condition; he had failed to find any copy whatsoever.

Undeterred by these fruitless exploits, Carter ploughed ahead with his usual combination of charm and bravado. He was hardly likely to discover a copy in the wild, he reasoned. Those would be long since gone, either fallen by the wayside or snapped up by the eagle-eyed book-hunters of previous generations. No, if copies of the *Sonnets* were to be found, they would be found in the trade itself, or in the libraries of rival collectors. The New York office had said that Mrs Blair was willing to pay a premium. Surely somebody could be found who would part with their copy for the right price.

Carter started with the usual reference books, briskly working his way through old sales catalogues and chasing up buyers until he had a clear idea of who owned what. His census of copies explained why Wells had not found success on this side of the Atlantic. The New York bookseller would have had an easier time looking on home turf, for, Carter discovered, all the known copies of *Sonnets* were already in America. All but two, that is. For it was well known that a matching pair was kept under lock and key in the famed Ashley Library of Thomas James Wise. Like a dragon guarding his hoard, Wise was unlikely to relinquish one of these treasures to Carter or his client. Better to keep searching.

Assuming he had missed something obvious or that another copy might yet be found, Carter began taking soundings among his fellow booksellers. Did anyone know of an uncatalogued copy floating around? Of a private collector whom he ought to approach? He made appointments with all his friends in the trade. Halfway through a casual lunch or evening drinks at the Garrick, just as the gossip began to flow freely, Carter would slip in that he was looking for a copy of the *Sonnets*. Reactions ranged from earnest shakes of the head to outright mirth. Nobody had anything useful to offer.

His options running low, Carter took to visiting all the most distinguished shops in Mayfair. He hustled around the premises of Maggs Bros. on Conduit Street, whose rooms resembled an ancient monastic library, with limewashed walls, vaulting arches, and leaded windows that dappled the shelves in cool sunlight. He made inquiries at Sotheby's, whose books department boasted some of the most keen-eyed and well-connected experts in the trade. Eventually, he arrived at the doors of that most august of antiquarian booksellers, Quaritch.

To call Bernard Quaritch a titan among booksellers would be to paint him too small. On his death in 1899, his obituarist for *The Times* proclaimed that it 'would scarcely be rash to say that Quaritch was the greatest bookseller who ever lived. His ideals were so high, his eye was so keen, his transactions were so colossal, his courage was so dauntless, that he stands out among men who have dealt in old literature as a Napoleon or a Wellington stands out among generals.'

Since his death at the end of the nineteenth century, the family firm had passed through several hands and several locations. The present custodian, Mr F. S. Ferguson, was an able enough bibliographer and the last person to have taken an apprenticeship under the old man himself. As for the present location, the shop now occupied a well-proportioned Georgian town house on the popular Grafton Street, open books and prints displayed in the ground-floor bay windows to entice passers-by. Through the thin voile curtains, they might glimpse the floor-to-ceiling cabinetry that dominated the interior of the shop, with neat rows of folios, quartos, and octavos lined up behind sliding glass doors. The air inside was still and quiet. No clock on the wall. It was as though time seemed to pause when one walked through the door, only to resume when stepping back outside.

At a large desk in the centre of room worked a man: short and stocky, but also curiously ageless. Carter had come to Grafton Street seeking his advice. Mr Mudie had been with Quaritch longer than most people could remember. New masters came and went, the firm moved from shop to shop, but always Mudie stayed put. He was almost a piece of the furniture, at one with the darkened oak of the shelves and desks and stepladders, a veteran of heady transactions in which medieval manuscripts and incunabula and Shakespeare folios exchanged hands for small fortunes. Mudie did not wear his book lore lightly; it was almost as though the book lore wore him. And so, when Carter came to ask about the likelihood of securing a copy of Elizabeth Barrett Browning's *Sonnets*, he placed immense weight on the response.

Recalling the encounter for his rapt audience, Carter explained how Mudie had peered across his desk and fixed him with that cold stare—a look they all knew well. He told them how Mudie appeared to ponder the question for a moment, cogs turning behind those thin, gold-rimmed spectacles.

'It's not likely.'

'Come now, Mr Mudie!' was Carter's jovial response. 'I know it's a rare and expensive book, but it's not as rare as all that.'

This prompted a bitter chuckle. 'That *is* true,' Mudie said. A long pause followed. 'But ... well ... it's a book we don't much care for.' He returned his attention to the tome open on his desk and with a gesture signalled that the meeting was over. His peculiarly enigmatic pronouncement left Carter feeling mystified. What on earth did Mudie know? Why so reticent?

'I couldn't get another word out of him,' Carter told his friends. But now here was Worthington, fresh from New York, asking the very same questions that had been keeping his brain whirring for the last six months.

Some of them he could answer quite definitively. 'Browning didn't own one,' Carter told the group, 'or at least there was no copy in the sale of his books at Sotheby's in 1913.' His enquiries had failed to unearth a single presentation copy signed by the author, and, he added, 'no copy ever appeared in the auction rooms before 1901', which he thought a suspiciously late date for a book purportedly printed in 1847. He had mined every source, looted every catalogue and bibliography, trawled through the entire published correspondence of the Brownings looking for hard evidence to confirm the authenticity of the *Sonnets*. But he had found nothing.

The real question was what the group was going to do with this information. As the fire dwindled and people began to filter away for the evening, Pollard spoke up. Had anybody actually *seen* a copy? he asked. His query was greeted with some bemused shrugs and shakes of the head.

'Now this is really interesting,' said Eddie Gathorne-Hardy. For while he hadn't found a copy of the *Sonnets*, he *had* seen a copy of one of the Ruskin fakes that Pollard had mentioned earlier in the evening. The book was included in a recent catalogue that had arrived in the post just the other day, as one of several pamphlets by Victorian poets like Browning and Swinburne. 'If they're phoneys into the bargain that would be too delightful.'

'Have you got the catalogue?' Pollard asked, looking serious. 'It would interest me to see it.' Grinning, Gathorne-Hardy sauntered over to the corner of the room and began rummaging through the waste-paper bin. After a moment or two, there was a triumphant yell and he returned to the group with catalogue in hand: creased and a little grubby, but otherwise intact.

As Pollard tucked the pages into his coat pocket, Carter gave him a knowing look. Could the *Sonnets* be linked to the fake Ruskin pamphlets? Perhaps there were others waiting to be discovered? Once outside, they arranged to meet for lunch later in the week, for the mystery had thickened again. Then they parted, Carter making a beeline for Mayfair and Pollard sauntering across Regent Street towards Soho.

There are perhaps as many techniques for detecting forgeries as there are for making them. In the realm of literary forgery, many of those techniques are as old as the hills. Since the very dawn of biblical scholarship, eagle-eyed monks and churchmen had used the techniques of textual criticism and philology to distinguish what they viewed as the true word of God from the later interpolations of men. Throughout the Renaissance and the Enlightenment, scholars of classical literature deployed very similar techniques in their studies of Greek and Roman texts. When in 1699 the keeper of the royal library, Richard Bentley, got into a spat about the disputed authenticity of the *Epistles* of Phalaris, a legendary king of ancient Sicily, he was able to prove with devastating efficiency that the language was packed with anachronisms, incongruities, and spurious allusions. The entire text had to be a later forgery—a revelation that piqued admirers of the *Epistles*, whose taste and judgement he had proved seriously deficient. But in all such cases these scholars were dealing with the forgery of a text, not of a book. And in the case of the *Sonnets*, where the text itself was wholly authentic, from the first comma to the last full stop, such techniques simply would not do. This ingenious fake would be detected not by looking at what the words on the page said, but only by paying attention to the look and feel of the ink and the paper.

By the time Carter and Pollard arrived on the scene, another group of scholars was already pioneering a totally new way of looking at books. The epicentre of this movement in London was the Bibliographical Society, which drew its membership from all corners of the book world. Carter and Pollard were both active members of the society, trotting along to its regular meetings in Bloomsbury, sitting together during lectures and exchanging mute commentary on the proceedings: a roll of the eyes here, a knowing grin there. They relished the uneasy harmony of collectors, librarians, academics, and booksellers.

Both would have been in the room for the inaugural address of the new president, Walter Wilson Greg, on 20 October 1930. His subject on that occasion was the present position of the field and how he saw it developing into the future—one calculated to provoke controversy. 'Unless I am mistaken a certain change of outlook is occurring among bibliographers,' Greg opened, 'while a certain change is also observable in the way in which bibliography is looked on from the outside.' No longer was the study of old books the sole preserve of wealthy collectors, obsessively listing and cataloguing and describing the rare editions in their libraries. The compilation of such checklists and catalogues was mere hobby work, Greg alleged, useful only to those who bought and sold books like any other commodity. But now, he excitedly proclaimed, the 'amateur and the dilettante are giving place to the expert and the scholar'. From their position at the back of the auditorium, Carter and Pollard would have been able to see Greg gesturing to some older gentlemen in the front row. 'And you may think that indirectly I am being hardly polite to certain eminent bibliographers, such as my friends Mr T. J. Wise and Dr Geoffrey Keynes. I assure you—I need hardly assure them—that I do the fullest justice to their bibliographical prowess.'

An independent scholar both financially and institutionally, Greg was the standard bearer for this new school of bibliography. Men such as Wise and Forman may have contented themselves with drawing up exhaustive catalogues of books, writing helpful notes on how to distinguish one edition from another, but Greg regarded this as the 'mere prostitution' of bibliographical expertise, nothing more than an 'adjunct to the collecting of pretty books'. Instead, Greg's generation of bibliographers sought to understand *how* these books had come into being. And their methods for doing so were, he believed, 'thoroughly scientific': paying meticulous attention to the designs of typefaces, the appearance of watermarks on paper, and the holes and rips and stains that revealed information about the journeys that books had taken since leaving the printing house. Such physical information could not lie. 'Upon this, as I conceive it, rests the future of bibliography and its claim to serious consideration' as a 'mature science', he explained. The only alternative being that bibliography should remain an 'amiable game' played by amateur collectors and the provincial gentry.

As for how these new scientific methods could be used to detect impostors and fakes, Greg had already given a virtuoso demonstration. Some two decades earlier, while Carter and Pollard were both schoolboys, Greg had stumbled on a mystery. Serious Shakespeare scholars had long known about a series of nine playbooks, all dated between 1600 and 1619, including standalone editions of perennial favourites such as *The Merchant of Venice*, *King Lear*, and *A Midsummer Night's Dream*. Sometimes these playbooks could be found in libraries or bookshops as individual pamphlets. But often they were bound together into a single volume, almost as though the original bookseller had taken unsold or remaindered copies of these separate plays and stitched them together into a collected set.

Working his way through one such assembled volume, scanning each page for minute variants in text and punctuation, Greg was struck by a 'curious similarity' in the appearance of the individual plays. Despite a gap of nearly twenty years between the publication dates of the earliest and the latest plays in the volume, and the names of different printers and publishers on the title pages, they all seemed to have been printed using the same decorative ornaments and fonts of type. The ornaments struck Greg as particularly important evidence. While slugs of type have always been cast in durable metal, these ornaments were carved by hand in blocks of wood, making them notably vulnerable to the ravages of use and time: to warping from damp, to cracks formed under the pressure of the press, to burrowing woodworms. From disturbances in the traces of ink left on the page, Greg could tell that the block used to adorn the '1600' quarto of *A Midsummer Night's Dream* exhibited signs of splitting along the grain, as well as a small notch in the outer rim of the design. But he also knew that when the very same block was used for a different pamphlet dated 1605, there were no such signs of damage. Unless this woodblock had somehow travelled backwards in time to the year 1600, there was simply no way the date on the title page of *A Midsummer Night's Dream* could be correct. The book had to be a later forgery.

Looking still more closely and combining the evidence of his eyes with that of his fingers and thumbs, Greg noticed that the plays all appeared to have been printed on the same mixed stock of paper. The watermarks matched, even though some of the plays were supposedly printed in 1600 and others were dated 1619. How would two different printers working nineteen years apart get their hands on identical sheets? Paper was a valuable and perishable commodity. It seemed highly improbable that bundles of the stuff would be left lying around for best part of two decades, Greg reasoned. The only logical conclusion was that all these books had been printed at the same time and by the same person. His chief suspect was the printer William Jaggard, who was known to have been using these fonts and ornaments around 1619, the latest date on any of the playbooks. The earlier dates were all false, he concluded. Jaggard had done an excellent job, closely imitating the house styles of those printers whose names he used on the title pages. Until now the ruse had gone wholly unnoticed.

Precisely why Jaggard decided to antedate these nine playbooks, making them look older than they were, was less certain. Perhaps the forgery had something to do with the 1619 injunction banning the printing of plays belonging to Shakespeare's old theatre company, the King's Men. By slapping false dates on the title pages, Jaggard made it look as though these playbooks had snuck onto the marketplace years before the edict was issued. Perhaps the deception sprang from the fact that Jaggard did not strictly speaking own the copyright to any of the plays. In every case the copyright belonged to the publisher whom he named on the title page. For everyday readers, these plays would thus seem like authentic publications and not the counterfeit piracies they truly were. When the authorised folio collection of Shakespeare finally appeared in 1623, there was a preface appended lamenting the many 'stolen and surreptitious copies' of the plays that had previously appeared in print. Doubtless the editors of the folio had these earlier forgeries in mind.

Greg's forensic handling of the false Shakespeare quartos was both deeply impressive and deeply inspirational. Pollard had already begun to follow in his footsteps, using similar methods to untangle the three 'first editions' of Thomas Hobbes's *Leviathan* and identify the two fakes. And yet it was not Pollard but Carter who must have detected the source of Greg's own inspiration. For there was something about the way that Greg would set up a puzzle and withhold his solution until the last moment, presenting it with all the flair of a circus performer; something about his delight in the thrill of the chase and the manner in which his scientific approach could invariably unlock each 'clue to the mystery'; something in the way he used phrases like 'our chain of inquiry is now complete' or 'in the course of an hour or so I had solved the puzzle', as though explaining his methods to a forgivably dim sidekick. The signs were obvious. Greg had been reading the adventures of Sherlock Holmes.

Because of his ongoing efforts to make detective stories a respectable field in book collecting, Carter must have recognised the influence at play. One of Greg's close friends once observed that he would submit detective novels to the 'same kind of scrutiny he gave to the variants in the first quarto of *King Lear*'. Another perceptive reviewer remarked that the bibliographer self-consciously displayed the 'intuitive and inductive powers of a Sherlock Holmes'. Just like Holmes, who could 'distinguish at a glance the ash of any known brand either of cigar or tobacco', so Greg was able at a stroke to discern specific fonts, papers, and binding varieties. For those of the 'detective mind',

Greg thought it 'pleasant to ponder over bibliographical and literary puzzles'. So too Holmes cannot let his mind rest until the puzzle is solved. 'Detection is, or ought to be, an exact science,' Holmes proclaims before his second adventure with Watson. And while Greg took issue with the phrasing—'Is not exactitude the aim of every science?' he asked—he likewise described his own work as a 'mature science'. The sentiment in each case was precisely the same. Here, at last, was a vision of the bibliographer as professional sleuth.

It is perhaps unsurprising that an expert in old books should take inspiration from Holmes, for the famous Baker Street detective was himself something of a bookman. On his first coming up to London, Holmes took rooms 'just round the corner' from the British Museum, where he spent his 'too abundant leisure time' in the reading room 'studying all those branches of science which might make me more efficient'. All through the 1880s he could be regularly sighted striding around the second-hand bookstalls of Charing Cross Road, hunting for jewels to fill the shelves at 221B. Indeed, in an alternative world, where it was possible to step quite simply and easily from fiction into fact, Holmes would have been one of young Wise's chief rivals. The two might even have rubbed shoulders at the Kensington shop of Alfred B. Clementson, one of Holmes's favoured dealers. So familiar was Holmes with Clementson and his peculiar personal quirks that in 1894, having feigned his death three years earlier at the Reichenbach Falls, he opted to disguise himself as the elderly bookseller while investigating a murder in London. The impostor *Sonnets* had been unveiled to the world just a few weeks before his return from beyond the grave.

Much like his junior competitor in the sport of book-hunting, Holmes displayed an uncanny knack for sniffing out 'impossibles'. His greatest treasure was surely his copy of a seventeenth-century Latin treatise entitled *De Jure Inter Gentes*, by the Oxford legal scholar Richard Zouch. Holmes showed the volume to Watson in his characteristically offhand manner. 'This is a queer old book I picked up at a stall yesterday,' he said, 'published in Latin at Liège in the Lowlands, in 1642.' However unassuming this quarto tome, bound in unpretentious 'weather-beaten' calfskin, it was a remarkable find. 'Charles's head was still firm on his shoulders when this little brown-backed volume was struck off,' Holmes remarked. And yet, before he fished this book out of the 'remnant box' where he found it, the earliest known printing was at Oxford in 1650, a full eight years later. No such 1642 edition was previously known to exist. Had he found the volume just a few years later, this pre-first edition could almost have come from the studio of Thomas James Wise himself. For all his unusual powers of deduction, maybe even Sherlock Holmes would have been fooled by that Moriarty of the book world.

9
The Moral Position

FOLLOWING the runaway success of the *Sonnets* in 1894, Wise stepped up the pace of production. He dragged Forman along for the ride. For the most part, Wise stuck to the tried and tested formula of reprinting minor works by major authors in standalone pamphlet form with false dates and publication details. The scheme had worked perfectly so far. Why change now?

Although he was getting the books onto the market much more quickly than before, often skipping the time-consuming process of sneaking copies into the major libraries and institutions, Wise never forgot about the importance of provenance. On the contrary, his lies became even more convincing. Consider his treatment of Tennyson's much-loved Arthurian poem *The Last Tournament*, which the two forgers printed in 1896 with a false '1871' date on the title page. Inside the front cover of Wise's personal copy was an elaborate handwritten notice, supposedly signed by the publisher, stating that 'not more than 20 copies were printed' of this 'private edition'. Of course, the note was added by Wise himself in a close imitation of the publisher's handwriting. When Maggs later sold a copy of the book, they included a reference to this very special copy in Wise's library, quoting information from its interesting manuscript addition. This was precisely the sort of detail that seemed to guarantee authenticity.

On other occasions, by way of establishing a high market price for the forgeries, Wise even started buying his own lots at auction. His method was characteristically sneaky. It went like this. Having anonymously consigned a fake or cluster of fakes to one of the major London auction houses, he would instruct a trusted agent to bid on the book on his behalf. As the seller, he could set a high reserve price to ensure the book did not go for cheap: say £52 for a faked-up 'first edition' of Tennyson's play *The Falcon*. At the same time, he instructed his man to bid up to the same amount. Because the sale went through a proxy, the auctioneer could have no idea that Wise was the buyer; and because the book was consigned anonymously, the agent remained unaware that Wise was the seller. And so, without the merest hint of his involvement, the forger created a legitimate market price for a deeply illegitimate book. Then the next time he wanted to pass on a copy of *The Falcon* to one of his American stooges, all he needed to do was point to the recent price realised at auction, telling them he would not take a penny less.

One of the fundamental problems with rediscovering 'lost' works of literature was that these books ought to have left some trace in the historical record: the ghost of a book that once existed; the visible absence where formerly a book had been. Wise understood the importance of creating convincing histories for his forgeries, and in 1895 he hit on a new idea. Previously he had inserted his fakes into the historical record only after announcing their discovery. The *Sonnets* was a perfect example. But, he mused, with a little planning might he not create his own gaps in the record? Gaps that precisely matched the size and shape of the forgeries he was manufacturing?

The vehicle for this dastardly scheme would be a multivolume series entitled *Literary Anecdotes of the Nineteenth Century*, the aim of which was to gather scraps of gossip about the literary titans of the Victorian era before they faded from living memory. By its very nature, the project was light on supporting evidence. And, as its editor-in-chief, Wise could sneak in whatever misinformation he wanted to see in print. When the first volume appeared in 1896, it was packed with ambiguous, misleading, and falsified details. It also contained lacunae that only the forger could fill.

A case in point was its treatment of *The Devil's Due*, the title given to a controversial letter sent by Swinburne to the editor of a periodical called *The Examiner* in 1875. 'It is said that concurrently with its appearance in the columns of *The Examiner*, *The Devil's Due* was printed in pamphlet form for private distribution,' explained Wise in his most authoritative tones. 'If such a pamphlet does exist, it must be of the utmost rarity, as no copy is known to the editors of *Literary Anecdotes*, who have instituted a lengthy search in the hopes of finding a stray example.'

Just a few months later, Wise was able to inform his friend Edmund Gosse that he had since been handed a copy of *The Devil's Due* by a 'gentleman, who called upon me in consequence of having read the note' in *Literary Anecdotes*. 'It really is vastly strange how things do crop up,' he remarked. Or perhaps not so strange when one considers that the forger kept a stash of copies under his desk. The pamphlet was yet another fake.

With the appearance of *Literary Anecdotes* in 1896, the rift between Wise and his co-conspirator grew deeper. Although he enjoyed a little trickery, Forman had never intended to deceive: or at least, not on the scale of Wise. He was a shy sort of a man, who preferred the four walls of his study to the cut-and-thrust world of the public man of letters. His bookplate, etched for him by the Scottish artist William Bell Scott, shows him buried in his work, old-fashioned quill in hand, surrounded by a haphazard mountain of Shelley paraphernalia: portraits, a marble bust, many volumes of poetry—his 'household gods', as he called them. If Wise's ambitions were set on shaking down the dusty world of the bibliophiles, Forman was more interested in scooping up relics of the authors who so fascinated and enthralled him.

Unlike Wise, who was interested solely in books, Forman would latch on to anonymous portraits at auctions and estate sales, convinced he had come across a true likeness of Shelley or of Keats. Occasionally he would manufacture them himself. In his edition of Shelley's notebooks, he presented a falsified portrait of the poet—in fact based closely on a sketch by Leonardo Da Vinci—as a previously unknown original from life. He delighted himself with 'relics culled from far and wide', as the verses on his bookplate proclaimed. Beneath his desk he even kept a cardboard box filled with what he believed to be a portion of Shelley's ashes, brought back to England after his cremation. Forman was not the first man to lose himself so thoroughly in bygone literary worlds. But such was his imagination that, in printing backdated 'first editions' for his collection, he was deceiving nobody more than himself.

The appearance of *Literary Anecdotes* forced a wedge into what was already a significant fissure. As editor of the volume, Wise had strong-armed Forman into contributing material on those poets whom he knew best: ranging from his beloved Tennyson, Browning, and Shelley to lesser-known poets such as Thomas Wade and Richard Hengist Horne. He had done so grudgingly. In the past, he had been treated poorly by the editors of such volumes. Many were the editors who had promised Forman fair credit for his contributions; many were the editors who had gone back on their word. So when Wise assured his friend that there would be no such 'scurvy treatment' this time round, he ought to have known better. Within minutes of receiving his copy of the book, Forman came to realise his error. Besides the briefest of mentions in the acknowledgements, everything in the book was anonymous. Nobody was named, not a single source given for a single poxy anecdote. Forman scribbled a note to Wise. The pair of them had arrived at a 'distinct understanding' that 'ultimate credit of everything' would be printed, he reminded his friend. 'Now the distinct understanding is a perhaps, and the anonymous system is actually said to be the universal rule, and to have been so from the first! Well! Well!'

That Wise sought so brazenly to deceive Forman caused much grief and wringing of hands. That he sought to deceive others was the final straw. Looking through the information contained in *Literary Anecdotes* at greater length, scanning the pages for the barest mention of his contributions, Forman grew increasingly piqued by what he described as a general 'appearance of *dishonesty*' in the volume. He noticed, for instance, the calculated imprecision regarding 'limited edition' books that Wise had himself published. Never would he state precisely how many copies were printed, always preferring to say 'a few' or 'strictly limited' instead of giving an exact number. This equivocation enraged Forman. 'You are reluctant to say how many are printed,

THE MORAL POSITION

and say *a few* because some will understand that to mean some ten or twelve, some twenty or thirty, and so on. There cannot on the face of it be an honest reason for wanting the number printed to be differently conjectured by different people,' he protested. He could imagine only one reason for Wise's haziness with the details and it was far from honest: 'printing thirty (more or less), you want someone to think you only print ten or twelve' and thus to think that the books are much rarer than they actually are.

These complaints all seemed rather immaterial to Wise. 'Quite so,' he replied coolly. 'And we print *Last Tournament* in 1896 and want someone to think it was printed in 1871! *The moral position is exactly the same!*'

It was a horrible situation. However benign his original intentions, and however repelled he was by the 'moral position' of profiting from forgery, Forman was now stuck in the same boat as Wise. He could not very well sink the vessel without going down himself, and from this moment on he seems to have been guided by a self-destructive impulse.

Forman was a great expert on the writings of William Morris, whom he had counted a close friend for some twenty-five years, since long before Wise arrived on the scene. Sometimes he would take genuine booklets from his Morris collection and add some decorative wrappers, printed on colourful paper. Admittedly, the original dates of publication would be printed on the new covers, as though they were an original feature of the booklet; but this hardly constituted distortion of the historical record and Forman always justified his actions to himself by noting that his old friend was never much bothered by the bibliographical fortunes of his own writings (a surprise from the founder of the Kelmscott Press). Even on those rare occasions when Forman adhered to the tried and tested formula for creative forgery, as with his pamphlet edition of Morris's poem *Socialists at Play*, backdated to 1885, he left hints and clues to the nature of the fake. Several copies of this little pamphlet were printed on paper with an '1896' watermark. It was almost as though he wanted to be caught.

When Morris died in October 1896, just a few days after the appearance of the noisome *Literary Anecdotes*, Forman embarked on an ambitious new scholarly project: a comprehensive, commemorative bibliography of all Morris's known writings, with lengthy descriptions of individual books of interest. It was in this capacity that the executor of Morris's estate, a bullish young man named Sydney Cockerell, contacted him towards the end of summer in 1897. Perusing a bookseller's catalogue early one morning, Cockerell had spotted a 'privately printed' edition of *The Pilgrims of Hope*, a short collection of poems that Morris had originally serialised in a socialist periodical. Despite having worked for several years as Morris's private secretary, Cockerell had never heard of such a book. Knowing that trusty old Forman was compiling the bibliography, he fired off a letter to inquire after its status. 'Do you know anything about a privately printed *Pilgrims of Hope*?' he asked. 'I have never seen a copy and begin to wonder whether it may not be an unauthorised reprint.'

Whatever he was expecting, Forman's response surely came as a shock. It was a partial admission of guilt. 'For *The Pilgrims of Hope* you see I am personally responsible,' came the letter, 'and I have much pleasure in sending a copy for your acceptance.' Attached to the book was the relevant entry from the draft of his bibliography, explaining how he had come to print this collected sequence of poems, originally scattered across several magazines: 'I could not persuade its author to reprint it: he considered it wanted more revision than he could give it at the time. I threatened to reprint it in a decent way myself, privately of course; and, as he did not forbid me, I did so.' Perhaps Forman thought this put him in the clear. Cockerell, however, smelled a rat and kept pushing. What about the rare 'first edition' of Morris's *Sir Galahad*, supposedly printed in 1858? 'I shall not believe in *Sir Galahad* until I find someone who saw a copy before 1860,' he said bluntly.

No doubt Forman was distraught with this latest development. He attempted to appease his interlocutor with another gesture. 'I will hunt through my cupboards and back rows,' he told Cockerell, promising to send copies of those precious little Morris tracts which he owned in duplicate—not just the suspect pamphlets but, as Forman put it, 'anything I have which you have not'. But in the very same letter he was forced to acknowledge that some of these books had indeed been 'run off expressly for me'. 'I think it is unlikely that they were sold in any quantity,' Forman added meekly, as though that might get him off the hook.

It did not. Cockerell responded the following morning. 'If, as you hint in your letter, you are responsible for the existence of some of these, I think there ought to be some statement of it in your bibliography or elsewhere, in order to separate these artificial rarities from duly published and authorised reprints—what do you think?' But no answer was forthcoming. Three days later, on 20 November, the leading arts weekly *The Athenæum* published a letter written by Cockerell and his fellow executor of the Morris estate, F. S. Ellis, cautioning bibliophiles against spurious editions on the market:

> A WARNING TO COLLECTORS
>
> As executors of the late William Morris, we think it right to warn collectors that unauthorised reprints of some of his contributions to the weekly and monthly press are now being offered for sale at high prices. It would be well for those concerned in the manufacture of such 'rarities' to remember that they are engaged in an act of piracy and that they lay themselves open to proceedings under the Copyright Act.

Though the letter did not openly name Forman, this public shot across the bow was enough to send him scuttling back to his study. He had no desire to respond to the notice in *The Athenæum* or in any way draw attention to himself. Even if he did, what was there to say? Whatever scheme Wise had planned next, Forman would take no part in it. He was out.

That was just as well, for early in the new year Wise would face a public challenge of his own. On 8 January, another letter appeared in *The Athenæum*, wherein Thomas and Archibald Constable, the father-and-son duo of Edinburgh publishers, questioned the authenticity of one of the Robert Louis Stevenson forgeries. 'It appears to have been printed to catch the collector of first editions,' they claimed; 'it is not a first edition—merely a pirated reprint, of which the sale is illegal.' Wise had little patience for provincial interlopers and used his contacts at *The Athenæum* to print a rebuttal: an entirely fabricated account of the pamphlet's genesis, citing 'several of Stevenson's most valued friends and correspondents' as his authorities.

He had no such advantage when, later in 1898, similar doubts began to emerge from America. A pair of well-known New York booksellers, Alfred James Bowden and George D. Smith, published a letter questioning some purported 'first editions' of Tennyson. 'There is an uneasy feeling among collectors on this side regarding the numerous little privately printed pamphlets by celebrated modern authors that are being offered from England. Grave suspicions are entertained that some of these are being manufactured—but that these suspicions are well grounded cannot be said.' One of the books they called into question was *The Last Tournament* by Tennyson, the 'morality' of which Wise had asserted in his back-and-forth with Forman. 'Maybe *The Last Tournament* by Tennyson *is* worth $300,' conceded Bowden, 'but it is curious that every Tennyson collector of note has been supplied with one lately.'

Bowden and Smith developed their suspicions against a backdrop of spiralling demand for modern firsts. By the close of the century, clusters of Tennysons and Brownings were raising hundreds of pounds in auctions at Sotheby's and Hodgson's. Over in New York, Bangs and Co. was doing a roaring trade in forgeries, with plausible fakes of Stevenson, Browning, Swinburne, and Thackeray selling for hundreds of dollars. Tennyson books did particularly well in New York. In January 1900, a copy of his play *The Cup*, supposedly 'PRINTED FOR THE AUTHOR' in 1881, was advertised by Bangs: an immaculate copy in original paper wrappers, consigned by an anonymous seller. The auctioneer did not bring down the hammer until bidding had reached an ecstatic $280. Just like *The Last Tournament*, the book was a fake.

Bowden renewed his cries of foul play in March 1901. 'Does the reader remember a period about two years ago when "rare" privately printed little pamphlets by Tennyson and Swinburne were being boomed?' he asked. 'It is significant that all these high-priced and "rare" privately printed items are of the pamphlet variety and of modern date—few being over twenty pages and of an earlier date than 1865. They are easy of fabrication and we believe they have been fabricated.' Nobody was in the mood to listen, though. For, later that same spring, the bookman extraordinaire William Henry Arnold was to unload the bulk of his library in an auction of staggering proportions.

The catalogue and its contents were the common gossip of book-hunters on both sides of the Atlantic. Arnold had been hard at it for years and had built up a collection that turned most of his rivals green. Among the modern treasures for sale was the original proof copy of Browning's *The Ring and the Book*, with annotations and corrections in the hand of the master himself. More than a dozen first editions of Elizabeth Barrett Browning were to be included. There was Coleridge's personal copy of Chapman's translation of Homer—the famous text which prompted those oft-quoted lines of Keats, travelling 'in the realms of gold'. And, for admirers of Keats, the auction was a once-in-a-lifetime opportunity to acquire a presentation copy of the first edition of his *Poems*, signed by the author, alongside manuscripts and letters written in his hand.

But there were also a good number of forgeries throughout the collection. And, when the day came, they continued to grow in value. The real star of the sale was a beautiful copy of the fake *Sonnets* by Barrett Browning. Wise himself had privately sold this volume to Arnold for $115, cooking up yet another fanciful backstory about the provenance. It was now the very first copy to come up at auction. After a furious round of bidding, the hammer price was an outrageous $440. 'It is rarely, indeed, that good poetry is worth money,' reported the *New York Times* with an approving, if perplexed nod. Even Wise was taken aback. 'I had expected this book to sell for about

£50,' he confessed. 'But it is a most interesting little piece, and very scarce indeed.'

Once the dust had settled, a reissue of the Arnold catalogue with hammer prices went to the printers. It quickly became the new benchmark against which all future sales were to be measured. If a gentleman acquired a book for less than the 'Arnold price', he could rest in the knowledge that he had secured a bargain. 'Collectors owe Mr Arnold a debt of gratitude,' explained the preface to the catalogue. 'An amateur who, with the help of these figures, cannot defend himself against his wife ought to give up book collecting at once. Armed with the facts so eloquently given here it will no longer be necessary to smuggle books into the house. A husband can throw the newly acquired volume down anywhere and look his wife in the eye as composedly as if he had just taken out some more life insurance.' According to this new gospel of standard book prices, Wise's forgeries were worth many hundreds of dollars.

Genuine rarities, too, were on the up. With the exception of rare works by Edgar Allan Poe, which had long fetched absurd prices in the thousands of dollars, no modern book was more desirable than Browning's early poem *Pauline*—the same little volume which Wise had spotted among the poet's scrap papers all those years earlier. In 1902—on April Fool's Day, no less—a copy sold for the record sum of $720. Nor was it even a perfect copy, having slight damage to one of the leaves. The *New York Times* reported the sale as 'an event of importance to all collectors of nineteenth-century first editions'. If anyone still doubted the merit of collecting modern firsts, or persisted in thinking of their collectors as modish amateurs, this sale proved them wrong. Wise had initially begun collecting this kind of material because he could not afford older books. Now the more established collectors of ancient poems and plays lusted after the very fare they had once scorned.

In this rapidly ascending market, Wise's expertise was increasingly in demand. Collectors, dealers, and auctioneers alike sought his opinion on the authenticity and financial value of modern firsts. He no longer merely reported on auction sales for the *Bookman*. In 1897 he had published authoritative bibliographies of both Swinburne and Browning, establishing himself as the go-to expert for booksellers. Outside working hours, he continued to plug away on a massive catalogue of Tennyson editions, with full descriptions and facsimile illustrations. Through these useful reference works, Wise was stamping his final say on the publication histories of those poets. Needless to say, he included his own forgeries alongside the legitimate editions, drawing attention to the authentic-looking copies he had been planting in prestigious libraries and private collections. Part of the problem for collectors and booksellers was that Wise was truly an expert on these authors. And the fact that he knew the books so much better than almost everybody else made it difficult for them to challenge his judgement. It was as though a trained, respected physician was confidently prescribing snake oil.

Some people bought into the scam more eagerly than others. One man proved shockingly vulnerable to Wise's salesmanship. Soon after Wise first began sourcing tricky books for John Henry Wrenn, the pair of them had struck a deal. In the spirit of camaraderie, they would not compete against each other. The American stockbroker would have first call on books by the authors he prized most dearly, namely Pope and Dryden and Tennyson, while Wise would be free to keep all the Browning and Shelley rarities that did not already line his shelves. And whenever he spotted a precious bargain which would be a mere duplicate copy in his own collection, Wise would send it over to Chicago and Wrenn would reimburse his costs.

It was an honest arrangement and, through his London friend, Wrenn secured many treasures of poetry, ranging from important works by Milton and Pope to the modern first editions on which Wise was so famously expert. The whole thing was no bother, Wise would explain in that offhand way of his: 'I am devoted to hunting up and buying books, and every additional volume I buy for you is an additional pleasure secured for myself.' There was simply no need for

Wrenn to thank him, let alone in that profuse American manner. 'Do, please, believe that the pleasure I obtain from the task is far greater than I can tell you.'

Some of that pleasure, at least, sprang from the sensation of deceit. Scattered among the genuine works were the forgeries. Wise was a master storyteller and strung his mark along with concocted tales of books that had unfortunately slipped through his fingers. Consider the following yarn. In their earliest correspondence, Wise had boasted of acquiring the 'horribly rare' trial edition of Tennyson's *The Promise of May*. Just before Christmas in 1897, he learned of another copy, this time in the hands of an unnamed theatre man who, Wise complained, 'had the cheek to ask £90 for it' when the record price was £84, 'and this price was paid only for an autographed copy'. Despite his efforts to negotiate a more reasonable sum, Wise regretfully told Wrenn that he had not won the book. It had gone over to America, he declared. How frustrating must it have been for Wrenn to learn that such a jewel was now in the hands of one of his domestic rivals?

And so when, in the following spring, Wise claimed to have spotted another copy on the market, at the bargain price of £40, Wrenn jumped. 'At this price the book is exceedingly cheap,' and, Wise reminded him, it had been 'some months since £90 was demanded for a copy'. But the low price was also of some concern to Wise. 'Would it be in any way improper if I were to ask you to refrain from making public the fact that you got the book for £40?' he asked. 'The market value of the book is £60 or £70, and if it became known that an example had been sold for £40 it might influence in some degree its value.'

How could Wrenn refuse such a reasonable request? He willingly entered into Wise's conspiracy of silence. His friend in London was sending him so many excellent books at such decent prices, he reasoned, and all without accepting a penny in commission. Keeping quiet about the price he paid for a book was the very least he could do in return. After all, time and again Wise's stories made it clear that he alone had the connections, the tenacity, and the taste to find this kind of book. Perhaps the request for silence would seem dubious coming from someone else. But in the cut-throat world of book-hunting, Wise alone could be trusted. The truth was rather different: Wrenn was paying good money for yet another dud from the forger's private stash.

Under Wise's guidance, Wrenn learned to invest only in books of impeccable provenance, which was, he naïvely thought, the best way of avoiding modern fakes. Such a strategy left Wrenn hopelessly vulnerable to Wise's fantasies and tall tales. Telling Wren that he had sourced a new cache of books from Forman, Wise passed on 'four little Browning volumes of great interest'—all of them fabricated first editions. Before they came to Forman, these 'four books were once the property of R. H. Horne', he lied, 'and were no doubt all given to him by the Brownings, as he was very thick with the Brownings in all those years, and worked in collaboration with Mr Browning and was never likely to have bought the books'. On another occasion Wise sent over the purported 'very rare trial issue' of Tennyson's *Morte d'Arthur*, supposedly obtained directly from the nephew of Tennyson's publisher, Edward Moxon, but in fact another forgery.

When in 1901 Wise pawned off an antedated fake of a minor essay by William Makepeace Thackeray—one of twenty-five copies printed 'for the Author's Use', according to the title page—he dreamed up a remarkably compelling account of the book's history. This very copy had once belonged to George Dolby, a lesser-known figure who had acted as secretary to Charles Dickens during one of his public reading tours across America. 'Dolby died not long ago in the workhouse, having sunk into abject poverty, the result of drink,' Wise told Wrenn. Before being pressed into service, Dolby had been forced to sell all his worldly goods for a few shillings. And among those goods was this little Thackeray first edition. 'It seems almost pathos, does it not? That a poor devil should go to the workhouse to die, and at the gates almost of the workhouse sell for practically nothing a valuable piece of property.'

It was precisely the kind of sentimental tale by which Wrenn had been so entranced on his first visit to Ashley Road, albeit tainted here with a cold, callous edge. Every word was a calculated lie. Wise expressed no sympathy for Dolby. He seemed more delighted than appalled by the irony of a man sinking into abjection while also possessing a great literary jewel.

So far as Wrenn was concerned, 'Tommy' Wise was his dear friend, perhaps even his dearest friend. When Selina Wise walked out on her husband in 1895, leading to formal divorce proceedings two years later, Wrenn had been there to lend a sympathetic ear. And when Wise remarried in 1900, he had sent his warmest congratulations and a beautiful glass lamp as a wedding gift.

Selina Wise could not have found the marriage easy. When he wanted to be, Wise could be charming and affectionate. But behind closed doors he was too often dogmatic, petulant, and cruel. From time to time, visitors to Ashley Road would remark on his unchivalrous behaviour. After a pleasant dinner one evening, guests were dismayed by his 'considerable brusqueness' to Selina after she forgot to bring out the cheese board. It was almost 'as though Selina had omitted the pagination in a book collation', joked one of the party. In the end, it seems, she lost patience with her husband's social climbing, with his churlish behaviour, and with his unrelenting, all-consuming, maddening bibliophilia. She left him for another man.

Frances Louise—or Louie, as the new Mrs Wise preferred to be known—was altogether more accommodating of Wise's quirks and shortcomings. They were the price she paid for a comfortable, respectable lifestyle. Her father, recently deceased, had been a bank manager, and 'Tom' provided for her just as well as her father had done. Interestingly, on the marriage documentation Wise had put down his own late father's rank as 'gentleman'. Though her husband's junior—just twenty-five to his forty-one—Louie was canny beyond her years and was, by general assent, charming company, though it seems she did not question Wise's social pretensions. Unlike Selina, she enjoyed rambling about the town with her husband, venturing forth on shared 'book-hunting expeditions', searching for treasures. Such patience was not commonly sighted among the spouses of book-hunters.

With his second marriage, Wise was moving up in the world. No longer the upstart collector of Holloway, he and Louie moved into 23 Downside Crescent: a substantial redbrick with large bay windows only a short walk from the heart of fashionable Hampstead. When Wrenn visited in 1902 and again in 1903, he spent the springtime exploring London with the couple, dining late into the night with Dr Furnivall, Edmund Gosse, and other luminaries of the literary world. 'It is a delight to us to know that you have enjoyed your visit to London,' wrote Wise. 'I need not assure you that it has been a very great pleasure to us to meet you here.'

The following summer Wrenn invited the Wises to join him in Vienna, where he was meeting his son Harold on vacation. And, in the summer after that, the two families embarked on a joint road trip across France. 'We shall be able to carry very little baggage with us in a car!' Wise had warned Wrenn. 'Just a change, and sufficient linen, that's all. No evening dress, or anything of that sort.' Perhaps this came as a shock to the Wrenns, who were used to a certain level of luxury in their Chicago mansion. More likely, though, it was a welcome change of pace, an exciting old-world adventure. Wrenn enjoyed the younger man's energy and Louie was a delightful and sprightly companion for Mrs Wrenn; from the back seat of the motor car, the pair of them could scoff and joke about their husbands' bookish pursuits. On their return home, the couples exchanged family photographs and, when young Harold married and fathered his first child, Wise asked his friend to give the baby a kiss from himself and Louie, who longed for a daughter of her own. Wise, in truth, could not have imagined anything less agreeable.

For all the overtures of friendship, beneath the surface Wise was simply a dealer conditioning a wealthy client. His relationship with Wrenn skilfully blended the personal with the transactional. When Bowden raised doubts about the authenticity of the Tennyson books that Wise had recently sold on to Wrenn, the forger pounced on his warnings as the delusional grumblings of a crank, an embittered 'second rate New York bookseller, who cannot get copies of the rarer

Tennyson pieces, and so tries to put his customers off them by crying sour grapes'. Wrenn ought to have known something was wrong. He ought to have spread his custom across numerous booksellers and dealers instead of entrusting everything to one man. And yet, blinded by greed and delusion, this giant of industry could not resist the hypnotic charms of the snake he called his friend. Like a thirsty man offered a glass of salted water, the more he drank the more thirsty he became. He coveted books, wanted them, needed them. Wise was happy to oblige.

10

The Kernless f and the Curious ?

Lunch was set for Brice's in Soho, an easy-going bistro serving passable French fare at a reasonable price: the kind of restaurant where lunch could quite easily slide into coffee and coffee into drinks and drinks into dinner and dinner into more drinks. Normally Carter would have preferred to dine at his club, where the linen was reliably starched and the cutlery silver; but he accepted that his friend could not easily drag himself away from the bookshop, which lay a mere hundred yards around the corner, on Gerrard Street. And besides, the unassuming, anonymous atmosphere lent itself to plotting.

One imagines the two booksellers laying out their plan of attack over a bottle of light burgundy followed by a pot of strong black coffee and a well-tamped pipe. Each of them had drawn up a list. In neat columns, under clearly delineated headings and subheadings, Carter enumerated some two dozen little first editions in the mould of the 'Reading' *Sonnets* that he thought equally worthy of investigation. Pollard's list was more haphazard, with the titles and dates of books scrawled, seemingly at random, up and down and across the pages of his notebook. But, in substance, the two lists were nearly identical.

Pollard pulled some folded papers out from inside his jacket and laid them on the table. It was the catalogue that Gathorne-Hardy had fished from the bin earlier that week. The pair of them looked at the cover, which was printed on flimsy orange paper. 'Catalogue of a Miscellaneous Collection of Books, Pamphlets, etc., including many Interesting and Rare Items', ran the title, to be sold by 'Herbert E. Gorfin' of Lewisham. Each looked at the other blankly. Despite their combined knowledge of the trade, it was not a name either of them had encountered before. Inside the catalogue was a different story. Among its contents was very nearly every single one of the dubious books that Carter and Pollard had jotted down on their lists, plus a good deal more.

Could this man, this 'Gorfin', have acquired all these books from a single source? Might he be a front for the forger? Or even the forger himself? The pair of them decided to use the catalogue as a rough guide to their terrain. If a rare first edition was included, they would scrutinise it. By the time Carter settled the bill and each of them pottered back to work, their list had swollen to some forty suspects. Each would need to be investigated.

Early progress was slow. Within days of that first lunch, Carter received an urgent cable from the New York office, summoning him on the next boat out of Liverpool. For him, the investigation would have to wait. And for Pollard, alone in Soho, there were other distractions. The mood in London was tense. Although some eighteen months had passed since the collapse of the American stock exchange, the crash cast a long shadow. Mass unemployment across the industrial heartlands of northern England lent new urgency to cries for revolution. Up and down the country, the working classes were increasingly receptive to the message of the *Daily Worker*.

Maxwell Knight could taste threat in the air. As director of M-Section, he had been actively planting new operatives inside the British Communist Party. But these agents were a long-term investment. Like apple pips planted in the ground, eventually they would grow and bear fruit; but for the moment they were fragile and best left undisturbed while they put down roots. Adding to his frustration was the simple fact that party members were growing ever warier of strangers. 'Efforts are being made to send spies into the party,' revealed one story in the *Daily Worker*, following a bungled operation by M's rivals in Special Branch. It was only a matter of time before one of the new recruits put a foot wrong. In the immediate term there was nobody to match Pollard's access. In short, Agent M/1 was needed.

His mission during that spring was to keep tabs on Reg Bishop, a dissident *Daily Worker* journalist rumoured to be conducting underground work for Soviet Russia. Pollard kept to his usual routine: attending editorial meetings of the newspaper and reporting back to M once a week. At first there was not much to pass on. Bishop was surprisingly candid in the meetings, one evening mooting an assault on the Japanese embassy in retaliation for its anti-Soviet activities. Evidently he did not suspect a spy in his midst. But for the most part his interventions were strictly editorial.

Things started to change after the return of Douglas Springhall from the Lenin School in Moscow. An Englishman by birth, 'Springy' had gone to Russia to undergo training in the clandestine techniques of subversion, disinformation, and sabotage. He had snuck back into the country without a passport, via agents in Berlin and Paris. At first, he had confined himself to the industrial regions around Newcastle-upon-Tyne, causing all kinds of nuisance under the alias 'Zanoff'. Now he was sitting tight in London with Bishop.

Precisely what they were plotting in Bishop's flat remained a mystery. Another MI5 agent overheard Springhall claiming that his latest Russian mission had been strictly propagandistic. He had been sent out east to Vladivostok simply to 'interview some people connected with the Chinese Theatre Movement' and 'persuade them to work more propaganda into their plays'. Perhaps he had returned home on a similar assignment, to disseminate Soviet agitprop on English shores.

Nobody with any knowledge of Springhall's earlier activities thought this story very likely, though. The Red Army did not spend years training its agents only to send them home for propagandistic grunt work. And so M pressed Pollard to do a little more digging and see what turned up. It took him less than four days to find information. On 7 March, he passed on what he had learned: 'Springhall is known to be conducting investigations for the party with regard to ships which might possibly be conveying munitions to the Far East,' where enemies of the Chinese Communist Party were gathering strength. As for his earlier mission to Vladivostok, that too must have been on high-level military business. Yet for all Pollard's digging, Bishop's connection to the whole affair remained hazy at best.

Espionage is often a business in which nothing seems to happen for vast swathes of time. An agent can sit and wait and watch for weeks, months, years. Then, suddenly, everything begins to move very quickly. So it was. On 19 May, Pollard learned that Bishop and his wife would be leaving for Russia, supposedly on holiday. The information was time-sensitive. Bishop would be setting off within two days. If M wished to keep track of his activities among the Soviets, he would need to act immediately. Pollard did not even wait for his usual weekly debrief but instead sent the news via urgent telegram. His quick thinking was to prove crucial. Another M-Section agent did not even hear about the trip until two days after the Bishops had skipped town.

One month later, with all M's other agents still seemingly in the dark, Pollard passed on further news. The Bishops did not travel alone. On the ship to Moscow they had been joined by a small group of aeronautics experts from the British government's experimental aircraft facility in Aldershot. Apparently these men 'took a great interest in Russian affairs' and seemed 'very sympathetic to the Russian regime', Pollard reported. More disturbingly, they did not return to the country at the same time as Bishop. 'It is not known how long they were going for' and it is quite 'possible that they are still there.' Was it also possible that Bishop had been entrusted with bringing these engineers into the Soviet fold? Could he and Springhall have been part of a conspiracy to steal British military secrets for the Russians?

Pollard learned much about the principles of detection from his clandestine work. Although the primary duty of an MI5 operative was to keep an ear to the ground and report back on suspicious individuals, M liked to employ people with a flair for investigation. 'Detective work means the use of one's eyes, ears and even one's nose,' he would later write; 'it means that observations must be accurate; it means having a great deal of patience and, most important of all, avoiding hasty conclusions without being able to prove them.' This was advice that his agents would do well to heed.

Yet Pollard, alone for all those weeks in Soho, perhaps could have learned even more from his neighbours. Next door to the bookshop on Gerrard Street, in two adjoining rooms upstairs at number thirty-one, met the Detection Club. Its members were well known to most booksellers, in name if not in person. Between them, Dorothy Sayers, Agatha Christie, and G. K. Chesterson—to name but a few—had sold hundreds of thousands of books across the English-speaking world. The club was founded on the premise that writing, so often a lonely business, can be improved by a little company. The solitary writer of detective stories has nobody off whom to bounce ideas, when the intricate conundrums of the genre positively demand to be tested on an intelligent audience before being put to print. And so, two or three times a week, having staggered back from a long and drink-fuelled dinner, and slalomed through the sleaze of the Soho backstreets, the premier detective writers of their day would congregate in the rooms next door to Birrell and Garnett to pick holes in one another's plots and devise abominable new methods of murder.

Sayers was the natural leader of the group. She was also a loyal customer of Pollard's, stopping by the shop in search of raw materials to inspire her books. For several years, Sayers and Pollard corresponded on the finer points of Wilkie Collins printings, and the Birrell and Garnett account books show her buying numerous Collins first editions and autograph letters. That the Detection Club should have a base in central London had been her idea and the two rooms on Gerrard Street cleaved to her vision: in one corner, a small collection of reference books on crime and criminology; comfortable, beaten-up leather armchairs by the windows, looking out over the street; a 'dark and ancient staircase' that took visitors 'past the haunts of industry, pleasure and mystery which made up the remainder of the house'. It was an environment in which her protagonist, the worldly Lord Peter Wimsey, would have been right at home.

Unlike Christie's dumpy Belgian sleuth, Wimsey was a debonair creation who had the tact and charm of an intelligence operative and a forensic eye for detail. The latter skill was of course a prerequisite for any detective. When confronted with a body, it was essential that he or she should be able to spot any clues that might help track down the killer: how the shape of bruising round the neck might determine the size of a strangler's hands; or how a mystery poison might be identified as cyanide by the tell-tale whiff of bitter almonds. Such run-of-the-mill puzzles posed no difficulty whatsoever to Wimsey, whose early adventures are awash with displays of virtuosic deduction.

There was the time when, called to examine a body found in a bath, Wimsey pointed out that the man could hardly be the famous Jewish financier the police believed him to be—on account of his not being circumcised. Or that occasion in Scotland when he identified an artist as the killer of another local artist by an errant tube of oil paint in his studio: a brand used by the victim but not the suspect. He was never too proud to ask for assistance when a crucial piece of evidence demanded expert scrutiny. Investigating a suspected murder at the Bellona Club in 1928, Wimsey called in a favour from an analytical chemist who, with nothing more than a glass tube, a Bunsen burner, and a phial of hydrochloric acid, was able to demonstrate the presence of arsenic on the victim's shoe. 'Enough of the stuff to kill an elephant,' announced the chemist; 'it's surprising how wasteful people are with their drugs.' Equally importantly, Wimsey was an enthusiastic and highly competent collector of rare books! He was precisely the sort of man with whom somebody like Carter—charming, urbane, sharp—would have rubbed along extremely well.

Beneath the surface, though, Wimsey perhaps had more in common with Pollard. During the First World War he had been recruited as an intelligence agent and sent on numerous missions behind enemy lines. On one occasion, he had even infiltrated a German officer's wardroom, gathering valuable intelligence on enemy movements. From time to time he was still called away on urgent diplomatic business for the Foreign Office, the precise details of which always remained unclear.

Sayers believed the skills nurtured by espionage and intelligence work could be invaluable in the detection of crime. Not simply because any detective would need a rudimentary knowledge of codes and ciphers, nor because they would need to exercise extreme discretion until they were ready to play their hand. What Sayers recognised was that spies could link raw detection and the meticulous handling of evidence with profound psychological insight. To a great detective, the people surrounding a crime contained more useful clues than anything he or she could find with a magnifying glass.

Here lay Wimsey's real talent: his ability to put people at ease, to coax information like a turtle from its shell. Solving a murder is rarely a simple intellectual exercise in which all the evidence can be neatly slotted together. Detectives encounter deception. People are not always who they claim to be. The real task is to filter good information from bad, to chisel beneath the façade, to peek behind the curtain. There is tremendous irony in the fact that, all this time, several members of the Detection Club were themselves leading double lives. To all the world, Sayers seemed to epitomise the childless public intellectual, when, in secret, she was mother to an unacknowledged son, and wife in a dead-end marriage. Even Agatha Christie had an alter ego in the romance novelist 'Mary Westmacott'. Had he ever bothered to pop next door and climb that 'dark and ancient staircase' to the rooms of the Detection Club, the bookseller-spy of Gerrard Street would have found himself among kindred spirits.

Carter did not return to London until the second week of May—just as things were heating up for Agent M/1—and on his arrival home was promptly dispatched on a book-buying jaunt to Europe. Summer was creeping into autumn before the investigation could begin in earnest. The next time they sat down together, the two booksellers divided the tasks between them. Each would play to his strengths.

Having already devoted several months to retracing the provenance of the *Sonnets*, Carter continued to poke holes in the official version of the story. He spent weeks combing through auction records and published correspondence, pencil in hand, searching in vain for traces of a presentation copy or any mention of the book by the Brownings or one of their friends. He wrote letters to librarians and private collectors on both sides of the Atlantic, politely asking them to check their volumes of unpublished Browning letters—but to no avail. Time and again, he went over the official story, as initially reported by Edmund Gosse in 1894 and elaborated by Thomas James Wise thereafter, each time spotting new inconsistencies.

Quite simply, there was nothing to back it up. In his bibliography of the writings of Elizabeth Barrett Browning, the standard work on the subject, Wise asserted that Gosse had heard the story directly from the poet's husband. But, according to the original version, Gosse heard the story from an anonymous source to whom Browning had told it eight years before his death. Carter did not know what to make of this discrepancy. He assumed he must be missing some overlooked piece of information that would help make sense of it all. He wrote to friends of Gosse, none of whom could recall from whom the vain and notoriously muddleheaded critic had learned the story of the 'Reading' *Sonnets* so many years earlier.

As a last resort, he penned a courteous note to Wise himself, who was by this time, as he liked to remind people, the 'sole remaining man who broke bread at Browning's table'. If anyone could shed any light on this mystery it ought to be him. 'In making some notes on the history of the privately printed edition of Mrs Browning's *Sonnets from the Portuguese* 1847 we find on page seventy-two of your bibliography, "The history of the volume has already been so fully told etc." Would you be kind enough to let us know where the story can be found?' Carter asked. 'With apologies for troubling you.' A response arrived the following day. It was as good as useless. Wise simply directed Carter back to the standard sources that he had already consulted.

Meanwhile, Pollard was entrusted with the forensic side of the investigation. He spent his evenings and weekends at the British Museum, working his way through the list of suspect books and coaxing them to surrender their secrets. In some respects, Pollard's approach to these suspicious little volumes mirrored that of Poirot or Wimsey when faced with a corpse. As Sayers habitually remarked, the human body is 'only so much organic matter with a known chemical content, and it will conform to the ordinary laws to which all organic matter is subject'. Better to approach a corpse with the 'cheerful materialism' of the detective than allow it to loom in the imagination. However sentimental our attachment to certain books and stories, at the end of the day they too are 'only so much organic matter'. Paper made up of pulp and flax and rags; ink from various natural oils and pigments; all bound in boards covered by skin from goats, sheep, and calves.

To most people the composition of paper and design of a typeface were uninteresting details. Yet in the right hands they could be clues. 'The detection of types is one of the most elementary branches of knowledge to the special expert in crime,' explained Sherlock Holmes when confronted with an anonymous threat pasted together with letters cut from the newspaper. He could instantly recognise the 'leaded bourgeois type' of a leader in *The Times*; 'these words could have been taken from nothing else'. It took him mere seconds to locate the precise page from which the letters had been clipped.

Following in Holmes's footsteps, Pollard had already made the analysis of typefaces something of a speciality. For the past five years he had been kept on retainer by the Langstone Monotype Company, advising them on the finer points of type design. His early Birrell and Garnett catalogues were particularly strong in books printed in fonts of historical importance. If there was anybody qualified to engage in a little typographical detective work, it was Pollard.

The problem was getting his hands on the clues in the first place. Quite a few of the forgeries had made their way into public collections over the years, but the prize items were more difficult to access. Finding a copy of the *Sonnets* was always going to be especially challenging. In lieu of an original copy, Pollard tried at first to make do with the photo-facsimile commissioned by William Andrews Clark: the one that Wise had speculated would be admired by Barrett Browning herself for its 'magnificent form'. But this proved wholly inadequate to the task. It was like asking Poirot to establish a cause of death from a mere photograph of a body. He needed eyes on the book. And not just any eyes, but those of a *bona fide* expert, sensitive to each flick of serif and coil of ligature. Thankfully he knew just the man.

Ever since he had first dropped by the Birrell and Garnett bookshop in 1926, Stanley Morison had mentored young Pollard in the typographic arts. A lifelong Marxist and a conscientious objector during the first war, he could often be found in the shop on Gerrard Street: tall, thin, and clad in a baggy black suit, as though he had just stepped out of an L. S. Lowry painting. His dour appearance belied both a clubbable wit and a concentrated sense of practicality. The suit was purchased from a supplier to the clergy, known for making cheap, hard-wearing garments. His wide-brimmed hat, adopted as a reaction against the preferred bowler of the brokers and bankers, even had a hole bored through the crown so that it could be more securely mounted on a hat-peg. This practical attitude carried over into his professional work as a type-designer, where he had a strong preference for clean, uncluttered, easy-to-read fonts over the decorative flourishes favoured by most of his rivals.

When Pollard and Carter learned that Morison was due to sail to New York on business early in the new year, they told him about their conundrum. During his latest round of research, Carter had discovered that the great American banker John Pierpont Morgan had bought a copy of the *Sonnets* from Quaritch in 1907. And, ever since his death, Morgan's grand library on Madison Avenue had been open to the public. Carter had learned about the copy only very recently, too late for him to consult it while he was stateside in spring. It was an imposition, Pollard knew, but while he was in New York would Morison swing by the Pierpont Morgan Library and take a look at the book for them? Of course, he agreed.

It is simple enough to recognise the features that differentiate one font from another. Typographers talk about letterforms in anatomical terms: they have legs and arms and shoulders, ears and tails and spines. Every font is to some degree unique. They can be distinguished by the tiniest of details: by the swish of the tail on a capital 'Q' or the obtruding bar of a roman 't'; by the loop and link of a lower-case 'g' or the bulging shoulder and bowed leg of a capital 'R'. Each serif, terminal, and swash makes an individual letter like a fingerprint. They are easy to tell apart at a glance, though it is often difficult to explain precisely why. The real trick is knowing which part of which letter may help to identify and date the font in question, a feat that requires a keen eye, considerable expertise, and extraordinary powers of visual recall.

When Morison came to New York that January and settled behind his desk in the Pierpont Morgan reading room, he was able to sit with the book for quite some time. His process was patient, methodical. He looked first at the binding: supple morocco boards and spine, dyed an extraordinary shade of ocean-blue, with gold tooling, stamped by Riviere and Son. He counted the pages—forty-seven plus a blank—and ran his fingers across the lettering to feel whether the type had bitten into the page or merely kissed the surface. Everything looked and felt just as it should.

Then he looked a little closer. It took him a while to see it, but there was something not quite right about one of the letters: the lower-case 'f'. Among all the letters of the alphabet, this one is unusual. To ensure that each letter is spaced evenly within a word, typographers historically designed the arm at the top of the 'f' (not its central bar) to arch out into the space beyond the body of the type. When the individual slivers of metal are arranged together into words, this arm interferes with the next letter in the sequence. Sometimes it will collide with the next letter—as in 'finite' and 'fluid'—for which printers use a single piece of specially designed type known as a 'ligature', which includes all the letters in question, such as 'fi' and 'fl'. More often, though, in traditional typefaces the arm of the 'f' will simply slot over the blank space above the face of the following letter. As in 'fabulous' or 'fool', the 'a' and the 'o' will be neatly tucked under its canopy.

In the world of typography, this overhanging arm, extending beyond the body of the type, is known as a *kern*. And yet Morison could see that the 'f' used to print the *Sonnets* had no kern. Instead of arching up and out in the usual manner, the stem of the letter bent very slightly back on itself before hooking sharply over and down, terminating in a bulbous teardrop. It looked almost broken-backed, Morison thought.

Although kernless designs were not unusual, he had always assumed them to be a recent invention. Because the kern projects outwards from the main body of the type, it is exposed and fragile. This had not been a problem on older printing machines, controlled as they were by hand. But with the mechanised, high-speed presses one found in modern printshops, it was easy for kerns to bend or break. Hence the demand for new kernless typefaces. So what was a kernless 'f' doing in an 1847 book?

Even more curious was the curling 'meat-hook' question mark used throughout the book, for Morison could tell immediately that this did not properly belong with rest of the font. It was at least one size too small. And the whole design appeared to tilt forward in a most curious manner. If he did not know better, Morison would guess that the face for an italic question mark, usually set slanting on the body of type, had accidentally been punched upright onto a roman body. An eccentric hypothesis, perhaps. But such an odd design demanded an odd explanation.

Morison was not a hasty man. Just as he took his time in the reading room, so too he spent several days digesting all he had learned in New York. He was steaming back across the Atlantic, four days into the crossing, before he sat down in his cabin and picked up a piece of the writing paper they provided on board, adorned by an image of the liner ploughing through the waves, ensign flying, steam and smoke pouring from the funnels. In his studied calligraphic hand, and with characteristic modesty, he elucidated the peculiar quirks of the font used to print the *Sonnets*, complete with diagrams of its kernless 'f' and curious '?'.

'I may be all wrong,' he wrote, 'but I have not noticed the broken-backed "f" as early as 1850 and if I had been asked I should have said that it was evolved in order to prevent broken kerns occurring on high-speed presses, of which there could have been few in Reading or anywhere else in 1847.' It would not be easy, but Morison guessed that, with some research, Pollard would be able to identify the font with even greater precision. From here, it was going to be a simple matter of finding the type-founder and deducing when the font had first been sold to the public. If that date was later than 1847, the book had to be a fake.

After a year of sitting and waiting, it was just the break the investigation needed. Pollard dropped everything else. His reports to M dried up. The bookshop would be left to run itself for a while. There was serious work to be done.

Eight major foundries had been producing type for the English printing trade over the past century and Pollard knew precisely where he could find samples of all their work: half an hour's stroll from the bookshop, tucked down a narrow alley off Fleet Street, in the St Bride Foundation Library. The foundation had been set up forty years earlier to train young printers for a life of work on the 'street of ink'. Though classes had long since moved to larger premises south of the river, the building remained a dedicated repository for the typographic arts. On the lower floor, straining against reinforced beams and struts, were tonnes of metal punches, matrices, and fonts, neatly stacked in box upon box upon box. Lining the shelves upstairs were all kinds of books of interest to the student of typography: catalogues and historical treatises ranging from the grandest of folios to the slimmest of pamphlets.

Of special importance was the library's collection of specimen books. These volumes were prepared by type-founders as a way of showing off their range to customers. Each year, the specimen books would grow fatter and fatter as demand for new fonts grew: blocky sans serifs, huge poster fonts, neatly cut decorative typefaces. Pollard was already very familiar with these specimens and samplers, having compiled a catalogue of examples for the bookshop five years earlier. But never before had he ventured to discover the identity and date of an unknown font by systematically going through the books. In truth, it was the kind of Sisyphean task that nobody had ever thought to attempt.

The parameters were broad. Magnifying glass in hand, Pollard would need to consult every specimen book he could find from between 1847, when the *Sonnets* had supposedly been printed, and 1895, by which time the book had been announced to the world. From the eight larger foundries, there were precisely 152 specimen books that fitted the bill, plus another twenty-one from the smaller firms. The work was slow and tiring on the eyes. Nowhere in the earlier specimens was there any sign of the broken-backed 'f' or of the tilting question mark. Indeed, kernless designs were wholly absent from the books. Until, that is, Pollard arrived at the specimens dating from 1883. For in that year alone, three different foundries introduced no fewer than eight separate kernless fonts.

One of those new designs from 1883 was a near-perfect match: Long Primer No. 20, from the P. M. Shanks type-foundry in Holborn. All the standard letterforms were identical to the ones used in the *Sonnets*. The font even had the same broken-backed 'f' that made it so distinctive. On closer inspection, Pollard saw that the lower-case 'j', too, seemed to be of a kernless design. Morison had not mentioned this detail in his note. Instead of looping roundly to the left, the tail of the letter jutted sharply back on itself before coiling around in a tight curl, just like a buttonhook.

If this font was first produced in 1883 and the *Sonnets* was printed in this font, how could it have been printed in 1847, as the title page claimed? It was just the sort of paradox that Holmes delighted in posing to Watson. 'How often have I said to you that when you have eliminated the impossible, whatever remains, *however improbable*, must be the truth?' he would chide his sidekick. 'You know my methods. Apply them.' In this case, applying Holmes's methods could lead to only one conclusion. The 'Reading' *Sonnets*, that most coveted of all Victorian first editions, must be a fake.

Except for one snag. The curious question mark was nowhere to be found. Although the example that came with Long Primer No. 20 was superficially like the question mark found in the *Sonnets*, the proportions were distinctive enough to set it apart. And so Pollard continued to search the archives of the St Bride Foundation for this errant piece of punctuation, tracking down twenty-seven different varieties of kernless type manufactured in the twelve years following 1883. Each design had its own question mark. None of them was a match.

Frustrating though this was, the fruitless search confirmed his suspicion that this oddly tilted question mark did not properly belong to the font. At some point the correct question mark for Long Primer No. 20 must have become lost or damaged or been misplaced by the printer, leading him to swap in a spare. In other words, the *Sonnets* was printed in a unique hybrid of two different fonts. And the chances of two different printers mixing these two specific fonts in such a peculiar and particular manner were vanishingly small, Pollard rationalised. Logic dictated that only one printing house could be using this idiosyncratic typographical mixture. If the same combination could be found in another book, one with an authentic imprint, that would be a 'direct clue' to the real printer of the forgeries, whoever he may be.

Clues come in all shapes and sizes. Some take months of patient sleuthing to unearth. Others simply appear when they are least expected. While Pollard was a born detective—meticulous, tenacious, thorough—it was to be a happy accident that would provide him with the final clue he needed. Early in spring, as the hardened bark of London's plane trees gave way to green-skinned shoots and buds, he found himself in the British Museum looking over an unexpectedly important book. It was a type facsimile of the 1840 first edition of Matthew Arnold's short poem *Alaric at Rome*, privately prepared as a keepsake for collectors in 1893. 'PRINTED FOR PRIVATE CIRCULATION ONLY', explained an ominous notice on the title page.

Skimming his way through the pages, certain patterns began to form before Pollard's eyes. The broken-backed 'f'; the buttonhook 'j'; the curious tilting question mark. All were there. This facsimile of *Alaric* had been printed in the same unique combination of fonts as the *Sonnets*: in the same workshop, certainly, and very likely on the same press by the same hands. There could be no doubting the evidence.

Pulse quickening and thumping in his ears, Pollard turned to the final sheet of the booklet. 'Printed by Richard Clay and Sons, Limited, Bread Street Hill, and Bungay, Suffolk, 1893.' He flicked back to the title page. He already knew what it said. For his own peace of mind, he needed to check again. There, below the title, in pompous, unyielding capital letters, was a name:

EDITED BY THOMAS J. WISE.

11

Sticky Fingers

The forging could not go on for ever. At some point it would have to stop. Now in his forties, Wise had a beautiful young wife, a large home in a desirable part of town, and one of the finest private libraries in the land. The essential oils business went from strength to strength. Money continued to roll in. His position in the book world was as secure as could be, with admiring letters arriving in the post every day, showing all the respect that was due to the pioneer of modern first editions. In a very real sense, the forgeries had served their purpose.

Criminals are sometimes content to drift off into retirement, to invest their ill-gotten gains in a modest country house where they might quietly bring up a family and indulge their hobbies and interests: gardening, perhaps, or horses. Wise was not that sort of a man. As his interest in the forgery game began to dwindle, so his crooked impulses would lead him down another shady avenue. It was time to diversify.

It all happened easily enough. Around the turn of the century, having clambered his way up the rungs of the book world, Wise turned his attention to the older volumes which had been beyond his reach as a novice. Not for him the pleasures of incunabula or medieval manuscripts, which demanded greater scholarly aptitude than he could ever attain. Nor the well-trodden path of the Shakespeare collector, whose interests were altogether too predictable, too obvious, and, ultimately, too expensive. Instead, Wise developed an interest in the marginally cheaper playbooks of Shakespeare's contemporaries and juniors: authors such as Christopher Marlowe, Ben Jonson, Thomas Heywood, and Thomas Middleton. Like the ephemeral nineteenth-century pamphlets that Wise had started by collecting and then forging, these individual quartos were fragile things. Frequently stitched together crudely without a protective binding, over the centuries their pages would have become stained by damp and mould or gone missing altogether. To find an example in fine condition was precisely the sort of book-hunting challenge that Wise and his contemporaries relished.

Yet condition could be manufactured, a fact that Wise knew only too well. In the early days of the Browning and Shelley Societies, he had regularly found copies of his legitimate facsimiles being touted as authentic first editions: corners creased and folded, paper smoked and rotted. He may even have been responsible for dressing one or two of these new books in old clothes. Who can say? The opposite, too, was possible—to take an old, damaged book and restore it to original condition, with seemingly untrimmed margins and pages unspoiled by the passage of time. In the right hands, even a frog might become a prince.

And frogs there were aplenty. During the heyday of book-hunting it was a common occurrence to stumble upon damaged quartos while trawling the back shelves of even the most ordinary bookshops. Men of taste usually steered clear of such examples because of their incompleteness. Indeed, Wise himself always cautioned neophyte collectors to keep away from imperfect books, to invest their money wisely. From time to time, though, an imperfect copy might come in useful. Imagine for a moment that one owns such a book—a Jonson quarto, perhaps—sad, lonely, sitting shamefully on the library shelves among its better-preserved fellows. For the most part, the volume is in excellent shape; it could almost have come off the press yesterday. But, frustratingly, at some point over the centuries the final pages have become detached and lost.

Now imagine stumbling upon another copy from the same edition, albeit in even worse condition: title page missing, dust packed into the gutter, margins eaten away by worms. But the same pages that are missing from the book at home are in this copy complete and surprisingly clean. There is a simple choice to be made. Either leave the volume to be picked up by a rival book-hunter. Or take it home, carefully snip the stitches holding this second copy together, remove the last few pages, and have them bound into the first copy. From two defective and unloved books one will have created a single perfect specimen—a book that might sit proudly on the shelves of any library.

This practice of fixing a damaged book with leaves taken from another copy was common enough among the bookmen of Wise's generation. Although such 'made-up' copies were frowned upon by bibliographical purists, most collectors had one or two on their shelves. Some went to extraordinary lengths to disguise the fact that their most prized volumes were monstrous hybrids.

Returning to our hypothetical Jonson quarto, even the untrained eye would be able to detect where the pages from one copy ended and those from another began. Because of the different conditions under which the two copies had been kept, each would have accumulated grime at different rates. The pages from one might be peppered with ruddy brown foxing; those from the other might be thick with unsightly scribbles and doodles. The margins of one might have been trimmed down, like nails to the quick, by some overzealous binder, while those of the other might be left uncut, in their original state.

How, then, to take pages from two different books, each bearing the scars of many lifetimes, and make them appear to belong to a single pristine copy? The answer involves skill, ingenuity, some chemicals, and a sharp blade. On the binder's workbench, both books would be carefully unstitched and assessed. If the margins of the additional sheets were drastically cropped, it might be necessary to have them bulked out to correspond to the remainder of the book. Matching sheets of paper would need to be found and carefully cut and pasted around the surviving pages. Even the unique spacing of the chain-lines, formed during the manufacture of the paper, could be made to match. When done well, the seam between new paper and old would be near-invisible, imperceptible under even the most sensitive fingertips. Only when the page was held up against the light could the very faintest scarring be discerned. If the replacement paper did not have the requisite watermark, an exceptionally skilled restorer would be able to supply a false one, scraping the outline of the necessary shape before washing the paper clean and pressing it flat. 'Magic or other secret means are not involved,' explained one practitioner of these dark arts, chuckling at the incredulity of his customers. 'When I explain that it is really only the knife that does it all, almost nobody wants to believe me, and yet it is the truth!' Any holes or rips would receive the same treatment.

Now that the sheets were complete, they would need to be gently bleached in a dilute solution of chlorinated lime, a potion for which each restorer had his own secret recipe. After two or three hours, they would be bathed in a weak vinegar solution, stopping the chemical reaction. To guard against crinkling or creases, all these disbound sheets would be individually pressed flat and placed on a rack to dry. At the end of this lengthy process, they ought to have faded to a uniform ivory. All that remained was to fold them, stitch them, trim them, and clothe them in a suitably fancy binding.

Only a handful of artisans were capable of such intricate restoration work. There were perhaps three in London with the requisite skills and experience. Luckily, Wise knew all of them: Mr Marlow at the Zaehnsdorf bindery in Covent Garden, experienced and esteemed for refined, stylish handiwork; the young upstarts at Sangorski and Sutcliffe, whose penchant for studding leather with precious metals and gemstones resulted in flashy and expensive but also rather tasteless bindings; and, of course, the firm of Riviere and Son, where a small team of skilled workmen quietly transformed a steady stream of defective old books into unblemished perfects, patching up wormholes, fixing torn margins, and adding facsimile pages. Unlike other binderies in town, Riviere's craftsmanship did not draw attention to itself. Good taste, unsurpassed technique, discretion—those were the qualities that made their work so special.

Although some of these high-class binderies kept 'hospital copies' of early books in stock, incompletes that might be dismembered to make up perfects, there was no guarantee that they would have the correct pages from the correct edition immediately to hand. For the customer, the difficulties of sourcing multiple copies of the same book, one containing leaves missing from the other, are obvious. Such discoveries require significant amounts of time, patience, and luck. A collector might go years between finding their first copy and chancing upon a suitable candidate for sacrifice.

Wise expended huge reserves of energy in tracking down appropriate 'hospital' leaves to make his imperfect books perfect. Frank Maggs recalled him often rummaging through the firm's damaged stock: 'I think we were able to help him here and there,' he said. Sometimes he would trade leaves with his fellow bibliophile George Aitken, who was more tolerant of defective copies and happy to accept some of Wise's cast-offs. But when push came to shove, Wise was not getting any younger, and he preferred to make his own luck. That left him with two options. While authentic leaves were of course to be preferred, he could always pay his friends over at Clay and Sons a visit and instruct them to print facsimile leaves to fill the gaps. But even their very oldest fonts would never be anything more than a rough approximation of the original seventeenth-century presswork. Pen-and-ink facsimile, where somebody meticulously copies out each letter on the page by hand, would be a more convincing and conventional approach. Legend even has it that one of the most celebrated facsimilists of the previous generation, a miniaturist called John Harris, had trouble detecting his own handiwork. At one point conservators at the British Museum had to call him out of retirement to point out the leaves that he had supplied for them, so indistinguishable were they from genuine print; 'it was only after a considerable search that he was able to detect them,' according to one amused eyewitness.

There was of course another path. If Wise could not find the necessary raw materials on the market, then he might steal them: whether that was a single page surreptitiously sliced from another copy or an entire gathering of leaves unlaced from a binding. The only question was where to find copies ripe for pilfering—and that was a question easily solved. After all, pristine copies of all these playbooks could be found within a mere twenty-minute bus ride of his house in Hampstead, in the national collection at the British Museum. The book forger would become a book thief.

Nobody knows precisely when the thefts started. Back in the early days, when he was just a young enthusiast researching literary curios on his days off, Wise would often have trudged past a display of mutilated books in the museum lobby: a trio of volumes with pages torn from their bindings, kept behind a screen next to the well-oiled doors of the reading room. The exhibit was accompanied by a note urging readers to join the librarians in 'condemning those who have thus so disgracefully abused the privilege of admission' while urging them to help 'prevent the occurrence of a similar outrage' by keeping an eye on their desk-mates. Far from warding off potential crooks, this cautionary display may have given Wise the idea for what was to come.

Or perhaps he learned from the gossip about sticky-fingered members which was perpetually bouncing around the reading room. There was the case of the well-known and highly esteemed journalist who, during a protracted spell of archival research, had opted against copying lengthy passages of text by hand and instead took to slicing them from the newspaper albums with his penknife. 'He was discovered and punished,' recalled one librarian with relish. Or the down-and-out artist who had been stealing prints and engravings from illustrated books. When his lodgings were searched, the constables recovered a large scrapbook bursting with plates which had been 'abstracted' from the museum volumes.

Reading privileges would of course be revoked from any thief caught in the act. Even more serious was the threat of prosecution. According to an 1845 statute, anyone caught stealing books from the national collection could face up to six months in prison, during which time he or she would be either put to hard labour or whipped. It is quite astonishing to think that Wise, so shrewd as a businessman, thought it worth the gamble. The overweening confidence that had served him so well was now pushing him to the edge of folly.

Yet this confidence was not entirely misplaced. Over many years of working under its vast dome, Wise came to an intimate understanding of security arrangements at the museum. Just as he had developed strategies for getting his fakes accepted into its collections, so too he identified weaknesses that might help him sneak material off the premises. There were two chinks in the museum's otherwise impregnable armour. Although the most precious tomes were kept under lock and key with a record of each time they were issued to a reader, that was not true for most of the quarto playbooks that Wise found so enticing. Even if a librarian were to discover that leaves had been stolen from one of the books, without this documentation there would be no way of tracing the damage back to him.

More perniciously, he learned that trusted scholars were sometimes granted their own desks in the large chamber north of the main reading room. As a junior reader, he would never have qualified for such treatment. Like all the others, he was forced to work under the watchful gaze of the superintendent, a severe-looking top-hatted individual who was, on a good day, equal parts 'a scholar, a gentleman, a police-constable and a boatswain's mate'. It was the responsibility of the superintendent and his staff to keep readers in line. To this end, his kiosk was mounted on a raised dais with unobstructed views across the rotunda. Not much escaped him.

But the north room operated under different rules. Desks were tucked into alcoves that studded the edge of the room, offering a space for quiet study without constant interruption. Footfall was minimal. By the turn of the century, with Wise firmly established as one of the nation's pre-eminent bibliographical authorities, he was as welcome in the north room as any member of staff. All the evidence suggests it was here that he would go about his foul business. If anyone spotted what he was doing, they kept their lips sealed. The most eloquent witnesses to his crimes are the books themselves. And the pattern they suggest is deeply shocking, both in the extent of the vandalism and the coarseness with which it was executed.

One theory holds that Wise must have taken the books home in the evening, where he could remove pages in the seclusion of his study. Because readers of Wise's stature were permitted to leave books out on their desks overnight, 'nothing would be simpler' than to sneak a quarto out of the library in one's pocket before returning it the following morning, leaves removed. The chances of anybody checking the desk overnight were practically nil. And yet the crudely torn stubs in the museum quartos paint a different picture. Their leaves were not removed with the surgical precision of the scalpel, as one might expect if they were taken home. Instead, Wise ripped pages from the books by hand. He did not pull them out in one clean motion, rather inch by inch, as though pausing to listen for footsteps on the marble floor behind him. Finishing the last tear and checking over his shoulder, he would flatten the leaves between the pages of his notebook, slip it into his jacket pocket, perhaps dab a bead of sweat from his brow, and calmly, confidently return the books to the issue desk and walk out of the front door.

Although the first few thefts had been committed so that he might perfect rarities in his own collection, Wise was soon palming off stolen material on his American dupe. By 1903 John Henry Wrenn had followed Wise deep into the terrain of early quarto playbooks. His London friend had promised to keep his eyes peeled for specimens worthy of his shelves, just as he did with the little Victorian pamphlets. The books soon came flooding in.

As usual, the purchases were all backed up by a first-rate provenance. Many of them came through a young dealer called William Calder, who, according to Wise, used to be an assistant at one of the big firms before recently setting out on his own. Under Wise's instructions, Calder was dispatched to look for bargains in the English provinces, trawling local auction houses and estate sales for books of interest. In this task he was even more successful than his employer could have hoped. 'This young fellow is proving a most useful chap,' Wise informed Wrenn. 'He is advertising for books, he tells me, in local papers in the country-towns, and is finding success.'

Many of the books he unearthed would have been either impossible to locate or wildly overpriced in London. There was, for instance, the copy of Thomas Dekker's *The Wonder of a Kingdom*, printed in 1636, which as Wise pointed out was a 'play of excessive rarity, and of the front rank of importance' to any serious collector. 'Calder asked me £25 for this copy, saying that it cost him £21. I paid him his price without demur, as it is very reasonable, and I have no reason to doubt his statement as to its cost to him.' Wrenn reimbursed him in full. On another occasion, Calder had come to Wise with a parcel of Alexander Pope first editions, supposedly the very copies that had been kept back by the original publisher. One of the books, a first of Pope's celebrated 1733 poem *An Essay on Man*, though 'soiled and slightly torn', was an astonishing copy: seemingly a previously unknown state of the original printing. Wise, thrilled by the discovery, kept this book for himself. 'If only I could live five hundred years', he joked, 'and compile a hundred bibliographies!!!'

It seems almost redundant to say that Calder did not exist. Years later, Wise would claim that this young bookseller had been conscripted in 1914, never to return from the western front. In truth, 'Calder' was a front for damaged books made whole with stolen leaves. The Dekker play had been completed with six stolen leaves; as for the Pope volume, Wise had taken very nearly the entire book from the museum, leaving behind only the title page. If one looks closely, it is possible to detect the spot where ink from the museum stamp had bled from inside the title page onto the first page of text, only to be scraped and bleached from the paper by the team at Riviere.

There were other personae, too. For instance, the mysterious 'Mr Hartley' from whom Wise claimed to have bought a cache of rarities in the spring of 1903. 'I had some difficulty to induce Mr Hartley to part with these plays,' he explained to Wrenn, recounting his techniques of persuasion. The hoard included a first edition of *The Bride*, a work of 1640 by the minor playwright Thomas Nabbes. This was a 'very fine' copy 'with no blemish of any kind', Wise assured his friend. The truth was rather different. He had picked up a damaged copy of the play at a knockdown price a few months earlier, before stealing the leaves needed to complete the copy from the museum. As for Mr Hartley, there was no such man.

By this point, Wise, now older than his mother at her death, was stealing to order. He knew precisely what he needed and would visit the museum specifically to take it. In 1906 he gleefully announced that he had snapped up a job lot of sixty-four playbooks from an enigmatic and deeply private individual calling himself 'Mr Wilson'. Wise would be keeping only four of the books for himself, all first editions that he did not already own. The remainder would be going to Wrenn for £640—according to Wise a 'fair, moderate, and reasonable price (not a bargain, but fair and reasonable)', especially so when the condition of the books was taken into account: 'vastly superior to the ordinary market copies', he gloated. This was a lie.

Among the collection was a handsomely bound first edition of Christopher Marlowe's famous tragedy *The Jew of Malta*, printed in 1633. It was a desirable volume. Only a few years earlier, the distinguished London bookseller Sotheran and Co. had accidentally advertised their copy at a mere three pounds and ten shillings: a mighty blunder from a firm that was already notoriously gaffe-prone. Within hours of the catalogue going out to customers, Sotheran's was inundated with offers for the book. Their reputation for having a 'bargain in every catalogue' was on this occasion perhaps a little too close to the bone, as it had been that time they mistakenly listed Browning's *Pauline* for a mere shilling when the average price was approaching a thousand dollars.

Six months transpired between Wise reporting his purchase and Wrenn eventually receiving his copy of *The Jew of Malta*, leaving plenty of time for the book to undergo major surgery. In this instance, the work done was no simple matter of inserting pilfered museum leaves into a damaged volume before dispatching it to Chicago. Wise wanted to keep the very best for himself. And that meant a degree of mixing and swapping. Whenever he bought a new book for Wrenn, he would assess the condition against his own copy. If the new copy had certain leaves in better shape than the one already on his shelves, he would quietly switch them over before patching the gaps with material purloined from the museum.

Wise often pulled this trick, swapping inadequate material from his own books into those he bought for Wrenn. In one instance, he even pinched leaves from a book that Wrenn had personally shipped over to him, entrusting him with having it repaired and rebound by the binders in London, whose craftsmanship was superior to their Chicago counterparts. That is precisely what happened with the American's new copy of *The Jew of Malta*. Various leaves were transplanted by Wise into his own copy of the book, on account of their superior condition, while some of the inferior leaves from Wise's copy found their way into the new one. The remaining gaps were filled in the usual way: by theft. Far from the 'vastly superior' volume crowed by Wise in his correspondence, Wrenn was buying a patchwork quilt of stolen and discarded second-rate materials.

As usual, the actual work of restoration and rebinding was outsourced to Riviere and Son, which Wise entrusted with this kind of special work. In most cases, there is nothing to suggest that the staff at Riviere thought these jobs out of the ordinary. Making up perfect copies was a major component of their business. It was quite normal for a customer to come in and instruct them to reconstruct a perfect specimen, especially a longstanding client like Mr Wise, who liked to see his books uniformly decked in gilt morocco.

But in the case of *The Jew of Malta*, at least, someone must have turned a blind eye. Because unlike all his earlier commissions, in which the additional material could have come from anywhere, here the closing leaves were taken from the museum copy. And on the very last page of the book, next to the concluding 'FINIS', was the official British Museum stamp. Naturally, the stamp had to go. Wise could not afford for his golden goose to suspect him of dishonest behaviour, let alone of so petty a crime as theft. He instructed his binder to have all trace of the museum stamp razored from the sheet. The cut itself was neat and the repair near-invisible. On one side of the page, the missing text was supplied in pen-and-ink facsimile. Any difference between this and the surrounding printed text was imperceptible to all but the most discerning eye—such an eye as Wise knew Wrenn did not possess.

Wise was not in the habit of trusting people on faith alone. Although the manager at Riviere, one Mr Arthur Calkin, enjoyed a reputation for discretion, the forger must have had some hold over the man, some firm assurance that he would keep his mouth shut. Maybe that hold was personal: perhaps a family secret or knowledge of illicit dealings. Maybe it was a bond of friendship. When, in 1928, Wise presented the binder with one of his own books, he inscribed the front endpaper 'For Arthur Calkin From his best friend Thos. J. Wise'.

Or perhaps Wise simply allowed his money to do the talking. His custom was worth a good deal, after all. He was spending hundreds of pounds on the binder's services every year, not only on books for his own library but on those belonging to Wrenn and his other friends and clients. If Riviere refused to repair a book they suspected had been stolen, would not Wise have threatened to take his business elsewhere: to Zaehnsdorf or even to Sangorski and Sutcliffe? It is tempting to imagine Calkin sweating over the moral quandary of rebinding leaves that he knew to have been stolen from the Museum. But maybe he did not particularly care, so long as Wise continued to pay his bills in a timely fashion. Easier simply to pretend not to notice and to follow his most valuable customer's instructions.

What cannot be doubted is that Calkin knew everything that was going on. When one of the younger apprentices at the firm, later an employee of the British Museum, grew curious about where Wise was finding all these loose leaves, and finally plucked up the courage to ask Calkin, he received a shockingly blunt answer. 'He steals them, of course!' After several more days of 'anxious consideration', he asked the same question to Mr Strong, the chief restorer at Riviere, whose scalpel and paste had transformed a thousand ugly ducklings into swans. He received the same answer. This trainee binder, who later admitted that as a young man he had 'rather idolised Wise', did not tell a soul for more than thirty years. To this day, the secret of Riviere's complicity has remained just that—a secret.

Once his books had returned, immaculate, from the workshop, Wise would paste his bookplate inside the front cover. The finishing touch to any addition to the Ashley Library, this bookplate was also an unambiguous marker of ownership. At the centre of the ornate design are two beautiful winged angels: one blowing a trumpet, the other clasping a billowing scroll that reads 'THOMAS JAMES WISE. HIS

BOOK.' Except some of the reading material in the Ashley Library was not rightfully his at all.

One can learn a lot about a collector by looking at their bookplate. Forman's shows the man himself, head buried in a book, oblivious to the world around him. Wrenn put his Chicago mansion front and centre, supported by a deep-rooted bough of oak. The Pre-Raphaelite flair of Wise's design for the Ashley collection gestured to his love of Rossetti and Swinburne. But more telling were the verses at the bottom of the plate, plucked from a longer poem by Francis Bennoch, an amateur Victorian rhymester who was also, like Wise, a professional man of business:

> BOOKS BRING ME FRIENDS
> WHERE'ER ON EARTH I BE,
> SOLACE OF SOLITUDE—
> BONDS OF SOCIETY!

There are several ways of reading the lines. In the context of the full poem, it is very clear that the books *are* the friends, bringing comfort and contentment in even the most secluded of places. And yet this isolated extract seems to speak to the acquisitive, covetous urge that had long been burrowing its way through Wise's mind like some ravenous worm. Books *bring* Wise friends from beyond his study; they are his centre of gravity; people come to him to see them and to learn from him. People admire him, even love him for the library he has assembled. If only they knew the truth.

12

Chemical Wood, Traces of Rag

Cecil Clay leaned back in his chair and assessed the two young men sitting across the table. They made for a strange pair: one immaculately turned out in crisp tailored worsted and the other slouched in threadbare corduroy. A tobacco pipe could be seen poking out of the second man's breast pocket, crammed in alongside a grubby handkerchief that may once have been white but was now a drab shade of taupe. In a vague nod to decorum, he wore a scraggly knitted tie around his neck. Clay did not look too closely at the tie, but he would swear it bore traces of lunch.

Carter took the lead. With characteristic diplomacy, he explained to the present head of the Clay printing dynasty that he and his partner worked in the rare books business. Over the past year, they had been investigating some highly coveted Victorian first editions that they believed to be modern forgeries. They had recently discovered that one particularly desirable book was printed in a unique combination of two different fonts, and that this unique combination could be traced to Clay and Sons. Carter then explained that his friend Pollard here had now located the same font in other rare first editions, some of them supposedly printed as early as 1842 and in places from Manchester to Massachusetts. Pollard confirmed this with a nod. These 'first editions' included works by everyone from Browning to Tennyson, Wordsworth to Ruskin, Dickens to Eliot.

They had since written to the foreman at the Clay press, Carter added, and had earlier that week received a reply confirming several of their guesses. Pollard pulled the foreman's letter out of his pocket and placed it deliberately on the table. The letter thanked Mr Pollard for his inquiry and informed him that the font used to print their 1893 facsimile of Matthew Arnold's *Alaric at Rome*, as prepared for the press by Mr Thomas James Wise, was known in the workshop as Clay's Long Primer No. 3. The letter told how, in 1876, the firm had purchased a set of Long Primer No. 20 from the P. M. Shanks typefoundry. After encountering problems with the kerned letters breaking in their high-speed presses, they had replaced the 'f' and 'j' characters with a newly designed kernless set, and substituted in a different question mark, making the new hybrid No. 3. The foreman couldn't remember precisely when this happened but would hazard a guess it was at some point between 1880 and 1883.

Cecil Clay asked if he could look over the letter. Pollard gestured for him to go ahead. He read it through carefully before looking back up at the pair of them, brow creased. Granting all this was true, Clay acknowledged that his firm must indeed have printed the books in question. There was no arguing with the facts. But he was not sure what more he could tell them. 'I do wish I could help,' Clay sighed. If he knew the name of the person who had commissioned the books, he would gladly tell them. But, regretfully, the company ledgers went back no further than 1911. Everything from before that date had been destroyed when the workshop was relocated from London to the small market town of Bungay in Suffolk. The name of the forger— whoever he may be—was now lost. Clay pushed the letter back across the table and offered his visitors a penitent shrug. What else was there to say?

The two booksellers began to shuffle back on their chairs, but before they got up to leave, Clay wished to insist on one thing. There could be no suggestion of impropriety among his staff. Back when he had been a mere novice on the workshop floor some forty years earlier, he explained, there had been a tremendous vogue for little facsimile pamphlets and keepsakes, all of which had been perfectly above board. Respectable men of letters such as Dr Furnivall and Mr Wise were always stopping by with new commissions for the Shelley or

Browning Societies. Often these involved putting an earlier date or the name of a different printer to the title page. Carter and Pollard needed to understand that his staff were jobbing craftsmen and not experts in rare books. Perhaps the printers had simply assumed these forgeries were legitimate facsimiles or collectibles. Perhaps someone deceived them.

Conclusive proof that the books were all fakes followed later in the spring. It is impossible to say whether the idea for testing the chemical make-up of the paper came from Pollard or from Carter. While the former was the more astute bibliographer, the latter was the aficionado of detective stories. He would have known from his reading that any competent detective might use all manner of scientific techniques for the analysis of unknown substances: observing them under magnification or swabbing them with chemical reagents. Anyone familiar with the Sherlock Holmes stories understood that chemical tests existed for identifying traces of human blood; early in their very first adventure, Watson strolls into the laboratory to find Holmes mixing a substance that will react with haemoglobin. Might not the same be possible with different compositions of paper?

There was good reason to think that, in this instance, such a test would yield results. For hundreds of years, paper had been manufactured almost exclusively from cotton and linen rags. However, in the middle of the nineteenth century a scarcity of rag-cloth forced paper mills to begin using grass and straw as alternative ingredients. It was not a happy substitution. The resulting paper was thin, brittle, and ugly. So perturbed were the newspaper proprietors by this new printing stock that in 1854 *The Times* offered a thousand pounds to anyone who discovered an effective replacement. The prize went unawarded for six years until, in 1861, it was announced that Spanish esparto grass could be used to make paper that was more robust in feel and more elegant in appearance. Several years later, an American inventor discovered a method for dissolving woodchips into a synthetic pulp from which an even sturdier paper could be formed. Using sulphuric acid, a Swedish mill commercialised the method, introducing sheets made from chemical wood to the English market for the very first time in 1874.

Each of these substances—rag-cloth, straw, esparto, chemical wood—reacted differently when exposed to different chemicals. In their 1888 textbook on papermaking, which included an entire chapter on the 'determination of composition of papers', the celebrated chemists Charles Edward Cross and Edward John Bevan explained that while esparto turns blue in an iodine solution, paper manufactured from wood-pulp will turn a deep, mucky yellow. Under a high-powered microscope, chemical wood can be distinguished by its flat, ribbon-like fibres, with pitted indentations along the face, whereas cotton fibres will appear twisted and intertwined. Combined with a historical knowledge of precisely when each of these different ingredients was introduced to paper manufacture, the chemical tests outlined by Cross and Bevan might prove powerful evidence for dating the suspected forgeries.

Pollard already had an inkling that the *Sonnets* was not printed on old-fashioned rag paper, despite never having laid eyes on a copy. Before being fed into the press, rag sheets were usually wetted, better to take the impression of the type. This process results in a slight fuzziness around the edges of the lettering, barely distinguishable even to experts, where the damp paper absorbs the ink. Inspecting the Morgan copy of the *Sonnets* in New York, though, Stanley Morison reported that it looked as though it had been printed dry. The edges of the letters were crisp, almost as though the ink was sitting atop the paper and not absorbed into it. Since the method of dry printing became widespread only with the introduction of esparto paper in 1861, it stood to reason that the *Sonnets* could not have been printed before that date.

The logic was sound, the evidence less so. There was something discouragingly impressionistic about feathery letter-edges or the lack thereof. It was difficult to imagine persuading a sceptical jury with such slender evidence. If even experts struggled to identify the signs, what chance had the layman? But chemical analysis was another story. If the paper could be conclusively dated by scientific means, a conclusion of forgery would be inevitable. Who could possibly dispute it?

There was only one snag. The tests proposed by Cross and Bevan were, by their nature, destructive. And the books that needed to be tested were collectible rarities. Carter's survey had already established that there were only two copies of the *Sonnets* remaining in England, both kept under lock and key in the Ashley library. It was hardly likely that Wise would allow a sample to be snipped from the pages of either copy. And the prospect of a rival American collector permitting them to tamper with such a precious volume seemed equally slim. Pollard was resigned to failure on this front; if there was no suitable copy to be tested, he said, then testing would not be able to take place. It was that simple. Yet his partner had a plan.

While in New York the previous summer, Carter had made the acquaintance of one Flora Livingston, the rare books librarian at Harvard and a formidable bibliographer in her own right. The interesting thing, Carter explained to his friend, was that Livingston was engaged in a longstanding scholarly feud with Wise. In a series of publications on Swinburne, Kipling, and Robert Louis Stevenson, Livingston had respectfully pointed out small inconsistencies and deficiencies in Wise's bibliographical pronouncements, based on her own analysis of the books in question. Never one to take criticism lightly, Wise had retaliated by publicly denouncing her scholarship as 'hopelessly ill-informed and misleading'. It was the same scorched-earth policy that Wise pursued with all his critics.

What were the odds that Livingston could be persuaded to cut a paper sample from the Harvard copy of the *Sonnets*? Carter pondered. If he clarified to her that Wise might be implicated in the scandal, and that the results of a chemical analysis might very well prove the deficiencies of his scholarship, might not Livingston go along with the plan? It would not be easy, to be sure. But it was certainly worth writing to her, to explain what he had in mind.

It was the middle of April before Carter received a tremulous letter from the Harvard librarian. 'I have had the courage to trim off a little slip of paper from the bottom of a badly folded leaf of the *Sonnets*,' she told him, with the air of a whisper. 'It will never show, and if it does no one will know the who or the why.' No credit for her part in the investigation was necessary, she assured them. Indeed, it would be better for all concerned if nobody knew that she had taken scissors to one of the library books, a practice generally frowned upon in the profession. 'The scrap of paper came from America, that is enough,' she said, adding that the enquirers ought to investigate a pair of Rudyard Kipling pamphlets that she thought suspicious.

With this crucial new piece of evidence up his sleeve, and paper samples from the other pamphlets on the way, Pollard approached the lab of Cross and Bevan to conduct the necessary testing. The paper chemistry report arrived within a fortnight of these final pieces of the puzzle. It was divided into three parts. The first grouped together books which, when inspected under magnification, showed definite evidence of chemical wood pulp. The second grouped books in which esparto and small traces of chemical wood could be detected. And the third contained books printed on esparto paper. Twenty-seven volumes were tested in total. Half contained some trace of chemical wood. None of them was printed on pure, old-fashioned rag paper of the variety used before 1861.

The verdict on the *Sonnets* was definitive. 'Chemical wood, trace of rag.' The ruling might just as easily have comprised a single word. Fake.

Scientific confirmation of the forgery raised an obvious question. Who was responsible? Undeniably, the forgeries were all part of the same group: they often appeared together at auctions and in salerooms and could usually be found in the same libraries and private collections. Find the person who forged the *Sonnets* and one would find the person who forged the entire group. The dead end at Clay's was frustrating but, on reflection, no disaster. If the mastermind behind the *Sonnets* could not be traced from the print shop, there was always the possibility of following all the known copies back to a common source. And that was precisely what Carter had already been doing.

At the start of the investigation there were several suspects. In many ways, the most likely culprit was Richard Herne Shepherd—now dead—a man known for his illegitimate Tennysons. During his lifetime, Shepherd had scraped a living as a literary hack, editor, and general odd-jobber to the antiquarian book trade. It was a hand-to-mouth existence, with any spare pennies going either to books or to the bottle. Back in the early days of the trend for modern authors, he could sometimes be spotted lurking in the dingier corners of the British Museum: 'a tall, angular man, often shabbily dressed, with shoulders rounded from long nights of poring over books'. Friends recalled him as an eccentric but gentle soul, someone with the voice of an angel and the manners of a saint, and whose peculiar habit of walking in the middle of the road made him the sworn foe of London's cabbies and coachmen. In his later years, on those days when he did make it to the museum, he had either trudged or hitched a ride all the way into town from Putney, where he lodged in a draughty garret over a roadside inn. One suspects that if Shepherd had not existed, Dickens would have made him up.

Shepherd was, by profession, a literary scrounger. He would trawl through old magazines and periodicals searching for early trifles by major authors. He would then publish these pieces—usually scraps by Tennyson or Browning or Swinburne—as standalone pamphlets and pocket a few pounds from the sales. Such printings were, of course, entirely unauthorised and often done against the explicit wishes of the authors. But Shepherd viewed copyright less as a matter of ironclad legal ownership than as one of temporary custodianship. Once a poem or essay had been allowed to go out of print, what harm could be done by reissuing it in a little pamphlet? If indeed it was a crime, it was a victimless one. So far as Shepherd was concerned, such literary pickings were fair game.

This attitude often got him into trouble. By the letter of the law, Shepherd's pamphlets and facsimiles were all piracies, and to make matters worse, he wasn't always very honest with customers who assumed that he was selling pristine originals. In 1875 his activities provoked the ire of the Poet Laureate himself. Tennyson's poem *The Lover's Tale* comprises more than a thousand lines of laughably ambitious blank verse. He wrote it while still a teenager and, in a fit of hubris, privately printed the text in his twenties at his own expense, before suppressing the resulting booklet out of embarrassment. Through a friend in the antiquarian trade, Shepherd somehow managed to get his hands on one of the very few remaining copies of this little booklet and, before it went up for auction, transcribed the text. This duplicate then became the basis for his own unauthorised reprint.

Tennyson was protective of his literary legacy—and justifiably so, given his status as Britain's national poet. The news that this errant piece of juvenilia was now accessible in a fresh pamphlet edition put him into a great rage. He swiftly initiated legal proceedings against Shepherd, which Shepherd duly lost (although Tennyson, in a charitable mood and learning that the defendant was little more than a pauper, agreed to pay the legal fees). Shepherd ended his days in disgrace, an object of abuse in the literary journals, attacked by the very men of letters he had once so profoundly revered. In 1895, poverty-stricken and overwhelmed by madness and drink, he died in Camberwell House Lunatic Asylum.

If one squinted, the dates could just about be made to line up. The discovery of the 'Reading' *Sonnets* had been announced to the world in 1894, a little before Shepherd's final descent into oblivion. A man in his condition would have ample reason for fabricating literary rarities. There was also the curious geographical coincidence. According to the story told in his bibliography, Wise had first been shown copies of the *Sonnets* by the elderly Dr Bennett, whose home in Camberwell was only a few minutes' walk from the asylum where Shepherd found refuge in his final days. The question was this: could Shepherd and Dr Bennett have been in cahoots? With the former somehow arranging for the *Sonnets* to be printed and the latter duping Wise into accepting them as genuine? Saying that he had been given the books by Miss

Mitford? Disarming him with a generous supper of hot buttered toast and sausages?

It was possible, Carter supposed. But the longer he pondered it, the less likely it all seemed. Although Shepherd had been convicted of literary piracy, there was nothing to suggest that he had ever backdated a pamphlet—whatever Wise claimed. And that was, after all, the *modus operandi* of the forger. Then there was the fact that this cluster of fakes appeared to come almost exclusively from the press of Clay and Sons. Over his long and varied literary career, Shepherd had used the firms of Strangeways and Walden, Ogden and Co., and Brawn and Brawn for his printing; but never Clay. After discussing the matter with his older brother, Cecil Clay reassured Carter by letter that 'we are both of us practically certain that the firm printed nothing for Mr Richard Herne Shepherd'. How likely, then, that he should have turned to them for such a sensitive and potentially risky sequence of jobs?

The questions kept coming. If Shepherd was behind the forgeries, why hadn't he included any of them in his own bibliographies of modern authors? What about the forgeries that came onto the market only after Shepherd and Bennett died in 1895? Admittedly, it was possible that the books had all been printed before that date and that a third man continued to distribute them. But this seemed like conjecture of the most desperate kind. Possibility is not proof.

The final nail in the coffin was the discovery that one of the forgeries printed in the distinctive Clay's Long Primer No. 3—with its kernless 'f' and curious '?'—was a copy of *The Lover's Tale* from 1870, seemingly designed to antedate Shepherd's own piracy of Tennyson's poem. It seemed hardly possible, let along plausible, that Shepherd would forge his own handiwork; particularly so because this was an episode from which he had emerged in disgrace. Unless Shepherd was playing an unusually baroque game, loaded with twists and turns, someone else had to be responsible.

If not Shepherd and Bennett, then who? Carter had a theory. For him, it all hinged on the identity of the person who had leaked that apocryphal tale of the Brownings on honeymoon in Italy—Elizabeth slipping the manuscript sonnets into Robert's pocket; Robert persuading Elizabeth to allow them to be printed—to Edmund Gosse.

Gosse had never divulged his source, and in his later years he embraced Wise's version of events: that the story had come from Browning himself. Having chased up each lead and consulted every letter, Carter decided that this claim couldn't possibly be true. Browning had known nothing about such a book, he was sure—and how could he have done when the typography and the paper both confirmed the *Sonnets* as a much later fake? His hunch was confirmed by the discovery of a letter from Browning to the essayist Leigh Hunt, published for the first time in 1933, in which the poet explicitly stated that he didn't even know of the sonnets' existence until three years after they were written. All the evidence indicated that the romantic tale fed to Gosse was precisely that: a romantic tale. And given that the story was obviously intended to validate the fake *Sonnets*, it stood to reason that the person who conceived the story must also have made the book.

After much reflection, Carter believed that person to be Thomas James Wise himself. Who else could it be? In the first week of 1933, against a backdrop of frost and dwindling daylight, Carter prepared a rough dossier, running through each of the alternatives and dismissing each in turn. The logic was inescapable. 'Gosse's unnamed informant was Wise,' he concluded, 'and he is responsible for the whole thing. He waits till Browning is some years dead: tells Gosse this story, with the unconvincing bit about the promise to Browning not to divulge it while he was alive and a proviso that his own name shall not be mentioned: shows Gosse his copy of the book. Gosse swallows it readily enough—after all, it is plausible, and he would trust Wise to have verified its authenticity up to the hilt—and it makes a nice prologue to his article on *Sonnets from the Portuguese*.' From this point onwards, the authenticity of the book was bolstered by Wise's formidable reputation and the vested interest of those collectors who had already paid high prices for their copies. 'He has thus built up out of nothing an imposing façade of authority', explained Carter, putting the book 'on a pinnacle of eminence so secure that it has never occurred to anybody to question its antecedents'.

The document outlining these doubts was potentially incendiary. Carter kept it private at first, sharing the pages only with Pollard. On further discussion, a copy was sent to Mr Mudie, the dour bookseller at Quaritch whose scepticism had first prompted Carter to delve into this mystery. Mudie returned the typescript the following week. His comments were uncharacteristically encouraging. 'I agree with everything you have said,' he wrote. 'It is inconceivable to me that the book having been printed in 1847, Miss Mitford kept all the copies to herself. Was no copy given to Mrs Browning or to her husband or to anyone else?'

Mudie said nothing about the Wise theory, possibly because he didn't believe it, possibly because he wasn't yet ready to nail his colours to the mast. Pollard too remained on the fence. Certainly, he agreed that Wise must have been involved in some capacity. But whether he was a villain or a mere puppet was less obvious.

The pair of them spent many evenings in the back room of the Soho bookshop, huddled over the evidence, gas lamp glowing, sherry in their glasses and tobacco at their fingertips. Pollard would sit at the desk while Carter, having excavated a battered wicker armchair from beneath a mountain of loose papers and books, would recline and listen while his friend offered all the usual cautions against acting in haste and repenting at leisure. 'Even if Mr Wise's high character did not render it unlikely, there is absolutely no evidence that he forged them,' Pollard said. Nobody could deny that Wise had wrongly guaranteed the authenticity of the books, nor that he had purchased them in bulk and profited greatly from their sale. He had donated copies to libraries and gifted them to friends. He had done everything in his power to make them appear genuine. Those were not the actions of an innocent man. Even if Wise had acquired the *Sonnets* from Dr Bennett as he claimed, however unlikely that scenario now seemed, the same could not be said of all the other fakes to which he had given a clean bill of health.

At the very least Wise had been unforgivably stupid, Pollard told his friend. And yet, however tempting the leap, it did not necessarily follow that he was himself the forger. Occam's razor could be a dangerous tool. Best not wield it too enthusiastically lest one cut oneself.

At some point the two booksellers would need to confront Wise directly. But now was not the time. There remained one further avenue to explore. And it would change everything.

13
Putting on the Ritz

WISE was running late. Having enjoyed a pleasant Wednesday afternoon out and about town with Mrs Wise, he had returned home to Heath Drive in Hampstead to ready himself for a dinner that evening at the Ritz. Luck was working against him. The traffic had been awful on the ride home, leaving very little time to change into his formal attire. Panicked and puffing, he threw on a starched white shirt and collar, waistcoat, trousers, buffed up pumps. Pausing for a moment to knot his bow tie, he grabbed a jacket from his wardrobe and charged out the door to the waiting hackney.

Only once the cab pulled up outside the hotel half an hour later, and Wise thrust his arms into the jacket sleeves, did he realise his mistake. He had brought his morning coat and not his evening tails. The Ritz enjoyed a reputation as the stuffiest of London's grand hotels. Dress codes here were taken seriously. To 'ritz' was already in common parlance as a verb, capturing the haughty airs and high-handed condescension of the clientele. From a distance, it is almost possible to feel sorry for the old rotter, pushing past the doorman into the lobby, only to be greeted by contemptuous glances and mutterings. It was not the sort of mistake that the old Etonian Carter would make—nor even Pollard, whose insouciant sartorial rebellions suggested a surfeit of public school and Oxford college dining. But for Wise, a social climber whose snobbery was born of deep-seated status anxiety, the whole thing must have been quite excruciating.

To make matters worse, Wise had been invited to the Ritz for a very special occasion. The Roxburghe Club was without doubt the most exclusive and patrician of book collecting circles. Its foundations went back to the summer of 1812, when a group of bibliophiles dined together on the eve of the sale of the late Duke of Roxburghe's library—anticipated as the book event of the century, with many unique items coming onto the market for the first time in generations. Reluctant to let the event fade from memory, the diners decided to gather again the following year, and again the year after that. So the club was born. Each year, around the anniversary of the sale, the nation's premier collectors would congregate in London and toast 'the cause of bibliomania all over the world'. This year, on 27 June 1928, the annual dinner was to take place at the Ritz.

Like any club worth joining, the Roxburghe was exclusive. Membership was strictly limited to forty, with new entrants being invited only after existing members had died. Between them, they were generally acknowledged to possess the very finest private libraries in the kingdom. Most were plucked from the upper ranks of the aristocracy: gentlemen who had inherited their books from their fathers and from their fathers before them. Wise, by contrast, was the self-made man from Holloway, the man who had built his own collection from the ground up.

He had been elected to the club one year earlier, in 1927, a few months before his sixty-eighth birthday. At the time of joining, he was grilled by Sydney Cockerell, who had proposed him for the opening. The Roxburghe was a strictly amateur organisation, Cockerell explained. Professional booksellers and dealers were barred from its inner circle. He knew that Wise had done a lot of reprinting work over the years and wanted to confirm there was no possibility that he had ever profited from selling those books to other collectors. 'Oh no,' Wise assured him. 'No man has ever regarded his books in a less mercenary manner than I have throughout my active life.'

It seems quite astonishing that Cockerell, the same man who had warned collectors against Forman's dubious William Morris reprints all those years earlier, was so easily seduced by this blatant lie. But then again, Wise had proved himself capable of forging just about anything—and that included his own identity. At the Roxburghe Club dinners, Wise assumed the mask of a gentleman. The trick was convincing others as much as he had already convinced himself. Modulating his vowels, refining his manners, trotting out old anecdotes about descent from the ancient line of Wyse, he looked every inch the upper-crust bibliophile. Except, that is, for when he wore the wrong dress coat to dinner.

Membership of the Roxburghe crowned what had already been a decade of extraordinary energy and achievement. Wise's reputation had grown together with his fortune. In 1922, and to general acclaim, he had accepted the nomination for the presidency of the Bibliographical Society, perhaps the highest accolade in London's tight-knit book world. Two years later he was elected a Fellow of Worcester College, Oxford, in the course of which he was invited to view the shelves of some student bibliophiles, including those belonging to an ambitious but scruffy young man at Jesus College named Pollard. In 1926, this distinction was followed by an honorary MA from the university—an accomplishment for anyone, let alone a self-made man with no formal schooling. These accomplishments were enough, even, for him to get away with wearing his morning coat on an extravagant evening without any social ramifications beyond a few raised eyebrows.

Much of this success was founded on Wise's unassailable reputation as a connoisseur. The Ashley Library loomed over the book world, a monument to the ingenuity and scholarly integrity of its keeper. Visitors were invariably struck by the sheer perfection of the books that graced his shelves. 'From the first Mr Wise made it a rule never to procure a book that was not perfect, and he has consistently preached this doctrine of perfection to young and modest collectors who are more tolerant of the maimed and defective,' explained the Oxford scholar David Nichol Smith with a nod of approval. 'It is safe to say that no one who has seen the Ashley Library has ever seen another in which the condition of the books is so uniformly flawless.' In a more poetic vein, and alluding to Browning's famous lines 'Open my heart, and you will see / Graved inside of it ITALY!',

A. Edward Newton joked: 'I know the word which will be found graved on Mr Wise's heart when it is opened; it is the word CONDITION. Only books that are practically faultless need knock at Mr Wise's door.'

Time and money alone could never be enough to assemble such a collection without a profusion of knowledge, judgement, courage, and unwavering conviction. All were qualities that Wise possessed and in such a degree as put him 'in the front rank of the conquistadores', as one reviewer for the *Times Literary Supplement* put it in the spring of 1923. As for his unsurpassed profile as a scholar, 'Mr Wise has an unfair advantage,' continued this reviewer, allowing his envy to surface. 'Other bibliographers carry laborious notes from library to library, only to find that they have noted the wrong thing. Mr Wise has all the materials in one room, and has only to spread them out.'

Everyone could agree on the fact that, in the Ashley Library, Wise had shaped a 'great work of art', something more 'like a Palladian temple or an epic poem' than a common scholar's nook. With row upon row of old plays stacked to the ceiling, all bound uniformly by Riviere, the very walls themselves seemed to be clad in gilt morocco. Like the keeper of any great work of art, Wise liked to present himself less as the owner of these books than as their custodian for future generations. 'He considers their preservation as a kind of national duty,' wrote a close friend. 'Thus he has made out of his hobby a fixed life-work which gives it a real dignity, and which will carry his name down to posterity.'

Among the treasures of Heath Drive was one book of special beauty: a quarto-sized volume bound by Sangorski and Sutcliffe in crimson morocco, delicately lettered in gilt: 'A MEMENTO OF MR AND MRS ROBERT BROWNING'. Mounted inside the front cover of the volume, behind a glass panel framed by more gilt decoration, was a lock of Elizabeth Barrett Browning's dark chestnut hair, supposedly given to her beloved before their wedding day. Facing this relic, the accompanying sonnet (the eighteenth in the sequence) tooled into the leather in yet more gold:

> I never gave a lock of hair away
> To a man, Dearest, except this to thee,
> Which now upon my fingers thoughtfully
> I ring out to the full brown length and say,
> 'Take it.'

At the back of the volume was a companion lock cut from Robert Browning's hair after the poet died: short and silver-white. And, in the middle, tucked into a perfectly sized nook, with Elizabeth's lock before it and Robert's behind, an unbound copy of that most precious of modern firsts: the 'Reading' *Sonnets*.

With each passing year, questions mounted over where all these books would go once their present owner passed from this world to the next. To the British Museum? To Oxford? 'I do not know exactly what Mr Wise intends to be the future destiny of his books,' explained another friend, the French scholar Seymour de Ricci, 'but there is good reason to hope that they will be ultimately located in one of the national collections.' With American collectors paying over the odds in recent years, this could be 'England's last and only possible chance to secure a really first class series of its finest books to be preserved as a monument for future generations'. In the meantime, Wise was only too happy to share his books and his opinions with his peers. Never one to cloister himself away like some monkish pedant in his cell, Wise opened the Ashley Library to any respectable bibliophile who made an appointment. He always put on a goodly show for visitors. Nobody could deny his extraordinary powers of recall. The location of every book in the library was firmly committed to memory. A guest might express interest in one volume, only for Wise to zip across the room and up a stepladder to grab another, even more fascinating book from the shelf. As they sat together and admired the object, he would reel off those characteristic yarns about Browning and Rossetti and Ruskin. The library seemed perpetually to bathe in the twilight glow of the *fin de siècle*. Some guests developed a taste for his stories, returning often to absorb the wit and wisdom of Mr Wise. Others were understandably overwhelmed by the experience and never returned.

Wise liked nothing more than to preside over the book world, passing judgement on his rivals from the comfort of the Ashley Library. He had a terrifying reputation for summoning members of the antiquarian book trade to tea, over which he would school them on the fakes or piracies they had unwittingly listed in their catalogues. With high-handed aplomb, he would marshal all the thunder and righteous fury of the aggrieved scholar, excoriating negligent booksellers as scoundrels, thieves, and liars.

Inevitably, Wise's tales grew in the telling. One of his favourites concerned a lesser light of the trade, one W. T. Spencer, whom Wise had invited to Heath Drive to show him some original Shelley letters that Spencer had recently acquired for sale. 'I saw immediately that they were forgeries,' Wise chuckled. 'So I tore them up, handed the fragments back to Spencer, and said: Now then! You are at liberty to sue me for destroying your property!' In the book world this story had become the stuff of legend: the brave, honourable collector putting the unscrupulous dealer in his rightful place. 'In detecting the wiles of this class of deceiver, Mr Wise knows no rival,' one ally proclaimed. 'He is the terror of all fraudulent booksellers, and fakes are to him what rats are to a terrier.'

There was only one subject on which Wise was uncharacteristically silent: and that was the subject of Wise himself. Even close friends remarked on the difficulty of getting him to talk about himself and not his books. When questioned about his early years, he would spin into one of fifty well-oiled anecdotes about the meetings of the Shelley Society, or the first occasion on which he met Swinburne, or that time Dr Furnivall introduced him to Browning. His guests would naturally be regaled with his tales of aristocratic roots, but on the details of his upbringing, on the question of who he *was*, Wise was unable to be drawn out.

One of his closer companions around this time was the loquacious French collector James Bertrand de Vinchelés Payen-Payne. 'I visited him frequently—usually on Sundays,' he later recalled. 'I always found him most charming. He was very entertaining and full of talk. But somehow, when you had left him, and came to think over the talk, you realised that he hadn't told you nearly as much as you thought he had; that the things you expected and wanted to hear, especially about himself, never followed.' 'He was always charming to me,' remembered another frequent visitor, 'but there was always a veiled menace about him.'

Although he wouldn't acknowledge it, Wise's road to glory and the Roxburghe was paved by the deaths of three great men. Swinburne was first to go. The old poet went peacefully in his bed on 10 April 1909, the unswervingly loyal Theodore Watts-Dunton at his side till the very end. Wise was holidaying in Eastbourne when he heard. 'The gloom of today's news overshadows everything,' he wrote to Wrenn. 'Swinburne is dead, and in him has passed the last of the great English poets.'

Wise could not remain gloomy for long, though. With death, he knew, came opportunity. Swinburne had left everything to his most devoted friend. And Theodore, Wise guessed, would need to sell a good chunk of his new inheritance to settle his affairs. The possibilities ranged from the encouraging to the positively terrifying. A public sale of Swinburne's books would need to be avoided at all costs. The thought of such an event gave Wise the shudders: all those tussling bidders and underbidders; him stuck in the middle, trying to muscle his way to victory against wealthy American boors. The prospect of the collection going through an intermediary was very nearly as bad: someone skimming a profit on books that, in Wise's judgement, were rightly his for the taking.

No, the only acceptable option was that Watts-Dunton would sell him the books quickly and privately, before any rivals could catch the scent. A few days after the poet's coffin had been driven from Putney to Waterloo, and thence by train to the family burial ground on the Isle of Wight, Wise paid Theodore a visit. The old man looked anxious and pallid, Wise thought. Ill health had prevented him accompanying his friend to his final resting place. His moustache, normally dyed a deep shade of brown, was showing grey at the roots.

He unloaded on Wise all the trouble he had endured over the past week: earnestly attempting by cable and by telephone to convey Swinburne's last wishes to his relatives. The poet had remained a vicious freethinker to the very end, Theodore explained, and had bluntly requested that he was not to be buried according to the rites of the Church of England. This news had caused upset among the more respectable branches of the Swinburne family. Theodore shook his head sadly. Wise arranged his features into an approximation of sympathy.

As for The Pines itself, the place had not changed much over the years. Wise was chaperoned up the stairs and past the same imposing Rossetti paintings, now bespeckled with dust. After a moment of fiddling with the keys, Theodore shuffled him into the same book-lined study where, what seemed a lifetime ago, an excitable Swinburne had so eagerly thrust his favourite volumes onto Wise's lap. The room now was cold and quiet and still. Theodore wilted into a chair. Outside, through the study window, Wise glimpsed the marble Venus in the garden. It was stained green with algae.

Although the two men had lived under the same roof for three decades, certain parts of the house had been Swinburne's domain entirely, leaving poor old Theodore with the mammoth task of calculating what, exactly, he had inherited. The books, he knew, were valuable. So too the poetic manuscripts, which he had been carefully filing away ever since Swinburne first moved into the house. But precisely how many books there were and precisely how much they were worth was a mystery to him.

Would Wise be willing to help him go through the study? Theodore asked. After all, Wise was a man of integrity, an expert of the highest tier, a friend to the poet for some twenty years. Who else could boast such credentials? By way of thanks, he promised that, if he decided to sell, Wise would be granted right of first refusal on anything that piqued his fancy. The entirety of the books and manuscripts would be his to buy, if he wanted them. Without wishing to look too eager, Wise agreed. He did not need to be asked twice.

The pair of them settled down to work that very afternoon. At first, Theodore wasted much time in ferrying about the most notable treasures of Swinburne's library: mighty association copies, important manuscripts with the author's corrections, many of the same ancient books that Swinburne had shown off twenty years earlier. And yet, now as then, Wise was distracted by the bundles of enticingly enigmatic papers stuffed into the bottom shelves and cupboards. Plainly these parcels had remained undisturbed ever since his first visit. It took him a while to convince Theodore that they ought to open a few of them to see what they contained. Once they started unwrapping each dust-laden package—slowly, carefully—the process became difficult to stop. What they were finding went beyond either of their imaginings.

'It appears to have been Swinburne's habit from his Oxford days to destroy nothing that came from his pen,' Wise later reflected, basking in the thrill of the discovery. Letters, manuscripts, bills, notes, lists, posters, circulars, proof-sheets: all had been bundled together, wrapped in brown paper, tied with string, laid to one side, and forgotten about. Most of the material was ordinary rubbish, the sort of workaday jottings that usually end up in the waste-paper basket. But hidden among the dross was much of value and importance: a plethora of unpublished poems, short stories, and critical essays.

These writings were not, as Wise put it, 'the mere sweepings of the poet's work-room, or compositions discarded by him as not being up to the required standard of excellence'. At the height of his powers, Swinburne's verse had often been too shocking, too adventurous for many publishers and literary editors. Fired by an intense thirst that no quantity of drink could sate, and by a tripartite obsession with flagellation, cannibalism, and sapphism, much of his 'most virile work' failed to find a home. At the same time, Wise explained, the poet's 'intense and ceaseless energy rendered his output prolific'. As a result, reams of unpublished and perhaps unpublishable stories, poems, and essays would pile high on Swinburne's desk. Whenever more space was required, this mountain of pages would be bunched together and left in a corner. That is, until Wise came along.

The process of acquiring these manuscripts for the Ashley Library continued all through summer and into autumn. Two or three times a week, Wise would take the train out to Putney. And two or three times a week, he would return to Hampstead in a taxicab, boot packed with spoils. His technique for procuring literary treasures had lost none of its early artfulness. When Theodore dug out the original manuscript of *Hertha*, the 'mystic atheistic democratic anthropologic poem' that Swinburne ranked as his single highest achievement, he originally wanted to keep hold of it, asking Wise to have it bound for him by Riviere in the same manner that they bound Wise's own books. It took several hours of gentle persuasion for Theodore to loosen his grip on the manuscript.

'How could I let it remain there?' Wise brooded. 'I had to worry myself for hours, and it was like drawing a tooth blessed with a double allowance of fangs to get it out of him. But get it I did at last.' Likely thinking that he was getting the better end of the bargain, Theodore eventually relinquished the manuscript for the hefty sum of forty-five pounds. Wise made a goodly show of foot-dragging, but secretly knew he was getting a bargain. 'I would have gone much higher rather than left it,' Wise confided with a triumphant smirk. The following morning he sent Theodore a cheque.

Wise's old companion Edmund Gosse, who in 1896 had been manoeuvred into publishing the fantasy of how Elizabeth Barrett Browning supposedly came to have her *Sonnets* printed in Reading, and who was now writing a biography of Swinburne, was quite appalled by the sums of money being spent at The Pines. 'I lose all power of speech when I think of the gluttony and shamelessness of this old toad,' he told Wise, with an eye to Watts-Dunton. 'Why do you go on feeding him with money in this way? Surely the old manuscripts which he dribbles out to you cannot be worth half the money you so generously give him. Left to himself, he would have made only hundreds where you have paid him thousands.' But Wise disagreed. Whenever he was with Theodore, his guise was always that of the literary apostle—an ardent disciple of Swinburne who saw literary merit in even the poet's most meagre scraps. But, as ever with Wise, this was a mask. His hawkish eye was more finely attuned to matters commercial, his cast of mind firmly that of the commodities trader. Swinburne manuscripts were a 'gilt-edged security', he believed. In this he was to be proved correct.

While the plum manuscripts were all destined for the shelves of the Ashley Library, for lesser jewels this was merely a temporary stopover. Their eventual resting place was to be on the other side of the Atlantic, among all the other books that Wise had sold to Wrenn over the years. Later that summer, when Wrenn made his annual holiday to London, he accompanied Wise on a pilgrimage to The Pines: hallowed ground to Wrenn, but a hunting ground for his friend. Having told Theodore—poor, trusting Theodore—that he would be treasuring these manuscripts until his last breath, Wise immediately flipped them for profit.

As for the newly discovered manuscripts, Wise was far too canny to let them sit idly on his shelves when there was money to be made. Against the wishes of Swinburne's heir, and with the assistance of the perpetually eager Gosse, he set about printing these unpublished works in his own bijou editions. His scheme followed the usual pattern: attractively printed on fancy paper in strictly limited private runs, just like the early Shelley Society pamphlets. As before, they proved extremely profitable.

The betrayal stung Theodore. He tried as best he could to prevent further publication, writing ardent letters to the dailies denouncing all these new Swinburne books as piracies that tarnished the immortal memory. But there was very little he could do. 'Would not the greedy old gent at Putney *curse* us if he knew what we were printing,' Wise gloated in one of his letters to Gosse. 'He can stop publications, but the law gives him no power over private printing.' For a time, Theodore banished Wise from the house and began selling his inheritance to other London dealers. It was too little too late. Wise had already purchased vast numbers of Swinburne's books and manuscripts, spending the quite extraordinary sum of three thousand pounds. His profits from selling them on to other collectors and booksellers, combined with the proceeds from printing the newly discovered poems and essays, have been estimated at more than three times that sum. It was the transaction of a lifetime.

Wrenn would follow Swinburne to the grave two years later, in 1911. When Wise conveyed his condolences to the family, he told them how deeply the loss grieved him. He meant it. The American would be difficult to replace. Before the end, his custom was worth around a thousand pounds a year.

With Wrenn it had been easy enough for Wise to present himself as a helpful intermediary between the domains of the moneyed collector and the professional booksellers; equally at home in both camps and yet belonging truly to neither. As he continued to glide up the ranks of the book world, this guise would become more difficult to sustain. For all the excitement at The Pines, and although he had long since ceased production, not once had Wise forgotten about the bounty of old forgeries that remained in his cupboards, printed years earlier and now safely stowed away. With Wrenn gone, he would need to find a new way of selling them: a friendly bookseller, perhaps—one who wouldn't ask too many questions.

Luckily, Wise had the perfect candidate for the job. Over the past decade, he had enjoyed the assistance of a clerk, a sweet-natured, simple lad who had joined the Rubeck firm some twenty years ago as an office boy, much as had Wise himself. His name was Herbert E. Gorfin. Working for Wise was not like working for any of the other directors, Gorfin learned. It involved doing a good deal of personal work on company time. One moment he could be looking up the trading price of lavender oil; the next he might be packaging up books to be shipped to America, delivering carefully wrapped bundles to the workshop of Riviere and Son, or picking up fresh purchases from Maggs or one of the auction houses.

Gorfin displayed quite an aptitude for this kind of miscellaneous busywork. Industrious, enthusiastic, and extremely likeable—an important but often undervalued trait in the rare books business—he was also unfailingly credulous, innocently signing and backdating all manner of receipts and documents under various names whenever

Wise instructed him to do so. He was soon helping trade books from Wise's personal collection, including substantial numbers of forgeries plucked from the stash hidden in the locked drawers and back shelves of the Ashley Library.

Shifting books from one pair of hands to another was to prove both profitable and enjoyable, though for Gorfin never more than a side-gig. Within a year of Wrenn's death, though, it became a full-time occupation. Spurred by his mentor's ceaseless encouragement, Gorfin left Rubeck's for good in 1912 and set himself up as an independent bookseller on Charing Cross Road. Wise helped steer several important collections into his lap, including the library of Thomas Burnett Smart, late bibliographer of Matthew Arnold.

At the same time, he started offloading large numbers of forgeries onto this hapless novice bookseller. Often Wise would visit the shop and hand over only one or two copies of each forgery, suggesting an appropriate retail price. Occasionally, though, he would turn up with large stacks of the pamphlets: nineteen copies of George Eliot's *Agatha*, for instance, appeared within weeks of Gorfin opening shop, following on the heels of twenty-three copies of another Eliot forgery, *Brother and Sister*, and various old Swinburne and Tennyson fakes.

Sometimes several copies of the same book would trickle in slowly. Over the course of two years, Wise palmed off no fewer than fifty copies of Dickens's short ghost story *To be Read at Dusk*, all of them supposedly first editions printed in 1852. Perhaps Gorfin ought to have been suspicious. Until now this standalone edition of the chiller was thought to be vanishingly rare, so rare that few collectors, if any, could so much as hope of ever finding a copy.

With the benefit of hindsight, the quantity and condition of the books all seems too fantastic to be credible. Yet Gorfin was trusting to a fault. Everything he knew about old books he owed to Wise. When his mentor exhumed the old remainder story that had served him so well back in the early days—that the pamphlets had been found in an old publisher's warehouse when the premises were being cleared prior to demolition—Gorfin swallowed it whole. And when Wise told him not to advertise all the copies at once for fears of spoiling the market, he took the lesson to heart.

As a stooge for the forgeries, Gorfin was to prove surprisingly if unwittingly adept. He may have lacked the guile of his mentor, but he understood the basic principles of supply and demand. He knew, for instance, that it was better to consign a single book anonymously at auction than to advertise that he had a dozen copies immediately to hand. Better, too, to wait for prices to peak than to cash in on everything now. Gorfin was only in his early thirties, after all. It would be prudent to 'keep a few things under the bed' for his twilight years. Wise had assured him that prices were only going to go up. If he played his cards right, advertising a few pamphlets at a time in each of his catalogues and discreetly trading them with other booksellers, he might just set himself up for life.

Harry Buxton Forman was the last to die. Since upbraiding his former partner for his deceptions and distortions, he and Wise had grown only more distant. With distance came paranoia. Whirring always at the back of Forman's mind was the fear that Wise would blow the lid off their old scheme, that he would somehow be found out and drag Forman down with him.

Sporadically, the two men would send each other letters. Wise's were invariably and irritatingly jolly, packed with exclamation marks and false cheer. 'My dear Harry Buxton F!' he would open. 'How the devil have you been?!'

Forman always responded in anxious, pleading tones. 'I do not despair of dropping in on you and talking over many things that are *better to talk about than write about*,' he would say, before feeding Wise's indiscreet notes to the flames. When Wise informed him of his scheme for laundering the old forgeries through Gorfin, including the most precious forgery of all, Forman, confined to bed with a severe case of flu, very nearly exploded. 'I hurry this off to beg you not on any account to proceed as you suggest about the *Sonnets*,' ran his reply. 'I can give you excellent reasons,' he said, though would put nothing incriminating down on paper. The letter itself was signed in a most telling manner, with Forman professing that he was 'as at this present' a sincere friend to Wise—perhaps not for much longer.

By the time Forman died in the summer of 1917, he had largely withdrawn from the social scene: nervous, detached, reclusive, adrift. A lukewarm obituary in *The Times* devoted very nearly as much space to his career in the civil service as to his pursuits as a man of letters. 'I see Buxton Forman is dead,' Gosse wrote to Wise on learning the news. 'I had not heard anything of him for years,' he reflected, adding a greedy postscript: 'He must have left interesting books and manuscripts'. Soon thereafter, Wise was summoned by the family to help them sort through the bookshelves, weeding out duplicates and personal letters before the probate valuation could get under way. He was a long and loyal friend, they reasoned. If Tommy Wise could not be trusted, then who could?

Leaving Wise alone in a library was not a very sensible idea; there was no telling what he might walk away with. For Wise, the invitation to go through Forman's books and papers was doubly tempting. The old man had been in on the scheme at the beginning, after all. There was a chance, albeit a small one, that he might have kept some incriminating documents or letters. Under cover of helping the family go through Forman's books, Wise could search for any indiscreet papers and quietly winnow them from the shelves and boxes, ensuring Forman's secrets went with him to the grave.

But the ever-acquisitive collector in Wise would not be so easily satisfied. Over several days following the funeral, he was required to share the library with Forman's younger son, Maurice, and an independent assessor who had come to value the books for probate. This evaluation was to be performed by none other than Quaritch's resident expert, Mr Mudie. All through the early part of the week, the three of them toiled quietly together, stopping at midday for luncheon and for tea in the afternoon, brought in by the homely Mrs Forman. After another couple of hours, Maurice would make his excuses and head out for dinner with friends, leaving Wise and Mudie working late into the evening.

Such were the circumstances when, after a solid day of sifting through the bookshelves, Mr Mudie stepped out of the library and put on what he thought to be his coat. When he reached into the pocket, expecting the familiar clink of keys, he was much surprised to find not his keys but a book. Curious, he pulled it out to find a small, slim octavo bound in sage-green levant. Mudie opened the covers. It was an 1813 first edition of Shelley's radical poetic manifesto, *Queen Mab*, a most valuable item that ought to have been included in his evaluation of the assets. Turning the pages, Mudie saw this was no ordinary copy; each and every leaf was covered with the poet's own scrawled notes, with crossings-out and marginal jottings and interlineated alterations to be incorporated into a new, revised edition. It was enough to transform an already valuable first edition into a priceless literary treasure.

Mudie was still absorbed in the book when Wise shot his head around the door. He turned pale. 'That's my coat you're wearing,' he pointed out.

Mudie held up the volume and waggled it in the air. 'Were you taking that home?' he asked, raising an incredulous eyebrow, his tone that of a suspicious schoolmaster.

'Thought I'd look it over,' Wise shrugged. 'Quite forgot I had it,' he added with a chuckle, though the laughter did not reach those dark eyes. Mudie held out the little volume. Wise snatched it out of his hand and grudgingly returned the book to its shelf. He turned and fixed a shrewd look on Mudie as the latter wriggled out of the coat and placed it on the peg before pulling on his own. Only once Mudie had taken his hat and turned to leave did Wise half-nod him a good night and close the door.

14
From Pillar to Post

Finding Herbert E. Gorfin was easy. His address was printed on the front page of his catalogues. Inquiries for books were to be sent to '91 Lee High Road, Lewisham, SE13', on the outskirts of London. Carter and Pollard took the train out. The house was a short trek from the station: a scruffy Victorian edifice, sand-coloured brick held together with crumbling mortar.

Beforehand, they had prepared themselves for a possible confrontation with the forger himself, or at least with one of his lieutenants. It didn't take them long to realise that Gorfin was neither. He was a meek sort of a man in his fifties, hair thinning with a wispy upper lip and creases around his eyes. The earliest forgeries had slipped onto the market late in the previous century. Unless he had been a most extraordinary prodigy, Gorfin was far too young to have been involved. And the likelihood of his being such a prodigy appeared slim. He seemed altogether too naïve, too gentle, and, frankly, too dim to have perpetrated such an audacious scheme as a teenager.

When asked, Gorfin explained that he had formerly been a bookseller on Charing Cross Road. He told them wistfully about his small but handsome premises among the other shops of Book Row, with its neatly stacked shelves and window displays to entice passing trade. He had issued his first catalogue in 1913 and quickly gained some reputation among men of letters, he said.

In hindsight, it had not been the best time to go into rare books. Within a year of that first catalogue, Europe was consumed by war. Trade dried up. Gorfin told his visitors how, in 1915, he had been forced to quit the lease and move the bookselling business back to Lewisham, gesturing to the walls around him. The following year he had been called up by the army. About his stint on the western front, Gorfin was silent. All he would say was that, since his demob in 1918, he had held down a litany of small jobs in the city—he was currently working as assistant to a grocer on Lamb's Conduit Street—and continued to sell books on the side, both through the auction houses and by advertising in his catalogues, the better to save for retirement and support his two sisters, with whom he shared the house.

Presumably that was why Carter and Pollard had visited? About a book?

Not quite, Carter explained, and told him all about their investigation. As he went through the evidence, patiently and methodically, Gorfin's shock turned to confusion. Was Carter quite sure about all this? The man from whom he had bought the books—all the suspicious pamphlets anyway—was one of our foremost experts on modern first editions, he said, someone whose name was a byword for honesty and probity.

Who was that expert? Carter asked, though he could very well guess the answer.

Gorfin replied without missing a beat: the distinguished bibliographer Thomas James Wise, he said. And he had proof.

The first piece of evidence was a notebook, plucked by Gorfin from a confusion of boxes, files, and abandoned cups and saucers: a small, thick octavo, green cloth boards, buff wrapper. He thumbed back through the pages until, finding what he was looking for, he thrust it under Carter's nose. The pages were ruled and divided by hand into several columns. On the left were dates, in the middle titles of books and numbers of copies, and on the right three spaces for pounds, shillings, and pence. It was a ledger.

After another moment's inspection, Carter saw what Gorfin was pointing at. Beside each title, he had logged the name of the person from whom the book had been bought. Book after book after book in the list was recorded as having come from 'TJW'. Many of the titles were already familiar to Carter. They were fakes, condemned both by paper and by type.

The second piece of evidence was, if anything, even more conclusive. From one of his cupboards, Gorfin fetched a small linen bag fastened with a drawstring. He turned it up and emptied a flurry of what looked like tiny paper dockets onto the desk. It was several seconds before Carter and Pollard realised that they were looking at chequebook stubs. Another few minutes of rummaging and, with a triumphant yelp, Gorfin located the stubs recording his payments to Wise. The dates and sums on the stubs corresponded precisely with those recorded in the ledger.

While Carter and Pollard inspected the evidence and took notes, Gorfin told them his story. And all became clear.

Before setting up as a bookseller, Gorfin had worked for many years as a junior clerk at the Rubeck trading firm, where Mr Wise was a director. Early on he had been assigned to Wise as an assistant. Gorfin had been good at the work, and Wise had quickly come to depend on him. In return, when the opportunity arose, Wise helped Gorfin to establish himself as an independent bookseller. It was thanks to Wise that he had been able to secure the premises on Charing Cross Road, he said. He would always be grateful for that.

But the relationship quickly soured. Despite Gorfin's newfound independence, Wise continued to treat him as an errand boy, a lackey who existed only to do his bidding. Several times a week he would come to the shop and make absurd requests. Sometimes he would hand Gorfin bundles of books to sell that same day, skulking in a nearby café while the trades were done before making off with the lion's share of the proceeds. He would assure Gorfin that he was selling him 'all' his copies of a pamphlet, only to turn up with another handful later in the year, after a high price had been realised at auction. He would provide the titles of books to sell on commission only to back out once Gorfin had established a price and secured a buyer. He would even ask Gorfin to broker deals for books that he had not seen, for which he was able to give no assurances on condition or quality.

Although these instructions always came with the trappings of a polite request, Wise was an impatient man and his requests had the effect of a papal fiat. He was used to getting what he wanted. Besides, Gorfin added, he had this way of making you feel special when he wanted to: a wink, a nudge, a conspiratorial grin, as though, for a heartbeat, he was admitting you to his inner circle. But the warm sensation never lasted long. 'The moment we ceased to be alone, when it came to showing and proving friendly relations before others, then Wise's attitude changed. His manner became cold and aloof. He was the client and master; I was the servant,' Gorfin muttered. 'Before long I realised that I was merely regarded as a tool.'

Before the cracks in this relationship became visible, while they were still hairline fissures in the plasterwork, Wise approached Gorfin with an alluring deal. 'Look here, Herbert,' he said. 'As you know, I've been dealing in these pamphlets now for quite a long time, have made plenty out of them, and am getting a bit tired of them. What about taking the remainder over from me at a nominal price, and dealing with them in future on your own?' The pamphlets had been extremely lucrative and this might be an excellent opportunity for young Gorfin to invest in his future.

Having already handled many of these booklets for his former master, Gorfin required very little persuasion. That Wise was willing to relinquish the entire stash on such favourable terms seemed to be his way of saying thank you, an acknowledgement of and recompense for all the unreasonable things that he had made Gorfin say and do over the years. Even at a token price, though, this was still a large transaction. By the time they were done, Gorfin had laid down nearly all his savings and capital—a little over £400—in return for a few boxes of old pamphlets. If he hadn't been so completely and utterly sure that he was making a sound investment, it would almost seem foolish.

In the years since, Gorfin had drip-fed these books onto the market precisely as Wise had suggested: one or two copies at an auction house; some pamphlets to a fellow bookseller; direct to American customers via his catalogues. He had sold first editions of Swinburne,

Browning, Eliot, and Arnold to Quaritch and Sotheran's. Nobody ever asked any questions. In addition to the pamphlets bought outright from Wise, there were also several books that Gorfin had only ever been permitted to sell on commission. That was how he had facilitated the sale of some of the scarcer works of Tennyson: the 'privately printed' first editions such as *The Falcon*, *The Cup*, and *The Promise of May*. And of course more than a dozen copies of the 'Reading' edition of Mrs Browning's *Sonnets*.

Surely this was enough? Gorfin had given Carter and Pollard more than they could possibly have hoped for: a real, tangible link between the forgeries and the imperious book-hunter of Hampstead. The story was backed up with hard evidence—the kind of evidence that a Poirot or a Wimsey might triumphantly unveil before a gallery of suspects; the kind of evidence that might even be laid down in a court of law. The question was what they should do next.

The thought of storming Wise's home and confronting him with a bag of old cheque stubs was tempting. How that would make the old dog squirm! Except, as Pollard was quirk to warn his friend, this new evidence was not nearly so useful as at first it seemed. Showing Wise how all the clues led back to his door might easily backfire on the investigators. They would be playing their hand at precisely the moment it ought to be kept close to the chest. Such a move would give Wise ample opportunity to prepare a counterstrike. What if he persuaded Gorfin to retract his statement, by threat, bribe, or force? What if he pre-emptively slandered Gorfin's reputation, discrediting him as a witness before he could even take the stand?

Equally, however, if they published the evidence of Wise's involvement without confronting him beforehand, they risked provoking the ire of the literary establishment: hardly a sensible move for a pair of booksellers. To accuse a man of such crimes without allowing him the opportunity to defend himself simply wasn't done—especially when the man in question was a member of the Roxburghe Club and past president of the Bibliographical Society. It would be the easiest thing in the world for Wise to claim there were simple explanations for the inconsistencies that Carter and Pollard had spotted in his bibliographies. If only these two hasty young men had come to him first, had paid him the merest courtesy of a visit, then all this confusion and unpleasantness might have been avoided, he would say. He would make them look like cads. Or worse, fools.

Yet there was another, more subtle approach: a third way, by which Wise might be made to prove his own guilt. With the investigation into the forgeries reaching its zenith in spring and summer, Pollard had stepped away from all but his most pressing duties for M-Section. Come September, though, he was back reporting on communist activities and the traffic of Soviet agents between Moscow and London. Perhaps this set him thinking.

In his undercover work for the British government, Pollard had witnessed various covert operations. Usually an agent would be instructed to melt into the background and watch and report back to his or her handler, a duty that Pollard had performed ably over the past three years. Occasionally, though, it was necessary for an agent to perform a more active role. Pollard had seen how M would sometimes thrust a stick into the beehive and watch the swarm seethe and surge, using his network to feed information to his enemies and niggle them into activity. Amid the confusion, mistakes would be made.

The bait might be nothing more than a vague rumour. It might be something more concrete about military operations or government counterintelligence or a potentially compromised safehouse. Given such information, to whom does the suspect turn? Is there anything suspicious or unusual in their daily activities? Any deviation from established patterns? A different route home? A furtive conversation in the park? A sudden, unscheduled back-room meeting? Are there signs of tradecraft? Are they looking over their backs? Covering their tracks?

All those dingy evening debriefs with M had prepared Pollard for this moment. The bookseller-spy had learned much from his handler: about recruiting assets and putting them into the field, about playing the long game and knowing when to strike the lethal blow. Faced with the task of securing the final piece of the puzzle against Wise, he seems to have asked himself a simple question. What would M do?

The plan was this. Pollard would establish contact with the suspect. He would level with him about the investigation, about the typographic and chemical evidence of forgery, about the presence of these fakes in Wise's bibliographies and catalogues. He would ask Wise whence he had obtained the books in question and listen to whatever he had to say. But—and this was the most crucial point—he would divulge nothing about his sources, especially not Gorfin. Not the merest hint. Once the meeting was over, he and Carter would do what spies do best. They would sit in the shadows and they would observe.

Assuming the old scoundrel was guilty, how might he be expected to react? There was always the chance that someone at Clay's would remember Wise ordering the disputed books. It would be worth a visit to head office to ensure that Clay kept his silence. Otherwise, Gorfin was the last remaining loose end. Pollard suspected that Wise would want to snip that thread before it could be followed back to Hampstead. With Gorfin's help, they would be able to catch him in the act.

After a summer spent writing up the results of the investigation so far, Pollard contacted Wise on the twelfth of October 1933. An interview was arranged for the fourteenth.

Pollard arrived at Heath Drive in time for tea. It was a quiet sort of a road, lined with muscular redbrick houses and well-established plane trees, leaves slowly turning from orange-yellow to a drooping russet brown. Some had already fallen, rotting underfoot to mulch. A gleaming black motorcar was parked in the driveway to number twenty-five. Pollard marched past it and, with a deep breath, rapped loudly on the front door.

Mrs Wise answered and with a few friendly words steered Pollard along the hall. Before opening the door to the fabled Ashley Library, she stopped him in his tracks and issued a hushed warning. 'You must not excite him,' she whispered, nodding at the door. Her husband had turned seventy-four only a few days earlier and was still recovering from a prolonged spell of ill health. He was likely to grow agitated by anything that displeased him, she warned. Best to keep things brief and to the point.

The door opened and there he was, every inch the dragon in his lair: propped up in an armchair, buttressed by chenille cushions under the elbows, a much older man than Pollard remembered from his brief visit to Oxford or the meetings of the Bibliographical Society. His skin was pale and his face, always chubby, had drooped like a bag of boiled sweets left too long in the sun, so that his eyebrows sagged over those 'cruel, porcine eyes'. The deep mahogany of the bookcases loomed against the walls, framing him perfectly against a backdrop of gemstone leather. The gilt spines glittered in the afternoon sunlight.

Wise smiled at his guest and gestured to the empty settee. Pollard sat. While Mrs Wise pottered around with the tea and exchanged pleasantries, the two men took the measure of each other. It was once said that Wise had a way of looking at you 'as though reading the date on a title page'. And nobody knew better than Wise how such dates could mask the truths of a book as much as reveal them. 'Those eyes probed, fathomed, weighed up with the same intensity that revealed to him a book's bibliographical secrets.' For his part, Pollard had been schooled in the art of observing ticks and twitches, hesitancies and stutters. The interview at Heath Drive was no simple meeting of minds; it was a game of chess.

Pollard opened. In the most respectful tones he could muster, he explained to his host how, over the past year or so, he and his friend Carter had been considering the authenticity of certain nineteenth-century pamphlets. He was sure that Wise would agree with them that it was important to establish beyond all doubt the authenticity of such valuable books; after all, Wise had spent much of his own career rooting out fakes and denouncing piracies. They had begun their investigation with the assumption that this would be a simple matter. However, in the case of certain pamphlets by Browning, Tennyson, Swinburne and so on, they had encountered quite startling gaps in the provenance.

'I am very interested,' Wise responded, 'and I would be pleased to assist you in any way I can.' He knew exactly which pamphlets Pollard was talking about: the 'privately printed' keepsakes that had become desirable among true literary connoisseurs in recent decades. Contrary to Pollard's suggestion that these pamphlets had little by way of provenance, though, Wise had himself obtained his copies from only the most reliable sources: from friends of the authors; from their employees and assistants; from the warehouses of their defunct publishers. When shown copies of these little books many years ago, Swinburne and Browning had proclaimed their authenticity. Who were young Pollard and his friend to say otherwise?

As for telling them *precisely* where and when he purchased the pamphlets, this was an impossibility. 'They cost a few shillings each between thirty and fifty years ago,' he pointed out, gesturing to the cases behind him, 'and the copies I have in my library are frequently not the copies I received,' having swapped and traded those first copies for superior examples that had since come to light. His memory was not what once it had been, he protested. Even if it were, though, to recall such tiny details from so many years ago would be a remarkable feat indeed.

And here Pollard landed the killing blow. Taking care not to divulge his sources, he laid out the forensic nature of the proof. The paper on which the pamphlets were printed was incorrect, he explained: chemical wood pulp and esparto grass instead of rag. The font, too, was not manufactured until years after the dates on the title pages—in some cases decades. Pollard was paying Wise a courtesy in explaining to him their findings before they were put to print, but there could be no disputing what they had discovered. All that remained was to find the person responsible.

Wise began to turn puce. Mrs Wise, having perched herself by the window on another settee, discreetly shook her head at Pollard, eyes imploring him to step back from the precipice. But it was too late. Wise was burbling; then he was standing; then he was shouting. Mrs Wise leapt up and escorted Pollard out of the room and off the premises, scolding him for provoking her husband when she had specifically told him to be gentle.

It did not matter. The first stage of the plan was complete. Pollard went back to Carter to debrief his friend on the interview. Now all they had to do was sit and wait for something to happen.

They did not have to wait long. That same evening, Carter received word from Gorfin. He had been summoned to Heath Drive. The note from Wise didn't reveal much, he said, only that Wise wished to speak with him on a matter of the utmost urgency. It was dated 12 October, Gorfin told them, the very same day that Pollard had contacted Wise with his request for an interview about the forgeries.

Convincing Gorfin to accept the summons was not easy. The man was petrified. More than two decades had elapsed since he had left Wise's employ. He had witnessed the fire and rain and mud of the trenches, the death and pain and destruction of war, yet he feared that a condescending look from Wise would turn him once again into a subservient office boy. He would be useless, he protested. As soon as he stepped across the threshold, his legs would turn to jelly and his brains to mush.

But the two young booksellers soon put him right. There was nothing Wise could do to him now, they reassured him. And if only Gorfin would play his part in the operation, there was a great deal that the three of them might do to *him*—unmask him as the ruffian he truly was.

At ten o'clock in the morning on the sixteenth, Wise cabled to reschedule the appointment to lunch the following day. 'Gorfin told us immediately of Wise's invitation,' Carter would later reminisce; 'he kept in constant touch with us, and sought our advice on the replies he should make.' Their advice was simple enough. Go to Heath Drive, they told him. See what Wise wants.

His reception was frosty. Mrs Wise showed him to the dining room, where her husband was waiting, and left the pair of them to their food. It had been years since Wise and Gorfin had last been in a room together. They had much to catch up on. And yet the old toad jumped into business without so much as a how-do-you-do.

'Trouble has arisen respecting some of the pamphlets that you bought from me,' he explained. Three days earlier, he had received a visit from a young man named Pollard, who seemed to think that some of these pamphlets were modern fakes.

Gorfin affected bafflement. This was the first he had heard of it, he told Wise. Was the allegation true? And if so, where had the pamphlets come from?

Wise sat quietly for a moment, gazing into his plate, and then fixed Gorfin with a stare. 'I rather blame you for this, Herbert,' he spat. 'It was your indiscreet marketing of them in numbers that led to an investigation being made as to their origin and to the assertion that they are spurious.'

Gorfin shrank. The illness that had so evidently sapped the strength from Wise's body had done nothing whatsoever to his force of will. There was something in the old man's voice that would brook no disagreement.

'Something will have to be done,' he added. And then he proposed a plan of action. 'You will agree to the destruction of all the copies still retained by you,' he said. 'As they are now mere waste-paper, I should compensate you for the loss to the extent of £25 or £30.' In return, Gorfin would make a formal statement that he had bought all the fake pamphlets not from Wise but from the late Harry Buxton Forman. This statement would be sworn before a lawyer. Gorfin didn't need to worry about its content; Wise would provide him with a suitable draft and back it up in substance with a statement of his own.

Given that the current market value of the remaining forgeries was in the thousands of pounds, the compensation was insultingly low—especially when one considers that Wise was also asking Gorfin to perjure himself. He declined the proposal straight away.

No matter, Wise told him. Take forty-eight hours to think it over. They would meet again on Thursday afternoon—would half past four do?—and Gorfin could give him his final answer then.

Gorfin left Heath Drive in a hurry. He scuttled down to Finchley Road and jumped on the number thirteen bus which took him all the way to Carter's office in Bloomsbury. The two booksellers were waiting for him. On bursting through the door, he was, Carter recalled, visibly sweating.

He sat down and told them everything: the degree to which Pollard's visit appeared to have shaken Wise and how sickly the old man looked; how he blamed Gorfin for drawing attention to the forgeries; how he commanded him to destroy the remaining pamphlets before they could be discovered. He told them about the trivial offer of compensation and the shocking proposal that he lie about the origin of the books.

Gorfin had never seen Wise like that before, he said. He looked frightened, desperate, dangerous: a cantankerous lion in a book-lined cage. He had not dared to say anything to his face about working with Carter and Pollard, for fear of what he might do next.

The plan was working.

15

Giving Yourself Away

As Gorfin was shown out of the door, Wise slumped back into his chair. Deep down he was confident that, by Thursday, Gorfin would accept his proposal. He had always come good in the past. Shifting the weight of the blame onto Forman had been an unfortunate development, but these things couldn't be helped and he felt little guilt about it. After all, the old fool had been his accomplice at the start. He had known what he was getting himself in for. And, now that he was dead and buried, what harm could be done?

Regarding Wise's health, Gorfin hadn't been wrong. Physically, at least, Wise was a wreck. Eighteen months earlier, while loading his wife's luggage onto the motorcar for their summer holiday, he had sustained a nasty fall, landing him in bed for eleven weeks. It had been a shock to the system. Friends would visit his bedside for book-chat and Wise, in that characteristically boorish manner of his, would show off his various ailments with what struck one of his young protégés as a 'bibliographer-like zeal for demonstration'. Ever since, he had been able to hobble around town only with the assistance of a stick and by clutching the arm of his nurse, a prickly but capable matron named Woolhorse. By the time of Gorfin's visit, there was still a persistent and unpleasant twinge in his hips and left shoulder, a dissonant note against the background hum of all the usual aches and pains that accompany old age.

Now, though, all infirmities would need to be forgotten, all aches and pains cast out of mind. At last, Wise had things to do and people to see once more. And no one, not his wife, not even nurse Woolhorse, would be able stop him.

In the years since his father's death, Maurice Buxton Forman had grown rather fond of Wise. Although he was thirteen years Wise's junior, young Forman had remained in close correspondence with his father's partner-in-crime, even after he returned home to South Africa, where he worked for the post office. In his absence, Wise had promised to look out for his elderly mother, stopping by for tea several times a week, and to keep Maurice abreast of literary goings-on in London, for which Maurice had inherited his father's enthusiasm. The two men exchanged all kinds of gossip about which books and manuscripts had been bought by which collectors for what sums. When Maurice decided to revise his father's edition of Keats for publication, it was Wise to whom he turned for advice.

In the early 1930s, a sequence of personal tragedies prompted Maurice to return to England for good: first the death of his sister, then the death of his brother, and then, at the grand age of ninety-two, the death of his mother. On his return in the spring of 1932, the family home must have seemed a very empty place. Its happiest days were in the past. Maurice spent as little time there as he could.

On weekdays, he would go for long walks, from Hampstead right down to Kensington, striding through the parks and squares of the city and breathing in the cool English air. At weekends he would decamp to Heath Drive, where he spent every Saturday afternoon in the library without fail. He justified it as his way of repaying Wise for the countless hours that he had spent with his mother after his father died. The truth was quite different. He was lonely. With his parents and siblings gone, and his sons remaining in Africa, Wise was perhaps the closest thing he had to family in London, something like a favourite cousin or a trusted uncle.

It is difficult to imagine what he must have thought when Wise summoned him to Heath Drive to tell him the news. But imagine it we must, for neither party kept any record of the encounter—or if they did it has long since gone to the flames. Perhaps it went something like this.

Maurice turns up in a chipper mood and is welcomed into the library. Mrs Wise settles him onto the settee and brings his usual pot of coffee before leaving him and her husband to their business. Wise looks serious—uncharacteristically so. He has recently been visited by a troublesome young bookseller who is investigating the authenticity of several dozen nineteenth-century pamphlets. Many of these pamphlets were catalogued and given a clean bill of health by Wise himself. And many of them are, he still believes, quite genuine. But the nub of the problem is that, without exception, Wise received all the items in question from Maurice's father. Once news of the forgeries broke, he would have little option but to say so.

It is a most regrettable situation, Wise tells him. If only Forman were still alive, he would be able to prove the authenticity of at least some of the pamphlets: his friend had received the Swinburne items directly from Watts-Dunton, Wise explains; his Rossetti firsts from members of the poet's family; his Ruskin pamphlets from the author himself. Forman told Wise all about the provenance of the books, he says, but of course none of it was written down.

As for the small minority of books that now looked to be fake, Wise could not doubt that they were handled in good faith. There is no question of Maurice's father having been engaged in any wrongdoing. Only, Wise adds coyly, everyone knows how he loved a 'find' and how easily his heart could overwhelm his head. He was not always a very rational fellow, despite Wise's best efforts to keep him on the straight and narrow. Wise now suspects that some enterprising crook—perhaps Richard Herne Shepherd?—manufactured the pamphlets with the sole object of swindling Forman for a few pounds' quick profit.

The difficulty now is that, without Forman alive to confirm this version of events, all the blame is sure to fall on Wise. How unfair this will be! His reputation is at stake and none of it is his fault, he complains. If only there were some means of verifying this story, some independent witness to events.

Maurice was in South Africa in the years concerned and can't be expected to know any of the details, Wise acknowledges; yet would it be asking too much of an old friend to confirm the story anyway? That his father, before his death, told him about providing Wise with all the dubious pamphlets? Will he perhaps consider making a statement to that effect? Out of some fathomless combination of pity and loyalty, Maurice agrees.

There is, of course, another possibility. Wise summons Maurice; Maurice answers, only to find the dragon of Heath Drive at his most fierce. Wise tells him about the investigation and hints of what he knows: that the unimpeachable Harry Buxton Forman was in fact a liar and a forger and he is very well minded to say so. He even hints that he has the evidence to prove it. But Wise is a generous man. If Maurice wishes to save his family from this scandal, all he needs to do is issue a statement to the effect that his father bought the pamphlets in good faith and gave copies to Wise as a token of abiding friendship. Either Maurice could tell the world that his father has been a fool, or else Wise would proclaim that he had been a crook. The decision, Wise tells him, is his to make.

Whether browbeaten, bullied, or bewitched, by the time he walked out of the Ashley Library, Maurice Buxton Forman agreed to do Wise's bidding.

With young Forman on side, the only remaining chink in the armour was Clay's. Wise hadn't properly understood all Pollard's talk of kerns and hybrid fonts, but it was surely worth dropping in on the printers and warning them off the scoundrels. He telegrammed the office to arrange an interview with Cecil Clay—'young Cecil', as Wise called him, though the man was in his sixties. They met in the same London boardroom where previously Clay had met with Carter and Pollard. They were, Clay would recall, alone.

Once the usual pleasantries between the two old acquaintances were out of the way, Wise keenly brought up the subject of the forgeries. When he did, Clay stiffened. Clay knew all about the pamphlets in question, he explained. Messrs Carter and Pollard had already paid him a visit.

What had he told them?

Nothing more than the truth—that the firm's ledgers had been destroyed when the printing works moved out to Suffolk. That there was no written record of any commissions from before 1911.

Wise let out a sigh of relief.

From a technical perspective, though, Clay added, the typographic evidence of forgery appeared quite convincing. Before he met with them, Carter and Pollard had already been corresponding with the printers about the years in which certain fonts had been acquired by the press. Clay assured Wise that he had known nothing of this correspondence until the investigators informed him of their progress. But, to speak quite frankly, from his perspective the firm had nothing to lose by helping the booksellers in their investigation. Indeed, helping them might very well be the only way to detach themselves from this mess.

'Those monstrous fellows,' Wise muttered, shaking his head at their tenacity. 'Can't you say you had nothing to do with these things?'

A moment passed in silence, then another, before Clay responded. 'How can I when you know we printed them for you?' he said. 'Tom,' he added gently, 'aren't you rather giving yourself away?'

On Thursday morning, the news went from bad to worse. First there came the letter. It was addressed to Mrs Wise. Slicing open the envelope, she saw that it came from Gorfin. This was odd, she thought. Tom had told her to expect Gorfin for tea that afternoon. Why would he write in advance when they would be seeing him later on? And why on earth would he be writing to her and not to her husband?

Any mystery was dispelled by the contents of the letter. Gorfin had spilt his emotions all over the page, writing everything that he had been too cowardly to say to her husband in person. He told Mrs Wise the 'full facts of the case': explaining that he had been in communication with Carter and Pollard, that he was co-operating with their inquiry, and that he would no longer dance to Wise's tune. 'I had intended on telling Mr Wise at our interview that I had been in touch with Mr Pollard and Mr Carter, but Mr Wise was in such an excited state, and I was so shocked by his changed appearance and evident condition of ill-health that I considered it better to defer doing so,' he told her. 'I leave it to you to convey the information to him as and when you think best.'

He did not leave her long. At about half past ten, a telegram boy arrived with a ticker tape from the local telegraph office. He was a smart lad: dark coat, brass buttons, jaunty hat, trousers bagging at the knees from day after day of frantic cycling. The note was laconic; just five words. 'IMPOSSIBLE AGREE HBF PROPOSAL. HERBERT.'

Mrs Wise asked the boy to wait by the door while she took the note in to her husband. He was waiting there a good while. Noises from within the house were muffled. When Mrs Wise did eventually come back to the door, she handed over a scrap of paper on which was scribbled 'Wire received anyhow we expect you to tea', to be wired back to Gorfin. Giving the boy a shilling for the telegram and a penny for his time, she sent him off on his bicycle and the residents of Heath Drive settled into a waiting game. Their answer arrived shortly after lunch: 'POSITION IMPOSSIBLE SEEKING INDEPENDENT ADVICE DO NOT EXPECT ME TEA'.

The remainder of the day passed in silence, but on the following morning wires once again bounced back and forth. At five minutes past ten, a telegram was handed in at Hampstead. Though it was unsigned, the conciliatory tone as a good as proclaimed Mrs Wise's authorship: 'MR WISE CANNOT TRAVEL PLEASE COME TODAY YOUR REPUTATION AND POCKET PERFECTLY SAFE MR WISE HAS ALREADY STATED THAT THE GOODS WERE BOUGHT FROM FORMAN AND SOLD TO GORFIN'.

The note was enough to elicit a response from Gorfin: 'WIRE RECEIVED ARRIVING 3.30 TO 4 O'CLOCK. HERBERT.'

The weather that day was miserable. Unseasonably cold for October: no wind, just relentless drizzle punctuated by spells of intense, bone-drenching rain. Shortly before the clock chimed four, there was a sharp rap at the door. Wise had rehearsed this moment. He had just enough time to wrestle his face into an affable smile before Gorfin was shown in, hair quite soaked through.

'Herbert!' he proclaimed. Gorfin looked completely taken aback by this display of bonhomie. 'It is so unfortunate that we have seen so little of one another these late years,' he added genially. 'Why is that? If we can get over the present little difficulty there is no reason whatever why we should not again do good business together.' Gorfin took a seat and mumbled something in reply, while Mrs Wise settled into her usual perch by the window. Their little misunderstanding the other day had been most regrettable, Wise continued; he hoped Gorfin could forgive him. He had been unwell lately and was not himself. Besides, now that they were in this mess it was in everyone's interest to sort it out quickly. He had a proposal that he hoped might achieve just that.

'I would be quite willing on my part to pay you back whatever sum it was you had originally paid me for the pamphlets—£400 wasn't it?' Wise asked. His previous offer of £30 appeared to have been forgotten. 'And as you seem not to like the idea that you should say you purchased them from Harry Buxton Forman, that little difficulty can be surmounted by our agreeing that, although you actually paid me for the various items, it was fully understood all the time that I was acting as the agent of Mr Forman in the matter, and that the pamphlets were actually coming to you from Mr Forman *through* Mr Wise!' With this final statement, he stabbed the air with a chubby index finger, as though that settled the matter once and for all.

Gorfin was lost for words. He would not help Wise shift the blame onto Forman. He had said so at their previous meeting. Hadn't Wise understood the need for honesty? Gathering his thoughts, he spoke up. 'I will subscribe to nothing but the plain unvarnished truth respecting them or my acquisition of them,' he said firmly. As for refunding his money, that was the very least Wise could do. In fact, Gorfin believed he was owed a good deal more. 'The potential value of the property is now something like £2,000, had they been genuine, as I had every reason to believe them to be when I bought them from you.'

He was getting indignant now. 'I am now fully convinced in my own mind that the author of their existence is none other than yourself,' he snapped, pointing an accusatory finger at his host. 'I have been disgracefully treated in the matter.'

Wise had never seen Gorfin like this. He was normally so timid, so compliant. Something had changed. Just as it seemed that Wise was about to bite back, fangs to the jugular, Mrs Wise politely deflated the tension with a little cough.

'Perhaps Tom could give you books of a value to satisfy you?' she asked, gesturing towards the mahogany bookcases. Even in this gloomy weather, the spines glistened behind the glass.

'I do not *want* books,' Gorfin groaned. It was books that had got him into this mess in the first place. 'I consider myself entitled to the value of the property which *his*'—he jabbed at Wise—'action has destroyed.'

Wise sat stock-still for a moment, his eyes fixed on nothing in particular. He seemed to be thinking. The rain continued to pummel the window.

At length, he spoke. 'I could of course get young Forman to sell some of these,' he said, waving vaguely at the cases. His voice grew soft and sly. 'But it does not seem as though it is any good paying you anything at all, seeing that the pamphlets are now just so much waste paper.'

And then Wise did something unusual. He asked Mrs Wise to leave the room for a moment. What happened next is something of a mystery. Nobody knows what, precisely, was said. In his account of the interview, Gorfin recalled only that 'Mr Wise then made a remark about blackmail whereupon I indignantly rose to leave, protesting against so outrageous a suggestion'.

Before he could reach the door, though, Wise was heard to bark after him. 'Are you going away to stir up further mud?'

'The mud is all of your making and has been stirred up by you,' Gorfin responded, wrenching open the door and stepping out into the hall. He did not even say goodbye.

Wise remained wedged in his chair. He made no attempt to follow. He heard Gorfin pulling on his coat in the hallway. There were whispers and then the creak of the front door opening. A cold draught whipped through the house, an angry dog biting at the old man's ankles. Another few seconds passed and then, from outside, through the pattering raindrops, drifted the voice of Mrs Wise, who had splashed outside in her slippers and was now calling down the road after Gorfin.

'You *will* come, Herbert,' she said pleadingly. 'If I want you.'

16

Wisecracking

Just round the corner from Pollard's bookshop on Gerrard Street, upstairs in an unassuming first-floor bistro, a table is surrounded by familiar faces. How good it is to be with old friends! Here are Carter and Pollard, of course, holding court in the lamplight. The Elkin Matthews boys, too, are out in force: Percy Muir and A. W. Evans listening on, attentive as ever, while Eddie Gathorne-Hardy languishes in his chair and pours himself another glass. The publisher and rare book enthusiast Michael Sadleir, another Elkin Matthews regular, joins in the conversation. Bookending the generations are the boyish Simon Nowell-Smith, fresh out of Oxford and now working at the *Times Literary Supplement*, and old Percy Dobell, a shrewd veteran of the trade whose father, Bertram, had sold books to young Tommy Wise the barrow-scavenger more than fifty years ago.

These dinners had been a regular fixture throughout the investigation. Over bottles of cheap claret and plates piled high, the Biblio Boys would gather, gossip, and, once dinner was done, fill their glasses, light up their pipes, and listen to the latest updates from Carter and Pollard. Naturally, the table-talk on this night was all of Wise's latest antics. Between them, they told the tale excellently: how Pollard's initial visit in October had smoked out the rogue; how Wise's immediate response had been to cable Gorfin and arrange a rendezvous; and how the beleaguered bookseller had swung back and forth between Heath Drive and Carter's office, secretly keeping them abreast of everything that transpired. Wise had played into their hands from first to last, they chuckled. When Carter mentioned the proffered financial settlement—£400 for Gorfin's silence and the return of his stock—gasps were heard from around the table. The latest update was that Gorfin had, with their encouragement, taken the money, albeit on the condition that he would not help Wise deflect the blame. 'Although such a settlement as this takes no account of the serious damage to my reputation that must result,' Gorfin had told Wise, 'I am anxious to be clear of the whole very unpleasant business.' The pamphlets were duly shredded in the presence of a solicitor.

The last pieces of evidence were all now slotting into place. A healthy supply of notes and postcards was flowing in from friendly librarians, eager to help establish the provenance of volumes donated by Wise or to check for minor variations in the punctuation or typography of this or that pamphlet. Particularly fortuitous was a new volume of previously unpublished Browning correspondence, including the note to Leigh Hunt in which Browning stated quite explicitly that he knew nothing of the sonnets, not even in manuscript, until 1849—two years *after* the date on the title page of the 'Reading' *Sonnets*. (The most delicious aspect to this story was that the original letter in question was possessed by none other than Wise himself.) On the other side of the Atlantic, Flora Livingston had been back to the Harvard reading room with her scissors, covertly trimming samples from the margins of fake Tennysons and Swinburnes: 'I enclose a little snip of the paper from *Morte D'Arthur*,' she wrote on 11 December. 'I did not know it was so scarce. Those little suspicious Tennysons all came on the market about the same time. I am curious to know what Mr Wise thinks about it.' She harboured no doubt that 'he knows more about them than he has ever told'.

Throughout, the company clung to their every word. But one man was listening especially closely, for he had a stake in the investigation. Michael Sadleir, in his capacity as senior editor at Constable and Co., had already agreed to publish the resulting book. Carter had sent him a proposal with the piquant title 'Wisecracking: or, Have With You to Heath Drive'—'*very* provisional title', he sniggered—which would quickly be swapped for the seemingly innocuous *An Enquiry into the Nature of Certain Nineteenth Century Pamphlets*. But this title, too, winked to the cognoscenti. For Edmond Malone's 1796 exposé of the William Henry Ireland frauds had appeared under the title *An Inquiry into the Authenticity of Certain Miscellaneous Papers*. And the book denouncing John Payne Collier's Shakespearean discoveries as fake had been published in 1860 as *An Inquiry into the Genuineness of the Manuscript Corrections in Mr J. Payne Collier's Annotated Shakespeare*. The new *Enquiry* announced itself as a worthy successor to these illustrious forebears.

Much like the title, the text itself would strike a delicate balance of innuendo and forensic investigation. 'You'll enjoy it,' Carter told one friend. 'It's a sort of cross between a detective story and a procès-verbal.' Wise was far too powerful to accuse outright. Instead, they would need to ensnare him in a tightly wound web of evidence—so tight that he could not attempt to escape without entangling himself still further—but at no point actually accuse him. Although they would not name the forger, having studied his handiwork it was possible to determine something of his character, they would explain. His literary knowledge and bibliographical expertise must have been considerable, as must his operational understanding of auction houses and the trade; he must have maintained a substantial and longstanding account with Clay and Sons; he must have been in a position to lay clues that would later confirm the authenticity of the forgeries; he must have enjoyed the friendship of at least one esteemed but overcredulous bibliographer who would help authenticate the discoveries from a 'position of eminence so secure that there would be no chance of anyone asking possibly awkward questions'. 'There was one such man,' Carter and Pollard wrote, 'who is the hero (or villain) of the present work.' It was not too difficult to guess whom they meant.

Of all the names that pepper the *Enquiry*, none appears so often as Thomas James Wise. His index entry stretches over four columns. That is because although they would not name Wise as the mastermind, his authentication and dispersal of the fakes was a matter of public record. After all, he had triumphantly published the story of how he discovered the 'Reading' *Sonnets* and had included similar books in his own bibliographies and catalogues—many of them now proven to be dubious. At the very least, then, Wise had been unspeakably negligent in accepting the books as genuine. And, in emphasising the rarity of books that he knew existed in substantial numbers, his disingenuousness had 'inflicted damage in plenty on innumerable collectors all over the world, who have for years paid good money—and in some cases a good deal of it—for books which are, in fact, worthless'. 'But far more serious in its import and far-reaching in its extent is the damage done to the integrity of bibliography as a whole,' Carter and Pollard stated coldly. 'Mr Wise, by his credulity, by his vanity in his own possessions, by his dogmatism, by abuse of his eminence in the bibliographical world, has dealt a blow to the prestige of an honourable science, the repercussions of which will be long and widely felt.' How could this man not also be the forger?

With Sadleir's agreement—and with Cecil Clay still keen to tell the truth and distance his firm from Wise's antics—the book would be printed by Clay's. Because the printers still had the kernless Long Primer No. 3 in their warehouse, Carter and Pollard would be able to lay out the evidence in black and white. On facing pages they would print a photographic facsimile of a page from the *Sonnets* and, opposite, the same page mocked-up in Long Primer No. 3. Even under a magnifying glass, the two pages would be exactly the same: identical down to the last serif. (This was also a spectacular joke, for as their specimen they chose the third sonnet in Barrett Browning's sequence, with the opening line: 'Unlike are we, unlike, O princely Heart!') Even sceptical readers, indifferent to the technical details of bibliographical analysis, would not be able to doubt the evidence of their own eyes. This typographical exhibit would be every bit as damning as a fingerprint on a murder weapon or a trail of bloody footprints leading back to a suspect's door.

The final stage before handing in the typescript to the publisher was to gain a legal opinion on whether its content was libellous. Pollard ran it past a friend of his, James Lyell, who was both a lawyer and a prolific collector of books and manuscripts to boot. Lyell was full of admiration for the investigative work on show: 'a careful perusal of the document can leave no doubt upon anyone's mind that the authors have with infinite pains and unwearied research built up a devastating case against the authenticity of the pamphlets and books which they condemn as forgeries'. However, he wrote, the detectives seemed to think that by wrapping their accusations against Wise in insinuation and innuendo, they would be protected against legal proceedings. In this they were quite wrong.

'There is almost throughout a veiled attack upon the honesty and bona fides of Mr Thomas J. Wise,' Lyell decided. And in places the veil wore so thin that, for most readers, it might as well not be there at all. 'Can there be any reasonable doubt that they would inevitably come to the conclusion that the authors of this book have accused Mr Wise of forging and marketing for gain these forged pamphlets, however skilfully they have avoided saying so in precise words?' On the question of whether the *Enquiry* was libellous, Lyell was firm. 'You need not ask me to point out specific passages which are defamatory, as in my view from first to last the whole book, as submitted to me, provides ample material for Mr Wise to commence proceedings if he thinks fit to do so.'

The document made for bracing reading. It was not the outcome the authors had been hoping for. Criminal libel was punishable by fines and imprisonment: a prospect which neither of them relished. The thought of swapping his flannels for prison scrubs must have driven Carter quite mad with worry. However, Lyell concluded his report with an important caveat to which he and Pollard might yet cling. Defendants in libel suits could always plead justification. In other words, they would be permitted to demonstrate in court that the defamatory words were, in fact, true. And in Lyell's judgement, Carter and Pollard would be able to make a strong case. The last thing Wise needed was for their accusations and evidence to be aired in a courtroom. Even if the ruling went his way, the case would generate volumes of adverse publicity; and if the ruling went against Wise, that would be tantamount to a verdict of guilt. His reputation 'as a bibliographer and an honest man' would lie in tatters. For Wise to risk such a ruling would be foolish in the extreme. No, Lyell thought, far more likely that he would keep a low profile and plead ill health.

Meanwhile, some five miles north of Soho, Wise was already plotting his counter-attack. 'Mark my words,' he smirked to one friend, 'these egotistic young idiots will wish they had kept their stupid fingers out of this particular pie!' His first priority was to muster the troops: loyal dogs who would respond to his whistle. Willingly or not, Maurice Buxton Forman had already taken his place at the front of the pack. Right alongside him was Monsieur Seymour de Ricci, who would act as Wise's emissary in the weeks following Gorfin's fateful visit to Heath Drive. On the first day of November, he was sent to put the scarers on Pollard at his bookshop.

'As a Briton and an Englishman, it should never be said of you that you scared Mr Wise off presenting a library worth a quarter of a million to the British nation,' de Ricci cautioned, alluding to the uncertain fate of the Ashley collection after Wise's death. The warning only amused Pollard. 'I thought that good from a semi-Frenchman!' he joked to his father. 'As I know that Mr Wise has flaunted his library under the noses of the British Museum, Worcester College, and Sotheby's in turn, when he wanted something out of them, I told Mr de Ricci that I was not impressed by his suggestion.'

With Carter and Pollard proving themselves undaunted by these attempts at intimidation, Wise's options grew limited. 'I have heard nothing further either from or about the doings of this pair of rascals,' he wrote to his old Roxburghe friend, Sydney Cockerell. There is a whiff of desperation to the note. 'I fear they are right about the origin of this wretched Reading *Sonnets*, and it is perfectly fit for them to make the fact known. But when they go further and suggest that *I* was the person responsible for its production, and that my story of its acquisition was knowingly untrue, it is *abominable*.' The whole controversy was being contrived to knock him off his pedestal, 'gaining glory for themselves by defaming my character. In the long run such a dirty action can only result in proving themselves to be a pair of cads.'

Accusations of caddishness would doubtless have amused the two young detectives. But it must have come as a real concern when Sadleir started receiving letters warning him against publication. Among the more determined of Wise's supporters was a Scottish writer and critic called Richard Curle. 'Is it true that a book is to be published soon purporting to show that Mrs Browning's *Sonnets from the Portuguese*, far from having been printed in 1847, was printed relatively recently?' he asked Sadleir. 'It seems incredible, but I have heard that such a work is to appear. T. J. Wise believes the *Sonnets* to be genuine, as has every other collector believed for years . . . If such a book is to be published, I would like to break the news gently to the old chap.'

The publisher promptly forwarded these queries to Carter, whose responses were characteristically tactful. The facts of the case, disturbing though they were, had already been conveyed to Wise, he explained to Curle. 'It was no pleasant task, as you may imagine.' On the matter of whether their findings might be hushed up, Carter stood his ground: 'Quite apart from any question of bibliographical ethics or of public duty to the book collecting world, to suppress certain proof of a fraud is to become accessory to it, and this is a responsibility which neither I nor my collaborator, Mr Graham Pollard, feel disposed to undertake.'

More than a month elapsed between Carter's letter and Curle's reply. 'I know nothing about the matter save what you tell me and the vague rumours that are floating around, but I beg of you to realise that Mr Wise is a very old and a very sick man. I really do trouble to think what effect such a publication would have on his already precarious health.' On the heels of this letter came another. 'It occurred to me that you might quite naturally think that my long delay in answering you might be due to my having got in touch with Wise—more especially as you know that I am concerned about his health. But we have never exchanged a word on the subject and I don't suppose for a moment that he knows that I know anything about it.' There was a distinct air of special pleading to the letter, a sense that Curle was protesting too much. The most natural explanation for the letter, as Curle himself confessed, was that he had been put up to it by Wise.

'May I beg of you to listen to me once again?' entreated a final note. 'I feel that a book, which would give out disturbing news to the world, is a very different thing to the same news confined to a handful of people,' Curle argued. 'Could it not at least be delayed for a time? He has been my friend for thirty years and I have always found him high-minded and generous.' Yet there was nothing particularly high-minded or generous about Wise's behaviour now, about his capacity to exploit friends to his own advantage.

No friend was more exploited than Frederick Page: a fellow amateur scholar and, during the working week, a manager at the London office of the Oxford University Press. Wise often summoned Page out to Hampstead; Page would always pour the tea, resulting in the pet-name 'Auntie Page', which in typical Wiseian manner managed to be both charming and belittling. It was on one such visit that Page was informed about the investigation into the suspect pamphlets. His initial reaction was to laugh it off. Surely it would be easy enough to disprove such baseless accusations, he scoffed. He would immediately put his assistant, an enthusiastic youngster called Ralph, on the case. Hold tight, Page assured Wise, and see what the lad turns up.

'It is merely a matter of producing true facts to prove how rash and misguided these young men are,' Page told Ralph on his return to the office. From now on, Ralph ought to spend his evenings and weekends in the British Museum, hunting down contemporary references to the 'Reading' edition of the *Sonnets*, preferably by Browning or someone close to the family. 'This will be a good exercise in research for you!'

When, despite his best efforts, Ralph failed to turn up any new evidence, Page returned to Hampstead to tell Wise the bad news. He had expected some small gratitude from his friend—he was, after all, a busy man and could have used Ralph's help these past weeks—but instead was met with fury. 'Looking for contemporary evidence of the suspected publications is a waste of time,' Wise barked. Instead, the boy ought to be undermining the technical methods of the exposé. 'Concentrate on disproving the charges by shaking the evidence on chemistry of paper, and typography,' he ordered. Without that evidence, any accusations of forgery would simply fall apart.

Page was a little shaken by the encounter. There was something unnerving about Wise's insistence that no amount of research would turn up the necessary contemporary evidence of the *Sonnets*. 'For who could be dogmatically certain that no passage in an unpublished letter, memoir or journal existed, except someone who knew that it was impossible because, for instance, the 1847 *Sonnets* did not exist in 1847?' Nonetheless, Page put such doubts to the back of his mind and once again dispatched Ralph to the library, this time with instructions to look for anything that might unsettle the investigators' technical arguments. The best young Ralph could do was a quotation from the *Oxford English Dictionary* under the entry for 'pulp', which showed that wood pulp had been used in Sweden to make paper since 1862.

What followed this half-hearted counter-investigation was a long and rambling letter to the *Times Literary Supplement*, in which Wise attempted to steal a march on his adversaries. The letter was drafted on his behalf by Page (and typed up by the long-suffering Ralph). It explained that vague doubts had recently been cast upon the '1847' edition of Elizabeth Barrett Browning's *Sonnets* on the grounds of provenance and technical anachronism. But those doubts could be dismissed easily enough, the letter claimed. Yes, the newly published correspondence in which Robert Browning claimed not to have seen the manuscript sonnets until 1849 was a snag. But was it not possible that two years earlier Elizabeth had quietly sent a transcript back to Miss Mitford in England, to have them privately printed so that she might surprise her husband with a copy after their marriage, only for this private printing never to make it back to Italy? As for the supposed technical anachronisms, wood-pulp paper and kernless letterforms had been in use since the early nineteenth century, claimed the letter with casual certainty. There was little point saying anything more on the subject. 'I will leave further exposition of this and the lower-case f to those who have a more microscopic eye than I can boast of.'

Perhaps the most surprising aspect of this letter concerned the provenance of Wise's own copies of the *Sonnets*. Everyone remembered the story of how Wise came to find the books: brought out by the elderly Dr Bennett after a meal of 'hot buttered toast and sausages'—the kind of wonderfully evocative detail that lodged in the memory—before being purchased by Wise for £10 apiece and 'hurried' to the book-hunters of London. Now, Wise blushed, this story was all quite wrong. In fact, the 'sonnets' he was talking about in that passage was an innocuous little volume of poems written by Dr Bennett himself. 'The confusion of two such books may seem incredible,' he admitted, but there it was. In fact, he now claimed, both his copies of Barrett-Browning's 'Reading' *Sonnets* had come to him from Harry Buxton Forman. Where Forman had found them was, alas, a mystery.

This letter surprised Carter and Pollard, though perhaps it oughtn't to have. Obviously Wise would try to discredit their investigation before the results were published. The very next issue of the *Times Literary Supplement* included two further letters on the brewing controversy. The first came from the pen of Maurice Buxton Forman, though he seems just to have been copying out words dictated by Wise: it confirmed Wise's version of events in every particular, naming his father as the true source of the books.

The second letter was sent in by Pollard. It roundly disabused readers of Wise's bibliographical competence. The point about wood pulp was all wrong, Pollard explained. Wise was talking about *mechanical* wood pulp—that is, wood pulped by friction—whereas the *Sonnets* was printed on paper composed of *chemical* wood pulp, which was first imported into England in 1874 and first manufactured there in 1883. Likewise the typographical argument. It did not matter if similar fonts were manufactured at an earlier date; the hybrid Long Primer No. 3 was not in use until 1880 at the very earliest. 'A detailed description of these tests with enlargements and diagrams, as well as a full examination of the negative evidence bearing on the 1847 *Sonnets*, has now been completed by Mr John Carter and myself,' Pollard told readers of the *TLS*. 'The book is already printed off, and, under the title of *An Enquiry into the Nature of Certain Nineteenth Century Pamphlets*, will be published within the next few weeks.'

As a foreshock comes before an earthquake, so these rumblings presaged the convulsion that was to come. The brief exchange of salvoes had already set people on edge. In the middle of June, a mere fortnight before the *Enquiry* was due to hit the shelves, the library of famed collector Herbert T. Butler was to be auctioned off at Hodgson's. There had been few events on this scale since the crash of 1929. It was going to be a blockbuster, stretched out over three days, the second and third of which would be devoted to books from the eighteenth and nineteenth centuries, including, according to the title page of the sale catalogue, 'First Editions of the Brownings, Matthew Arnold, Fitzgerald, Meredith, Stevenson, Swinburne, the Rossettis, William Morris, Hardy, Kipling, and others', plus a sequence of 'first editions of Victorian poets and novelists' still in their original wrappers and cloth, precisely as issued, all in an 'unusually clean state'.

Any mention of books in such pristine condition ought to raise flags. One of the star lots was to be a copy of the 'Reading' *Sonnets*—the first to come up for sale in many years—a characteristically fine copy bound in crushed brown morocco, stamped in gilt. After the revelations hinted at in the letters page of the *TLS*, though, how could such a book now be sold? The auction house had no choice but to withdraw the lot. Such caution was a 'bore', Carter told Sadleir, but he supposed it couldn't be helped. And any disappointment was more than offset by the fact that the 'remaining twenty-five or so forgeries in the sale have not been touched'. If anything, this was an underestimate. The actual number was closer to thirty.

Sadleir was a good deal more understanding of the auction house's wariness; he was himself fraught with nerves. As publisher, his priority was to ensure the *Enquiry* saw light of day. By the letter of the law, it was theoretically possible for Wise to apply for an injunction even before the book was published, so long as he had access to a copy and was able to cite passages in his application. 'I want to take every precaution against the other side getting a sight of the text,' he told Carter. He proposed not sending any review copies to the newspapers until the very last moment, just in case someone leaked a copy back to Heath Drive. To do so would be 'unwise', he suggested, doubtless with a wink and a nudge.

The first few copies were secretly dispatched to reviewers in the wake of the Butler sale. For a while everything went quiet. And then, in the final days before publication, the reviews flooded in. To Carter's delight, the reader for the *Sunday Times* was none other than Dorothy Sayers herself (who must by now have realised what that odd young bookseller downstairs from the Detection Club had been up to all this time). 'If this book could be turned into a detective novel, called *The Catalogue Crimes* or *The Clue of the Crook-Backed F*, it would grace the annals of a Carrados or a Thorndyke; for it chronicles as pretty a piece of investigation as those heroes ever accomplished.' she proclaimed. 'Connoisseurs of detective method will find it more fascinating than any fiction.' The 'tireless investigation of detail and the close and impartial reasoning' was worthy of Sherlock Holmes, announced another reviewer. Meanwhile, writing for *The Spectator*, John Sparrow (an astonishing young scholar who would squander his talents on internecine Oxford politics) would praise the authors for reconstructing their investigation 'so luckily and excitingly that even those who know nothing of book-auctions and bibliography will share the thrill with which their story must inspire the expert, and ask, as eagerly as he, *who was the forger?*'

For that was the point of it all. Everyone could see that a plain answer to that plain question would have left Carter and Pollard hopelessly vulnerable to legal action. They knew to read between the lines. 'The reader arrives breathless at the very brink of disclosure; the curtain descends with a rush; the lights go out; the mystery is solved at every point except at this culminating point of identity,' wrote Harold Nicolson in the *Daily Telegraph*. But was a plain answer even necessary? Like any other reader, all Nicolson needed to do was follow his nose; and he, like all the other reviewers, could smell one person who more than any other emerged from the investigation 'with a faint brimstone scent of almost satanic humour'. Wise.

17

A Delicate Mission

'You know him well,' the older man barked. 'Can't you get him to make a confession of exactly what he has done? It would get the dreadful business off his chest and leave him in peace.'

The speaker was Arundell Esdaile, eminent bibliographer and Secretary to the British Museum. It was high summer and the *Enquiry* had been out only a few weeks. He was speaking with Wilfred Partington, a junior disciple of Wise who had spent a lot of time at Heath Drive in recent months. Esdaile was correct. Partington did know Wise well and what he knew only confirmed the improbability of persuading Wise to confess. 'It was easier to imagine a zoo spectator entering the cage of a bear racked with toothache, and trying to extract the molar with a motor-spanner,' Partington reflected. He kept the thought to himself, though, and responded to Esdaile with a noncommittal shrug.

Similar conversations were taking place on the other side of the Atlantic. In the back room of Max Harzof's bookshop in New York, the elderly collector and regular customer A. Edward Newton shook his head in sorrow. 'I asked those two young fellows not to publish their findings now,' he said. 'It will kill poor old Tommy.' Harzof, typically venomous, could not agree. 'The son-of-a-bitch needs killing.'

Reporters had already caught up with Wise. They had found him at the Queen's Hotel in Hastings, on the Sussex coast, recovering, he claimed, from yet another spate of poor health. Evidently the illness had not reached his silver tongue.

This whole forgery business had been a terrible misunderstanding, he told the journalists. The two booksellers who broke the story were overenthusiastic youngsters: out of their depth and motivated by spite. 'All my life I have been preaching against bad copies of books and teaching people to leave bad copies alone,' he explained. 'That has done small booksellers a lot of harm and so they curse me and hate me.' Many of the books condemned as forgeries were, in fact, genuine. And those that were not had nothing to do with him. 'I was only the vehicle,' he protested to a hack from the *Daily Herald*. 'I was the messenger lad who took the goods for delivery. They were planted on Forman and on me.' Furthermore, he would hazard a guess as to who was behind it all. 'Richard Herne Shepherd,' he spat, that odious rogue.

The newspapers lapped it up. Wise even managed to spin it so that reporters, contrary to all sense, described him as a specialist witness and not the prime suspect. 'EXPERT NAMES THE MAN HE SUSPECTS' ran the *Herald* in a sensational front-page splash. And that was only the start. If these fresh-faced ruffians had put him on the back foot, so much the better for him to throw forward a counterpunch.

That counterpunch was slated to appear in the *American Book Collector*, a monthly periodical published out of New Jersey. It took the form of a 'personal statement' establishing the supposed facts of the case: that the *Enquiry* was packed with trumped-up charges and *ad hominem* attacks on Wise's integrity; that all his copies of the suspect pamphlets had come to him from Forman; that he had played no part in their circulation or sale. Above all, the essay seemed concerned with refuting the charge that, for the last forty years, Wise had been a commercial bookseller in anything but name. 'If anyone will accept my word, here it is,' blustered Wise. 'I did not forge nor procure to be forged the pamphlets in question, nor any other pamphlets, nor anything, in all my life; nor have I put into circulation anything which I knew or suspected to be a forgery ... I am forced to conclude that I have been duped'. But then again, so had everyone else.

Wise showed the essay to a few close friends before sending it off with the sense of a job well done. Then, with impeccable timing, came news from that most trusted of his lieutenants, 'Auntie' Page. 'I have seen Carter and Pollard,' Page told Wise. He sounded winded, as though reeling from a blow to the stomach. 'I'm charged to tell you two things; very weightily charged indeed.'

The two investigators had consented to meet with Page in his unofficial capacity as Wise's man-about-town. Page had gone into the meeting hoping for a truce; Carter and Pollard were looking for unconditional surrender. They had been quite stern with him, giving Page a warning to pass on to his master. Unless there was some firm evidence to buttress his claims, Page told Wise, he was from this moment forth to cease any and all accusations against Gorfin and Forman: impugning the truthfulness of the former or naming the latter as the source of the forged pamphlets. If Wise broke those terms they would, in Page's words, 'crush' him. Just because the Clay ledgers had been destroyed did not mean that the firm had no recollection of the work done for Wise, they hinted. If Cecil Clay was to swear an affidavit, that would force Wise into an untenable position. 'Now you must understand that they are fully persuaded that they can prove a charge of fraud and forgery against you,' he told Wise. 'If you have not already sent off that article to America, you will do very well to suppress it, and to reconsider your position. You *must* reconsider your position, anyhow.' He closed the letter with a final piece of counsel—the last he would ever offer his old friend. 'I can give you no other advice in the matter than this: unless you know yourself to be innocent, you have only two alternatives: (1) silence; (2) a confession. Any lie on your part now means mate in two moves.'

Wise chose silence. He withdrew the piece from the *American Book Collector* before it could be published. On 30 August, a letter from Mrs Wise was printed in the *Times Literary Supplement*. It comprised a single sentence.

> I regret to inform you that my husband, Mr T. J. Wise, as the result of a nervous breakdown more than two years ago, arising from overwork, and the long and painful illness which followed, is utterly unfit to carry on any public correspondence or controversy, and his doctor has strictly forbidden him to do so.

*

For Page, at least, the choice of silence was as good as a confession. It struck him hard. After much careful thought and with melancholy weighing on his shoulders, he packed up his complete set of the Ashley Library catalogues, a gift from Wise, and returned them to Heath Drive. Enclosed was a note—which was 'angry from so gentle a man', recalled Ralph the office boy—telling Wise never to contact him again.

Wise's vow of silence was enough to shut down the journalists, but the bibliophiles were not so easily satisfied. Many could not shake the unpleasant feeling of having been duped. In some quarters denial was beginning to morph into righteous anger. 'Book collectors throughout the world are still waiting to hear from Mr Wise an explanation of the forgeries exposed by Mr Carter and Mr Pollard,' ran one letter in the *TLS*. 'Those of us who have bought the forged pamphlets for large sums of money cannot consent to leave the matter where it is.'

Among the duped collectors were several members of the Roxburghe Club. 'What an extraordinary exposure,' wrote Lord Rutland to Lord Mersey. 'Wise must be made to talk before it is too late.' Lord Lansdowne was particularly enraged. 'It seems to me, and to others to whom I have spoken on the subject, that a *book* club such as ours would make itself ridiculous if a member, who has been virtually convicted of forging first editions, is allowed to remain on its list,' he told Lord Hornby. He had been studying the club handbook and had found, under section twenty-one, provision for revoking membership based on a two-thirds vote. 'This makes it quite simple to get rid of Wise.'

Except it wasn't that simple at all. For all Lansdowne's protestations that the Roxburghe was a 'book club', it was in its soul a club for gentlemen. And the expulsion of a member by petty vote, however impartial or democratic, was simply ungentlemanly. It would not do, protested Lord Aldenham, the club president. 'Virtually convicted' was not the same thing as 'convicted'. Wise must be given a fair hearing.

The problem was that Wise seemed to be doing everything in his power to avoid such a hearing. 'I regret that I cannot give you the assurance you desire as fully as I should like to do,' he told Aldenham. 'My lawyer has forbidden me to write or say anything more.' To tell the Roxburghe everything that he knew about these forgeries, and about the people whom he believed to have been involved in their manufacture, would be to introduce nameless 'gentlemen of position' to the scandal, of whom one was still alive. 'This I could not possibly do.' As non-explanations go, it is quite extraordinary.

Aldenham tried everything. Would Wise consider speaking to a very small group of senior members in strictest confidence? If they accepted his story as genuine then, in the words of Sir Frederic Kenyon, former president of the British Academy and perhaps the most distinguished scholar of ancient palaeography ever to have lived, 'no dog could bark at him any more'. However, Kenyon continued, if Wise refused to give such an explanation, then 'the only inference must be that there is none to give, and we should have to ask him to resign'. This was the situation that Aldenham most feared. If the club decided to mount an investigation, and if the investigation were to find Wise guilty, the club would have no choice but to expel him and thus mire itself in scandal.

This back-and-forth between members of the Roxburghe went on for months. Eventually it was decided that an emergency meeting would be convened at Lord Aldenham's London residence on 12 December to discuss 'l'affaire de Wise'. At one point Lansdowne even mooted sneaking Carter and Pollard into the meeting—'concealed somewhere on the premises' within earshot, he said—presumably to feed him information that might either verify or refute Wise's defence.

Thankfully it never came to that. On 6 December, six Roxburghe men gathered for a secret dinner at Lord Hornby's house in Chelsea, including Lansdowne, Sydney Cockerell (now *Sir* Sydney Cockerell), and Lord Crawford. 'We were a very amicable sextet, and apart from the reason for it, we enjoyed the evening thoroughly,' recorded Cockerell in his diary. It had become abundantly clear that Wise would not jump of his own volition. And so, with the port slowing in its clockwise orbit, it was decided that someone ought to give him a soft push. 'Various degrees of severity were discussed,' wrote Cockerell. Just before the diners parted ways, it was agreed that he and Kenyon (who had proposed and seconded Wise for membership) should go out to Heath Drive and, 'in as friendly and considerate a manner as possible, try to persuade him to resign at once'.

The following morning Cockerell confirmed this arrangement with Kenyon and, on Monday afternoon, they met at Burlington Gardens and from there took a taxi out to Hampstead. 'Ours was a delicate mission,' Cockerell recalled, 'to persuade him to resign from the Roxburghe Club on grounds of ill-health, and to enable us to cancel a meeting of the club on Wednesday at 5 pm to deal with revelations made by Messrs Carter and Pollard in their recent book.'

As usual, they were greeted at the door by Mrs Wise, who showed them through to the library. Stepping inside, Cockerell assumed that Kenyon, as the more senior partner in their expedition, would take the lead; except as it goes the bashful Kenyon found it impossible to raise the subject. He kept waiting for Mrs Wise to leave the men to their business. But, to his dismay, having brought in the tea and cake, she parked herself in the window seat and kept a hawkish eye on the proceedings. 'The tea-party was agonizing,' Cockerell would recall, wincing at the memory. The conversation circled round and round until, eventually, with the teapot drained and the crockery cleared away and Kenyon fidgeting uncomfortably in his seat, Cockerell was forced to take the bull by the horns.

'Wise,' he said bluntly, 'you are under a bit of a cloud and some of us think you ought to resign until it blows over.'

Wise protested that a resignation would be tantamount to an admission of guilt.

Not at all, Cockerell assured him. That would be a most uncharitable interpretation of events. Consider it a temporary measure until the business clears itself up. The Roxburghe would be glad to have him back just as soon as he was able to provide them with the assurances they needed. Until then, he ought to prioritise his health.

It took much persuasion, but Wise duly agreed to tender his resignation. He did so verbally, there and then, and on one condition: that the club would provide him with a written guarantee that it regarded him as having admitted nothing—for, he claimed, he had nothing to admit.

By the time Cockerell and Kenyon left Heath Drive, it was dark. Scarcely daring to believe their luck, they made it to Lord Aldenham's townhouse by a quarter-to-six, only to find that he was yet to get back from a long weekend in the country. Kenyon excused himself—he had a train to catch—leaving Cockerell to wait it out alone. Half an hour or so later, Aldenham arrived home and, delighted by the news, gladly agreed to cancel Wednesday's extraordinary meeting, which had now become unnecessary. By seven o'clock, Cockerell was in Chelsea with Lord Hornby, sharing the good news over a quick dinner before the two of them set about notifying the membership. He was done just in time to catch the nine-fifty-five train back to Cambridge. Come midnight, he was home and, exhausted, in bed.

However Wise tried to spin it, his resignation from the Roxburghe was certainly regarded as a confession by many—and a disgraceful one at that. But Carter and Pollard had been hoping for something more substantial. Not just a confession, but an explanation.

To be sure, in the wake of the *Enquiry* some delightful new evidence had come to light. For instance, a copy of the forged Swinburne first, *Siena*, recently donated to the Bodleian. When held up against the light at a certain angle, this pamphlet displayed a strange phenomenon: at a jaunty angle across the title page was an oily residue of text that did not match anything in the pamphlet. At first the librarian at the Bodleian thought this must be offset: that is, wet ink accidentally transferred when one sheet is stacked against another in the printing house. But he quickly realised that this could not be possible. Offset ink appears back to front whereas these letters were the correct way around—and moreover, the ghostly text looked nothing like ink. There was only one way that such an oddity could be produced. 'It is almost certainly due to a thin film of oil transferred when a pile of unfolded sheets of *Siena* (of which the Bodleian copy must have been at the bottom) was put down for a short time on some type which had been set and locked up in the form but not yet inked.'

A quick visit from Pollard was enough to confirm these suspicions. And, with a little sleuthing, he identified the text in question: a prospectus for lectures towards the law degree at King's College London. For the last fifty years the regular printer for King's had been Clay and Sons. That meant *Siena*, too, must have been printed by Clay and not by 'John Camden Hotten' as the title page suggested. But the real nail in the coffin was a reference in the ghostly prospectus text to the eleventh edition of a legal textbook, which was not published until 1890. This made the '1868' date on the title page of *Siena* an impossibility.

Still more incriminating for Wise was news from the Huntington Library in California. Having eagerly read the *Enquiry*, one of the librarians there decided to check their 'authentic' copy of Arnold's *Alaric at Rome* against Wise's facsimile edition, just to see how close they were. After all, this facsimile was the same book that had enabled Pollard to trace the unique hybrid font to Clay. It would be interesting to retrace the steps of the investigation. Much to this librarian's shock—and, one imagines, horror—with the two books side by side it was obvious that they had been printed from the same setting of type. Certainly, there were differences. The 'authentic' copy was printed on yellowed old paper whereas the facsimile was on clean white sheets with an '1889' watermark; the leaves of the 'authentic' copy were gathered in a slightly different way; a few small printing marks had been changed; and of course the 'authentic' copy did not have the short preface that Wise attached to his facsimile reprint. But otherwise the two books were identical. More to the point, this was not a legitimate facsimile that had been faked up after the fact by some unknown malefactor; the differences between the forgery and the facsimile could only have been made during the printing process and thus, if one follows the logic, under the direction of Wise himself. 'I think that this clinches the question of who the forger really was, even if there was doubt before,' Pollard told his father.

But the books themselves could only reveal so much. Forensic analysis can answer the who, when, and where of a crime but never the why. And, with Wise having shuttered himself away in his den, it seemed that that last question would never be answered. Carter and Pollard could not stop, though. There had to be something they could do to draw him out: some leverage, some document, some proof of malfeasance that would get him to speak.

Unbeknownst to the detectives, the very thing they required existed and was on the other side of the Atlantic. It took the form of several letters that had gone back and forth between Wise and Forman in 1896, while the former was readying the proofs for *Literary Anecdotes of the Nineteenth Century*. The letters and marked-up proof sheets had come up for sale in 1920, when Forman's books were auctioned off by the family. Somehow Wise had missed them during his weeding through the back shelves and cupboards. The papers were bought by a wealthy American stockbroker called Carl Pforzheimer, who was at that time building one of the nation's great private libraries (in a few years he would spend the record sum of £9,500 on a Gutenberg Bible). Not very often do private collectors require the services of a full-time in-house librarian. Pforzheimer was the exception. It was this librarian, William Jackson—Bill to his friends—who made the discovery.

His attention had been drawn to the documents by one of Wise's few defenders, the New York bookseller Gabriel Wells, who had pointed out—quite correctly—that Carter and Pollard had misattributed an anonymous essay in *Literary Anecdotes* to Wise when in fact it was by Forman. While looking through the annotated sheets and accompanying correspondence, Jackson spotted it. Wise was a scruffy writer. He had responded to Forman's queries not on a fresh sheet of paper, but by scribbling between the lines of the original letter. Where Forman had complained about Wise's dishonesty in describing certain reprints as 'exceptionally rare', Wise had responded with a far more incriminating line: 'Quite so. And we print *Last Tournament* in 1896 and want someone to think it was printed in 1871!'

There it was in black and white: an admission of guilt in the forger's own hand. In March 1935, while Carter was over in New York on rare books business, he was invited by Pforzheimer to inspect the document. It was the very thing he had been hoping for. In his mind's eye he could already see Wise turning scarlet as the thing was unravelled before him, like the final clincher in a Sayers book or a Christie. How he would explode!

Unfortunately, this scene would never come to pass. Despite Carter urging on publication, backed by enthusiastic nods from Bill Jackson, Pforzheimer remained unmoved. For several months, he seemed to do little more than twiddle his thumbs. One suspects him of wallowing in denial. He had respected Wise as a book-hunter, revered him even, and taken his counsel to heart. He simply did not want him to be guilty. And, lest he be judged too harshly, one must recall that he was not the first man in this sorry affair to have buried his head in the sand. Three months after Carter was granted sight of the paper, with both enquirers growing tetchy, Pforzheimer wrote to say that he considered the matter closed. Now was not the right time to publish, he said. Maybe he would change his mind in the future. But for the time being everything would have to remain as it was.

Carter was disappointed. So too Jackson, who wrote to London to assure Carter that he would keep up the pressure on his employer. Pforzheimer was an arch procrastinator, he explained, with a 'constitutional dislike for doing anything he can put off till next week'. So far as Jackson could tell, Pforzheimer was deeply afraid of legal action being taken against him by Wise, however unlikely this situation seemed. Consulting with his lawyers, he mooted selling the document to Carter and Pollard for a dollar, and with it all rights and responsibilities, and once they were done with it they could sell it back to him for an equally nominal sum. What they decided to do with the document in the interim was none of his business, legally speaking. But the promised sale never materialised.

By Christmas of 1936, the bookseller-detectives were getting desperate. Something needed to be done to shake Pforzheimer from his perch. Having returned to New York, Carter contacted Jackson to remind him of his promised assistance, laying out the arguments in favour of publishing the incriminating document:

1. Because the truth is in general better than uncertainty.
2. Because there is always the chance that some full statement might be obtained from Wise by the publication of the truth.
3. Because Wise might die and later publication of the document would raise, however unjustifiably, tiresome questions as to why it had been suppressed.

Still Pforzheimer did nothing. The next surviving letter from Jackson to Carter whiffs of frustration: 'I did my best—gave all the reasons I could think of but to no avail. I shall try again at the first opportunity.'

Beneath the perfect dome of St Paul's Cathedral, if you whisper into the wall, your voice can be heard on the far side of the structure. The dome of the British Museum reading room contained no such architectural quirk, though it may as well have done; gossip here spread fast. In 1936, the story echoing round the reading room was that a document had been discovered, somewhere in the United States, which proved the guilt of Wise once and for all. For now, this was only a vague whisper, but Carter had an idea. The vagueness was precisely the problem, he explained. 'Once a piece of information of this character and importance begins to circulate, in however vague a form, it is impossible to stop it,' Carter told Pforzheimer. 'I am afraid, in fact, that this so far underground rumour cannot fail before long to come to the surface; and it would probably so do in such a way as to nullify your own efforts, with which we have every sympathy, to handle the matter with the utmost possible consideration for those concerned. Let a newspaper man run across the tail end of this story and you can imagine what an elegant lot of headlines would result.'

One detects the hint of a veiled threat here, as though Carter was issuing the American an ultimatum. Entrust us with the publication of the document and permit us to confront Wise, he seems to say, or else we shall allow it to be published in the most damaging way possible and your name shall be dragged through the mud. If Pforzheimer detected the subtext, he did not show it. His response, as usual, was to sit on his hands. Equally, if Carter had been putting the frighteners on then he did not follow through. Thus the business of the document reached an uneasy truce. Pforzheimer possessed crucial evidence in his library but would allow no one to see it; Carter and Pollard had the proof they needed to squeeze further information from Wise, but without Pforzheimer's say-so they could not use it.

Pforzheimer's decision to batten down the hatches was especially disappointing because the document raised all kinds of new questions about Forman's part in the scam—questions that could not very well be answered by anyone besides Wise himself. And who knew how much longer he would be around? Carter and Pollard wanted answers. And time, it seemed, was running out.

18

What a Lot of Books

Legend has it that, in the moments before his death, Wise was asked to come clean and confess to his role in manufacturing the nineteenth-century forgeries. The old man was weak, slipping in and out of consciousness, breath fluttering. 'Oh,' he murmured in a last flash of lucidity. 'It's all too complicated to go into now.' And thus he died. He had lasted less than three years following the publication of the *Enquiry*. He was seventy-seven years old with a history of poor health. That didn't stop people whispering that in the end it was the shame that killed him.

There were no children to inherit. Wise never gave Louie the family she yearned for. 'Children!' he had used to scoff. 'I can't afford children. They cost a thousand pounds each; and what a lot of books I can buy for that!' And so, in accordance with the final iteration of his much-revised will, the contents of the Ashley Library were offered to the British Museum at a knock-down price. His widow did not want for money. Even without the books, at the time of his death Wise's estate was valued at over £138,000 (some £10 million today). On the open market, the books were probably worth the same again. In the end, they went to the museum for a little under half their true value.

The decision was not without controversy. 'Exposed faker of books will have memorial at British Museum', ran one newspaper. *The Times* bent over backwards to justify the purchase as an 'outstanding event' in literary history. 'Wise was a bibliographer of the greatest skill and distinction, in spite of the scandal which attached itself to his name in his last years' was its verdict. Three years on from the *Enquiry* it was 'important to keep the incident in its proper perspective'. They did not, of course, want to admit that their perspective on the affair might have been distorted by the prospect of mountains of precious books going to their national museum, to be stacked like gold bars in a vault.

For Carter and Pollard, news of Wise's death came as a blow. Now they would never get their explanation. For some time they had been diligently compiling materials for a revised edition of the *Enquiry*, incorporating all the new evidence that had since come to light. But without Pforzheimer's co-operation, without him sharing the document that proved Wise's guilt once and for all, the work had proved impossible. For a time, Carter considered throwing caution to the wind and going to press with a draft that took Wise's guilt for granted. After all, there was nothing Wise could say about it now. And Pforzheimer would be forced to publish the document once reviewers asked what wrought this change in the enquirers' position. However, this came to seem a bad idea. Sensible booksellers, Carter reflected, did not aggravate wealthy collectors.

On top of that were all the usual distractions. At Birrell and Garnett, business continued to stagger on, with customers to see, books to sell, and bills to pay. In the aftermath of her favourable review for *The Times*, Dorothy Sayers had stopped by the shop on Gerrard Street to talk paper chemistry with Pollard, doubtless with the intention of weaving some such detail into a future mystery. The two of them would go on to form something like a friendship: she offering corrections and hints for the revised edition of the *Enquiry*, setting her detective mind to practical use; he advising her on matters of printing and typography. In her next and most successful book thus far, *Gaudy Night*, it would be revealed that even Lord Peter Wimsey was an admirer of the *Enquiry*. During a discussion about the fabrication of scientific results and the possible motives for forgery, Wimsey is prompted to remind his friends about the long and distinguished history of literary fabrication: 'Chatterton?' he asks. 'Ossian? Henry Ireland? Those nineteenth-century pamphlets the other day?'

In a delightful twist, late in 1937 Sayers and Pollard together dipped their otherwise impeccable toes into the turbid pond of forgery. The fake in question was planned as a Christmas jape: a fictitious account of one of Lord Peter's forebears, Lord Mortimer Wimsey, supposedly written soon after his death by an unnamed Church of England clergyman. The title page of this little pamphlet made no mention of Sayers and, to complete the illusion in true Wiseian style, was furnished with a false imprint:

BRISTOL:
Printed by M. BRYAN, Corn-street.

1816.

Pollard was tasked with making the pamphlet look as convincing as possible, guiding on the typography, paper, and the overall look of the page. He took the job extremely seriously. Mary Bryan was a real printer based in Bristol at that time, using similar fonts to those used for the fake. It almost looks as though Pollard wanted to prove himself a more capable forger than Wise. 'I have had a paper specimen which will not do' is a typical sentiment from one of his reports to the author. The only clue giving the book away is that Lord Mortimer Wimsey was a product of Sayers's imagination and not a real person.

When Sayers got round to sending a copy to Pollard, she inscribed the title page with a personal note from the fictitious 'author'. Pollard received the booklet with thanks, though his mischievous response speaks volumes about his desire to be thought of as a rival to Lord Peter. 'I must also ask you to transmit to the author my thanks for the presentation copy,' he winked. 'I am sorry that its inscription was written at least ten years after the pamphlet was printed, for I see that a metal pen was used.' His tone may have been jesting, but he was, as usual, correct. Metal nibs weren't mass produced until the 1820s.

Meanwhile, and much to everyone's surprise, Carter, the perennial ladies' man, had decided to settle down and marry. Her name was Ernestine Fantl, a young curator at the Museum of Modern Art in

New York. The two of them first met at a summertime house party in, of all places, the leafy Oxfordshire village of Berwick Salome, where Ernestine was spending a weekend during her first trip to Europe. Carter struck up contact on his return to New York later in 1936 and, on Boxing Day morning, the two were married.

The ceremony was small—just the pair of them and their witnesses—though the journey to the town hall was precisely as elegant as one would expect from Carter. 'A friend volunteered to provide the family Rolls Royce to get us and our witnesses there,' Ernestine would later reminisce. 'It had unfortunately a habit of breaking down, although, preserving its image, invariably on Fifth Avenue. It duly did so, but obligingly near a restaurant called the Caviar where, while we waited for the Rolls to be repaired, we had a pre-wedding breakfast—caviar and Montrachet.' It is a well-oiled story, burnished in the telling. One desperately hopes every word to be true.

Nobody could dislike Ernestine. 'She is young, small, dark, rather pretty, very bright, self-possessed, capable,' wrote Carter's employer with a combination of approval and, one suspects, relief. 'They seem blissfully happy and act as if they had been married for years.'

'I *am* very happy', Carter confirmed to Pollard. On the same postcard, and with perhaps a little more excitement than might be thought appropriate for a newlywed, he boasted of the wedding gift that his colleagues at Scribner had bought him—a book which just a few years earlier had proved impossible to find: slim, bound by Zaehnsdorf in boards of crushed blue morocco, stamped in gilt. His very own copy of the 'Reading' *Sonnets*.

Detective stories tend to follow certain patterns. It is in their nature to weave together loose threads, to wrap everything up in a final scene. All the suspects are gathered; the detective presents his or her evidence; the murderer (for it is usually a murderer) is prompted to confess. And, in confessing, the puzzle is solved—for what good is a puzzle without a solution? Real-life endings are seldom so neat. Threads remain loose. Suspects disappear. Felons profess their innocence contrary to overwhelming evidence. Thomas James Wise, when confronted with the ironclad proof of the *Enquiry*, chose to seal his lips. He never did confess.

Or did he? For in stipulating that the Ashley Library should be left to the nation, Wise must have known that his last and most egregious crime—the theft of leaves from the British Museum and their insertion into his own books—would eventually be discovered. All the clues were neatly laid out for the taking; now someone merely needed to come along and piece them together. Is this gesture not a confession of sorts?

If so, many years would pass before anyone realised it. Pollard came very close to uncovering the secret after the death of Mrs Wise in 1939, though he did not know it at the time. There was a final clearing out of Heath Drive that summer. Everything went: wardrobes, chests of drawers, walnut and mahogany cabinets, bedsteads in oak and brass, writing tables, chairs, chesterfields, an array of Persian and English rugs, decorative and domestic crockery, glassware, and silver plate, a sturdy iron safe, and an Austin Twelve motorcar. The bespoke cabinets from the library had already gone to the British Museum with the books they once housed. It is said that, when dismantled, their mahogany was discovered to be the 'thinnest veneer' over cheap hardwood. But there were still a few scraps from the Wise collection which hadn't made it to the museum: old unbound pamphlets and standalone leaves which had been forgotten or mislaid, the inconspicuous remnants of Wise's secret book hospital.

Pollard attended the sale. Going back to Heath Drive must have been a strange experience for him, revisiting the scene of that original confrontation, now stripped of its fixtures and fittings. One lot which caught his eye was a bundle of pages torn from seventeenth-century playbooks and pamphlets: more than a hundred in total. It was a tantalising hint that all those perfect specimens in the Ashley Library were perhaps not so perfect as their owner had claimed—or at least that their perfection was the result of surgery. He ventured a couple of lukewarm bids but relinquished the lot to a rival bookseller for just one pound five shillings. Had he taken the bundle home, perhaps he would have noticed that, among the rejects from Wise's book hospital were several mismatched leaves torn from books in the museum.

Two months later, in September 1939, war was declared with Germany. As gas masks, rationing, blackout alerts, and bomb shelters became everyday realities, the buying and selling of rare books came to seem a frivolity. Birrell and Garnett was an early casualty. The shop on Gerrard Street shut its doors for the final time that year. The Scribner office on Bedford Square, however, persisted, thanks in no small part to Carter's extraordinary determination and drive. He was busier now than ever before, busier even than at the height of the investigation. Within days of war being declared, he was recruited to the Ministry for Information as a press censor, ensuring that military secrets remained out of the public eye. It was a full-time job but the hours were irregular. Sometimes he would be working in the day, sometimes at night. It was usually possible to find one or two hours each day to keep the rare books side of business ticking over. So long as the Americans kept out of the war, he explained to his fellow London bibliophiles, the demand for rare books would persist. 'England needs American currency. The trade needs the American market. We'—meaning Scribner—'need good books.'

And yet, for all his bravado—'I look very odd with a rifle!' he would joke to his American employers—these were deeply frustrating and, one imagines, frightening years for Carter. Instead of cycling home to Ernestine after a busy night shift at the ministry, he would hole up in the Scribner basement and sleep under a makeshift bomb shelter constructed from stacked volumes of the *Dictionary of National Biography* and the *Encyclopaedia Britannica*. At the height of the Blitz, explosions repeatedly blew out all the windows in Bedford Square. 'I'm sick of it,' he told Percy Muir, who had sensibly retreated to the country: 'it always pours with rain immediately afterward'. While the rain was welcomed by the city's overstretched firefighters, who found themselves racing from blaze to blaze during a bombing run, it put Carter in a terrible mood. Damp is a bookseller's worst enemy. Most of the city was using sandbags and blackout curtains to ready itself for further bombardment; Carter was trying to prevent his stock getting wet.

Staff at the British Museum suffered the same problem. On 10 May 1941, with Luftwaffe bombs lighting up the London sky, a cluster of incendiaries struck the southwest quarter of the building. Many of the most valuable artefacts had already been stashed underground in abandoned tube stations or evacuated into the countryside. A decent quantity of precious books and manuscripts had been taken to the National Library of Wales in Aberystwyth. Removing most of the books had been deemed impossible, though, and so they had remained put. At first it was feared that the fire would claim everything; in fact, the hoses did more damage, ruining what the flames could not reach. By the end of the night it is estimated that over a hundred and fifty thousand volumes had been destroyed. There are stirring photographs from the days that followed: thousands of books lining the halls and corridors, propped open on the floors and atop display cases, drying in the air, windows open to let in the breeze.

Mercifully the Ashley collection survived the war intact. Three hundred of Wise's books were part of the first tranche evacuated to the countryside in 1939 and another two thousand followed the next year. The most valuable of the remaining volumes were moved to bombproof safes in the basement. Come the end of the war, though, the Ashley books were no longer the priority they once had been. Museum staff were too busy assessing the damage to the bombed-out reading rooms, managing structural repairs, and working out how they were going to fill the sinister gaps on the shelves.

It was 1955 before anyone took a serious look at the contents of the Ashley books. The job of incorporating them into the catalogue was assigned to one of the younger members of staff. David Foxon was only just out of his twenties but already counted among the museum's sharpest intellects. At nineteen, having secured his place at Oxford, he had been recruited to the government's code and cipher school at Bletchley Park, where he had joined and eventually headed up a small unit deciphering Italian submarine communications. After the fall of Italy in 1943, he had been seconded to a mosquito-infested intercept station in Ceylon, monitoring Japanese airwaves and coordinating cryptographic intelligence with the Americans. The work was exhausting but exciting, and no matter how exhausted he became, the excitement never left him.

Working at the museum nurtured Foxon's thrill for puzzles and made excellent use of his ability to identify and interpret patterns. The Ashley books posed a puzzle like no other. Suspicions were first aroused by Wise's copy of a play by Ben Jonson, *The Case is Alter'd*, from 1609. While cataloguing, Foxon noticed that four leaves at the end of this quarto had undergone significant restoration. Unlike the rest of the book, these leaves had been severely cropped at some point; a restorer had built back the margins with old paper and skilfully added the missing head and tail of each leaf in pen and ink. In other words, this was not a single, flawless specimen but two imperfects married together. Such practices were common enough fifty years ago, Foxon reflected, and ought not to be judged too harshly. When comparing the old museum copy to the new Ashley copy, though, he noticed that the former was lacking the very same pages that had been added to the latter. Moreover, the museum copy was cropped down to precisely the size those stitched-in leaves had been before the restorative margin-work.

Foxon set to the puzzle with the same relish as had Carter and Pollard twenty years earlier. Trawling the museum catalogue for damaged playbooks, he identified likely victims of vandalism and theft. Time and again he found that the Ashley books had been made up with the missing leaves. With characteristic ingenuity, Foxon discovered that he could detect an anomalous leaf in a number of ways: by looking for creases, folds, and imperfections in the paper; by mapping patterns of foxing or water-staining across multiple copies; by lining up the original stitch holes, made when the quarto was just another crudely threaded, unbound pamphlet to be hawked on the streets of seventeenth-century London; or by tracing the paths taken by hungry bookworms as they burrowed through a volume. If a grub had bored through page after page and then disappeared, only to resume its burrowing a few pages later, then those untouched pages had surely been snaffled from another copy. In an authentic, complete copy the holes would all line up. In one case the stolen leaf was not even properly bound in; Foxon found it tucked loose into a book, as though Wise had intended to finish the job later but had forgotten all about it. When lined up against the stub in the corresponding museum volume, a play by James Shirley, the tear line was found to match perfectly.

Was the decision to sell his books to the British Museum a small act of atonement for Wise? Or was he getting the last laugh, basking in the glory of his wickedness, adding insult to injury by flaunting the evidence of his pilfering? There has always been a subset of villains who wish for nothing more than to be caught so that they might openly boast of their exploits, especially those who pride themselves on the ingenuity of their crimes. Wise was not one of those men. After his death, it was suggested by some of his friends—most notably George Bernard Shaw—that the whole forgery business must have been a runaway practical joke, an elaborate prank conceived at the expense of gullible Americans and their cheque-books. 'His fictions hurt nobody, and gave keen pleasure to collectors,' Shaw claimed. 'Why should we be angry with him for making people harmlessly happy?'

The fact that Wise himself never attempted this line of defence is perhaps the surest argument against it. For him, far more was at stake. Everything he had accomplished rested on this edifice of deception: his scholarship, his reputation, his good name, his relationships. To be exposed as a fraudster—and a fraud—was his greatest fear. Having spent so many years cultivating a reputation as the greatest book-hunter of the age, who would trade that for the grubby laurels of a trickster?

In truth, the forgeries had been Wise's ticket into the upper reaches of bibliodom and the thefts had helped to keep him there. As a young uneducated clerk surrounded by university men, he had needed both money and something to make him stand out. Each new 'discovery' became a token of his prowess and his promise as a man of letters. The book world had given him a home and a purpose, and he would do whatever it took not only to remain a part of that world but to climb to its pinnacle. When uncovering the thefts from the museum, Foxon called Wise's sanity into question. 'Clearly there are irrational motives at work,' he concluded. But there is another possibility. Might his actions be entirely in keeping with the social anxieties of a man who does not belong? Wise was, in every sense of the word, a pretender to greatness. As the shark that stops swimming will sink and die, so Wise had to maintain the lie. The discoveries needed to keep coming.

It is, however, worth considering the charge levelled by Foxon in a little more depth. Bibliomania is a disease with many symptoms. In 1930, the journalist, bookman, and all-round good egg Holbrook Jackson devoted more than eight hundred pages to an 'anatomy' of this affliction. His book is a great compendium of learning: a tome that belongs on the shelves of any enthusiastic book-hunter, though as a caution not as a guide. Over the years, he had met bibliomaniacs who were otherwise men of great erudition and ambition; others, like himself, who with 'nerves frayed and brains dulled' had taken to books 'as sick souls take to drugs'. 'Some are wise, subtle, witty,' he wrote; 'others dull, sad, and heavy; some intelligent, some ignorant; they are moody and miserly, vain and bragging; but all mad.'

To his eyes, the only thread holding this loose group together was a kind of distorted, degenerate, destructive lust. 'Bibliomania is perverted bibliophily,' Jackson concluded. 'These perverts cannot see books without coveting, yearning, craving for them.' As another writer put it: the disease 'seizes hold of rational beings, and so perverts them that in the sufferer's mind the human race exists for the sake of the books, and not the books for the sake of the human race'. He gave the example of an eighteenth-century Dutch collector who was made so anxious by the thought of his library being soiled by ash or smoke that he refused ever to light a fire in the house, even in the depths of winter, 'and was often so cold in bed that he contrived to warm his feet by laying a folio on them as it were an extra blanket'.

There is, of course, a little of the bibliomaniac in every bibliophile. Each of us knows that ache, that urge, that craving. Only the greenest of collectors, having lent a book to a friend, ever expects to get it back without a struggle. And yet, left unchecked, such book-madness could permanently warp the brain, Jackson warned. Corrupted desire could twist a bibliophile into that most deranged and depraved of creatures—the biblioclast: cutting, slicing, or tearing pages to be mounted, rebound, or, heaven forbid, used to light one's pipe. It was not unknown for such ghouls to make a rare book rarer by acquiring all the extant copies and burning the surplus. Others would be driven to theft and, Jackson reminded his readers, few who started on that path ever changed their course. In Flaubert's earliest short story, written in 1836 at the age of fourteen, the protagonist is a reclusive bookseller, driven to murder by his lust for a precious incunable. It was based on the purportedly true story of a bibliomaniacal monk-turned-bookseller-turned-serial-killer, Don Vincente, recently captured and sentenced to death in Barcelona.

So far as we know, Thomas Wise never killed anyone (though the exposé of his forgeries must have brought one or two collectors close to heart attack). He was not a murderer. In the decades following his death, successive generations of bibliographers and dealers have speculated—both in print and over drinks—about the precise nature of Wise's book-madness. Was he a compulsive liar? A kleptomaniac? Or even a psychopath? And yet, granting that he does in some ways fit the pattern of biblioklept and biblioclast rather closely, a diagnosis of bibliomania raises more problems than it solves. Most of the time Wise's attitude towards books seems to have been not intemperately passionate but disconcertingly cool and calculating. His acquisition was guided by frosty self-interest. Wise never served his books; they always served him. The problem was not his sanity but his ethics.

Perhaps the most revealing book Wise ever printed was not among those that went to the museum after his death—though only because he had already donated two copies. In 1882, at the age of twenty-three and before his involvement with the Browning and Shelley Societies, he saw through the press a slim volume entitled, simply,

Verses. By Thomas J. Wise. The book was no fake. As a youngster, Wise had indeed tried his hand at poetry—with predictable results. There is almost something charming about the youthful naïveté of the writing. Individual poems are framed by epigraphs from Browning, Shelley, Morris, and Rossetti, and many of the poems are transparent—albeit unsuccessful—imitations of those heroes. They were the kind of poems that might have made his mother smile before her final descent into ill health eleven years earlier. But it is not the content of the volume that is so revealing. It is its form.

The booklet was printed by William Fullford of Pentonville Road near King's Cross, a jobbing tradesman better known for customisable diaries, postcards, and business stationery than for bijou poetry collections. He was likely selected by Wise for his cheap rates (the sign above his door read 'Cheapest High-Class Printers and Stationers') and the convenience of his workshop, which was located just a fifteen-minute walk from the family home.

From Fullford's perspective, a thirty-page octavo booklet of poems must have seemed a simple enough commission. However, Wise managed to transform it into a job of extraordinary bibliographical complexity. The title page alone features an inelegant mishmash of four different typefaces: traditional large roman capitals for the title; a clunky modern slab serif for the author's name; a standard old-style roman for the epigraph and date; and rounded sans serif capitals for the imprint: 'PRINTED FOR PRIVATE CIRCULATION ONLY'. It is as though Wise, overwhelmed by choice, opted for a little bit of everything. Instead of being left plain, the ruby red boards were printed from the same setting of type as the title page in gold—a fiddly task for even the most skilled of printers. Of the thirty-five copies produced at first, some were done on plain white paper, some on pale lavender paper, some on large pink paper, some on antique 'parchment' notepaper. Early the following year, six more copies were printed on ultraheavy, cardboard-like stock from Whatman Paper Mill in Kent, known for producing some of the finest papers in the world (for these later copies Wise added a decorative red border to each page, framing his verses like family photographs).

Especially tricky must have been the five copies printed on vellum, which was notoriously slippery in the press and consequently difficult to get a decent, smudge-free impression on. Not as slippery as Wise, though, for even at this early date he was telling untruths about his books. In the front of one of those copies Wise has written in pencil 'one of three copies printed upon vellum'; in the front of another he has written 'one of only four copies printed on vellum'. Elsewhere he says five.

Small wonder the relationship with Fullford did not last. Young Wise cannot have been an easy customer. As Carter would later point out, 'neither text-printing on cardboard-heavy Whatman, nor gold-printing on coloured paper boards, would be within the compass of the average printer'—let alone machining on vellum. Such an intricate job would have required Wise to be in the print shop, selecting fonts, inspecting proofs, supervising every step. He would have been constantly getting in the way, bossing the printer about, giving instructions, asking questions, considering answers, learning the strengths and limitations of the press.

As the epigraph for his *Verses*, Wise selected a quotation from Martin Tupper: 'Thoughts that have tarried in my mind and peopled its inner chamber'. Perhaps it was here, in Fullford's workshop, studying his selection of fonts and ornaments, that a fiendish thought became lodged in the chamber of his own mind. The thrum and whirr of the industrial presses, their cogs, chains, belts and cylinders ticking and rolling against the background hiss of steam; the proof sheets in Wise's hands, ink still oily and glistening, as he half-listened to the grumblings of his printer; ideas clicking into place like slivers of lead type.

Epilogue

In 1997 the Ashley collection of books and manuscripts was moved, along with all the other books held by the British Museum, to the new British Library buildings at St Pancras. If you go onto the online catalogue today and attempt to request one of the Ashley books in the usual manner, you will hit a dead end: 'Permission required. Please contact reference services.' Staff at the reference desk will look puzzled by this—nineteenth-century materials don't usually require special permission—and suggest you email the curator. Presuming you have a good reason up your sleeve for why you need to consult this particular copy of a book, and not any of the other copies in the stacks, then, all being well, a few days later it will be made available—albeit under strict terms. As surety, you will be required to surrender your library card at the issue desk. You will be directed to one of a small number of specific tables kept for restricted material. Tucked inside the front board of the book you will find a laminated red slip printed with a crossed-through camera and, in bolshy capital letters, 'NO PHOTOGRAPHY ALLOWED'. At no point is the book to be left unattended.

There is nothing unusual about this in itself. Many printed books are restricted for one reason or another. Some are fragile and need to be handled carefully. Others are legitimate treasures of the national collection: Shakespeare playbooks, early bibles, Caxton's Chaucer. Before my interest in Wise blossomed, I was required to sit in this section of the reading room only when studying books from the personal library of Alexander Pope, whose annotations elevated some otherwise unremarkable octavos to the level of jewels. It is also the section of the library in which printed erotica must be consulted, where the vigilant librarian can ensure you aren't enjoying yourself too much.

In most cases, though, it is only individual books that require permission. The Ashley collection is one of very few named collections to be restricted *in its entirety*. All five thousand seven hundred and eleven books with an Ashley shelfmark (the actual number of volumes is much higher because of multivolume works) require special authorisation before they can be consulted—and only then under close surveillance. Nearly four thousand of the Ashley books still haven't been logged in the general catalogue and exist in a sort of limbo, as though the sinners haven't yet been weeded out from the pure. One would be forgiven for thinking the library doesn't want you to see these books. Perhaps one assumes a certain level of institutional embarrassment. In truth, there is no shady conspiracy. After his discoveries went public, Foxon was reassigned. New books come into the library every day and it is difficult enough to keep up with those, let alone cataloguing large collections of old ones. Once celebrated as a triumphant acquisition for the nation, the Ashley collection simply fell through the cracks. Nowadays the books are forgotten by many and ignored by most.

Opinion among those who *have* recently studied specimens from the Ashley library is near-unanimous: the books look odd. Tastes have changed. Today we tend to be more accepting of books that show signs of their age—dirty pages, annotations, ink-splashes, dog-ears and the like—and not to focus so dogmatically on the 'virginal' condition and buttery leather that Wise and his contemporaries cherished. With that in mind, the early playbooks that Riviere patched up with stolen leaves, washed, bleached, and bound in fresh morocco, tend to look a little *too* clean, almost uncanny, as though they were printed yesterday.

There is something uncanny about the forgeries too. One of the more disturbing items in the collection is the so-called 'memento' of the Brownings: an elaborately tooled morocco case containing locks of hair from both poets and, sandwiched between them, a copy of the *Sonnets*. Accessing this volume requires an even higher level of authorisation than the other Ashley books. The overall effect of it is, as the bookseller John Collins writes in his account of Wise and Forman, both 'distasteful' and 'extremely bizarre'. It almost seems as though the locks of hair were intended to make the *Sonnets* appear more real, to bestow on the booklet the aura of authenticity. As things stand, the effect is quite the opposite: knowing that the *Sonnets* is fake makes us question the provenance of the locks of hair. Here we see the broader and more sinister impact of the forgeries writ in miniature. They undermine our confidence. We doubt our judgement, question our instincts. Is this the real thing? Or am I being deceived? What if I get this wrong? After a while, authenticity itself comes to seem an illusion.

There are, of course, collectors today who specialise in literary fakes, for whom the forgeries of Thomas James Wise are some of the most valuable on the market. Receipts for the sale of the Schimmel collection of forgeries at Bonham's in 2012, which included a good portion of Wiseiana, totalled more than £160,000. The last time Carter's personal copy of the *Sonnets* came up for public sale—at Christie's in 2005—it reached $19,200. Adjusted for inflation, that is substantially more than any price achieved while the book was still thought to be authentic.

For book-hunters with shallower pockets, one can still occasionally scoop an underpriced Shelley Society reprint or one of Wise's Swinburne piracies from the barrows and basements of Bloomsbury and Charing Cross Road. Last year I picked up a copy of Wise's facsimile edition of Shelley's *Adonais*, his second foray into facsimile printing, done for the Shelley Society in 1886 from his own copy of the original. Intriguingly, this copy of *Adonais* has been stripped of Wise's introductory essay and any accompanying material declaring it to be a facsimile. There is only the '1821' date on the title page and the cobalt blue wrappers duplicated from the original. At some point in its history—it is difficult to say when—this innocent facsimile was turned into a fake.

*

In retrospect, we see in the encounter between Wise and his young adversaries the collision of two markedly different worlds. A working-class boy made good, Wise was a paragon of late-Victorian capitalism, whereas Carter and Pollard were to the manner born. Perhaps the greatest contrast was in their attitudes towards their friends. For Wise, people were expendable. He used them and, once they had served his purpose, he discarded them. In that regard, his treatment of people was much the same as his treatment of books. Carter and Pollard, by contrast, stayed true to each other from first to last. Their dossier of evidence against Wise was built both on the application of their own technical know-how and on the willingness of friends to help: not only the Oxbridge-educated Biblio Boys, but also Flora Livingston and her scissors, the courageous Gorfin, and the typographer Stanley Morison.

Although the outbreak of war temporarily scuttled some of those friendships, by 1942 things were looking up. Pollard returned to London to take up a civil service job at the Board of Trade (a position that required him to make an awkward statement to the present director of MI5 explaining his earlier political conduct) and the Biblio Boys began to meet again on a regular footing. The following year Carter was sent to New York as the new division head of the British Information Services. As promotions go, this one was perfectly suited to his talents. His office supervised the production of snappy pamphlets detailing the British war effort for American readers. Naturally, Carter ensured they were stylishly written and, just as importantly, attractively printed. His experience with, sympathy for, and knowledge of America and Americans made him a wonderfully effective propagandist.

After the war, Carter returned to writing and bookselling full time. In 1950, while trawling a private collection in England, he discovered, and in the following year sold, a previously unrecorded copy of the Gutenberg Bible—'crisp and unmarked' and 'magnificently large', it was the find of a lifetime (flying the book over to New York, he observed wryly that he must have been the first person in history to take a Gutenberg Bible airborne). However, the gracious manners and political instincts he displayed during wartime had not gone unnoticed by his superiors in government and, in 1953, he was poached by the British Embassy in Washington for diplomatic service. Life as an attaché suited him and Ernestine very well: the speech-writing and schmoozing were counterbalanced by a rotating calendar of cocktail parties, gala dinners, and nights at the ballet. He returned home in 1955 to hearty thanks from the Foreign and Commonwealth Office and a CBE. Unquestionably his most successful book, the coyly titled *ABC for Book Collectors*, came out in paperback in 1961. It remains in print. There may be more up-to-date volumes out there, but none possesses the same mischief or sparkle.

The revised edition of the *Enquiry* did not materialise in the authors' lifetimes, despite a few privately printed 'working papers' putting together new pieces of the puzzle and several near-complete drafts (some of which are, delightfully, written on the reverse of sheets from the manuscript of Carter's pioneering essay on detective fiction). Both enquirers had too many irons in the fire and Pollard, in particular, was too easily distracted to see the project to completion. His name was often used jokingly—sometimes despairingly—as a byword for procrastination. 'Pollard's pace' was the common refrain. In their later correspondence on Wiseian matters, the notes, though never infrequent, grew shorter and the handwriting shakier. Carter died, aged sixty-nine, on 18 March 1975. Pollard survived him by eighteen months. On Carter's death, Pollard sent Ernestine a short note of condolence: sincere, simple, heartbreaking: 'John was the best friend I ever had and the first person who really believed in me. I have never really faced up to the thought of a world in which his steadfastness would no longer be a source of ultimate support.'

Wise, it seems, never had that kind of friendship. He had his house, his wife, his motorcar; and of course, he had his books.

Further Reading

The starting point for any reader interested in the Wise forgeries should be Carter and Pollard's original *An Enquiry into the Nature of Certain Nineteenth Century Pamphlets* (1934). It is an extraordinary book. Reprints of this edition were published in 1971 and 1983. Copies of either the first or the reprint editions are difficult to come by and often expensive, but well worth seeking out.

Although Carter and Pollard never saw the revised edition of the *Enquiry* to press, many of their subsequent findings were published separately. First there was *The Firm of Charles Ottley, Landon & Co.* (1948), which focused on a series of fake Swinburne pamphlets. Further revelations were made in the essays collected by William B. Todd in *Thomas J. Wise: Centenary Studies* (1960), which was followed by four short pamphlets intended as working papers towards a new edition: *Precis of Paden* (1967), *The Forgeries of Tennyson's Plays* (1967), *The Mystery of 'The Death of Balder'* (1969), and *Gorfin's Stock* (1970). These and other materials were incorporated by Nicolas Barker and John Collins into *A Sequel to an Enquiry into the Nature of Certain Nineteenth Century Pamphlets* (1983), which builds on the findings of 1934, elaborates on the typographical evidence, and describes a good number of forgeries unidentified in the original *Enquiry*. A good overview of the developing literature can be found in Donald Gallup, 'The Carter and Pollard *Enquiry* Fifty Years After', *The Papers of the Bibliographical Society of America*, 78 (1984), 447–60.

FURTHER READING

The main thread pulled in the *Sequel* is the degree to which Forman was involved. Back when the *Enquiry* was first published, the Pforzheimer document had not yet been discovered and it remained under embargo for a decade thereafter. The existence of this document, and the revelation of Forman's connection to at least one of the forgeries, was finally made public in 1944, though not by Carter and Pollard. That honour belonged to Fannie E. Ratchford, librarian at the University of Texas, which had acquired John Henry Wrenn's collection after his death. In *Letters of Thomas J. Wise to John Henry Wrenn: A Further Inquiry into the Guilt of Certain Nineteenth-Century Forgers* (1944), Ratchford firmed up the charges against Wise, published conclusive evidence of Forman's complicity, and accused Herbert Gorfin and Edmund Gosse of being co-conspirators. All these men were in cahoots, she claimed.

Carter's surgical critique of Ratchford appeared in a lengthy review in *The Atlantic* (Feb. 1945: 93–100), in which he set out for the first time the full backstory of the investigation. Gorfin is defended against baseless accusations of collusion. The charges against Gosse are shown to rest on the flimsiest of evidence. In the margin of a surviving proof sheet for the Browning fake *The Runaway Slave*, the word 'mangoes' is corrected to 'mangos'. Ratchford thought the correction was in Gosse's handwriting. It is not. The case against Forman was more difficult to answer: from the unpublished Pforzheimer document, Carter knew Forman to have been involved in at least one of the forgeries and very probably in several others too. Even conceding this point, there was no 'Wise-Forman-Gosse workshop', Carter showed.

In these pages I have followed the Carter line. Without doubt Forman collaborated, and some of the faked-up pamphlets and doctored books appear to have been contrived by him alone; but it was Wise who took charge in conceiving, printing, and publicising the vast bulk of the forgeries. It was he who had the standing account with Clay; he who corrected the surviving proof sheets; he who announced the 'discoveries' to the world; he who sold them for personal gain. By any reasonable standard, he was the principal forger. When questioned about the Morris fakes, Forman immediately came clean. Wise never did. A crude but more-often-than-not accurate test of whether a forgery was the work of Forman or Wise is whether it was printed by Clay. Forman preferred to entrust work to smaller operators whereas Wise was almost exclusively their client. The *Sequel* is a superb work of scholarship, but I worry that Barker and Collins jump at shadows: forgeries displaying even the merest degree of typographical sophistication are assumed to have been masterminded by the more assiduous Forman, even where the stronger connection is with Wise.

News of the thefts from the British Museum was broken by David Foxon in an article for *The Times* on 18 October 1956 and given thorough treatment in his short but explosive monograph, *Thomas J. Wise and the Pre-Restoration Drama: A Study in Theft and Sophistication* (1959). A supplement, co-authored with William B. Todd, followed in *The Library*, 5th ser., 16 (1961), 287–93. On Foxon's career, see James McLaverty, 'David Foxon, Humanist Bibliographer', *Studies in Bibliography*, 54 (2001), 81–113. An accessible introduction to the sophistication of the Wrenn books is given by Aaron T. Pratt in *Collated and Perfect* (2019).

Information on Wise's life comes from several sources. The first biography to appear was Wilfred Partington's *Forging Ahead* (1939). A prospective English edition was delayed by the war and, in part, by Carter, who advised Faber against publishing it (something about the text being 'written without distinction and often with vulgarity'). Eventually, an English edition appeared under the title *Thomas J. Wise in the Original Cloth* (1946). Despite Carter's stylistic objections, Partington's biographies contain some useful information and anecdotes drawn from life. From a bibliographical perspective, the most detailed account is John Collins's *The Two Forgers: A Biography of Harry Buxton Forman and Thomas James Wise* (1992). As his title indicates, Collins divides the blame equally between the pair. My own view of the relationship between Wise and Forman may be gleaned from the foregoing pages. In addition to these printed sources, I have also drawn on the very many unpublished letters in archives, libraries, and private collections across the world, but most particularly in the Harry Ransom Center at the University of Texas.

FURTHER READING

For information on Carter, the first port of call must be an erudite and very enjoyable biography by the American librarian-collector Donald C. Dickinson, *John Carter: The Taste and Technique of a Bookman* (2004). There are further snapshots of Carter's personal life in Ernestine Carter's autobiography, *With Tongue in Chic* (1974). But mostly I have worked from the large collection of Carter's working papers and correspondence at the Harry Ransom Center (MS 4564, boxes 15–25), at Cambridge University Library (MSS Add. 8230–8240), and at King's College, Cambridge (GBR/0272/JWC). Carter's classic essay 'Detective Fiction' can be found in *New Paths in Book Collecting* (1934), 31–63.

Pollard has no full-length biography, though there are two useful retrospective essays: Carter's 'Graham Pollard', in R. W. Hunt, I. G. Phillip, and R. J. Roberts, eds., *Studies in the Book Trade: In Honour of Graham Pollard* (1975), 1–9; and Esther Potter, 'Graham Pollard at Work', *The Library*, 6th ser., 11 (1989), 307–27. These sources have been supplemented by the Pollard papers in the Bodleian Libraries at Oxford (MSS Pollard 1–425), which together take up nearly fifty linear metres of shelving. A subject index to the papers, prepared by Esther Potter, may be found in MS Pollard 425. Additionally, the business ledgers of Birrell and Garnett are held by the British Library (Add. MSS 52862–52870). Declassified MI5 reports from agent 'M/1' are in the National Archives at Kew (scattered through the KV series). Henry Hemming first identified 'M/1' with Pollard in his book *M: Maxwell Knight, MI5's Greatest Spymaster* (2017).

There are several good accounts of book culture around the *fin de siècle*, including David McKitterick's magnificent *Readers in a Revolution: Bibliographical Change in the Nineteenth Century* (2022) and, of course, Carter's *Taste and Technique in Book Collecting* (1948; rev. 1970). The liveliest contemporary accounts of the 'first edition mania' on which Wise preyed are John Herbert Slater's *Round and About the Book-Stalls: A Guide for the Book-Hunter* (1891) and *Early Editions: A Bibliographical Survey of the Works of Some Popular Modern Authors* (1894). The best study of this radical shift in collecting habits is an unpublished doctoral dissertation by Madeleine Myfanwy

Thompson, 'Birth of the First: Authenticity and the Collecting of Modern First Editions, 1890–1930', submitted to Indiana University in 2013. It is a real shame that this dissertation has not been published and I encourage readers to seek out the text online. For a wonderful first-hand account of the London antiquarian book trade in the early twentieth century, look for Percy Muir's *Minding My Own Business* (1956). Muir's papers at the Charles E. Young Research Library in Los Angeles contain the draft of an unfinished autobiographical novel about a young man's entry into the antiquarian trade (Collection 1430, box 5). It is very funny.

On facsimile printing, the go-to book is David McKitterick's *Old Books, New Technologies: The Representation, Conservation and Transformation of Books since 1700* (2013). On the evolving relationship between literary forgery and the methods of philological detection, see Anthony Grafton, *Forgers and Critics: Creativity and Duplicity in Western Scholarship* (1990; rev. 2019). An intellectually satisfying account of Wise within the broader history of forgery and fakery can be found in Kevin Young's *Bunk: The Rise of Hoaxes, Humbug, Plagiarists, Phonies, Post-Facts, and Fake News* (2017). Ken Rendell's *Forging History: The Detection of Fake Letters and Documents* (1994) is an essential practical guide for would-be Carters and Pollards. And, for a riveting account of bibliographical detection in the modern era, readers could not do better than Nick Wilding's 'Forging the Moon', *Proceedings of the American Philosophical Society*, 160 (2016), 37–72.

Acknowledgements

This book is about many things: ambition, greed, deceit. It is also about friendship. Like Carter and Pollard's *Enquiry*, this book is itself the result of many friendships. Countless people have endured my chattering about Wise and his antagonists. When I first launched myself into this story, I was repeatedly asked, with no little sarcasm, why I, an upstart bibliographer in my late twenties, might be drawn to the story of two upstart bibliographers in their late twenties. Why, indeed. But after years of working through their letters and papers and notebooks, Carter and Pollard have come to seem like friends. I have come to admire their style, their intellect, their flair. If this story prompts even a single reader to go back and revisit the *Enquiry*, I will consider my job well done.

I have been extraordinarily lucky to work with some of the best in the business. My agent, Anna Webber, has represented the book with characteristic good cheer and enthusiasm. Clara Farmer immediately understood what I was trying to achieve and helped squeeze the book into its final form. To her, Rosanna Hildyard, Sam Wells, and the whole team at Chatto, I am hugely grateful. Among my colleagues at Newcastle, I must single out James Harriman-Smith, Jenny Richards, Michael Rossington, and Anne Whitehead for their support, and Laura Elliott for her wizardry with numbers. I count myself fortunate to have been able to talk Wiseiana with Nick Wilding and Henry Woudhuysen. Jim McLaverty shared memories of David Foxon, in addition to being the very model of a modern bibliographer. And Niall Allsopp has, as ever, been a trusty partner in crime.

ACKNOWLEDGEMENTS

Much of the research underpinning this book was conducted at the Bodleian Libraries, the British Library, Cambridge University Library, and the Harry Ransom Center in Texas, where the staff have been unfailingly gracious, hospitable, and ready to help. In particular, I would like to thank Aaron Pratt at the Harry Ransom, Tanya Kirk at the British Library, Owen McKnight at Jesus College, Oxford, and Michael Meredith at Eton College, all of whom dug out special bits and bobs from the stacks (and their desks), shared their own formidable expertise, and indulged my curiosity. Library time was made possible by grants from Newcastle University, the British Academy and, in the final stages, the Leverhulme Trust and the Arts and Humanities Research Council. I would like to thank those bodies here.

In a sense, these pages are a love letter to the book trade, to the barrow-scavengers and the shelf-trawlers, to the joys of analogue book-hunting in an age of digital convenience. None of this would be possible without the judgement and courage of today's antiquarian and second-hand booksellers, many of whom are working, like Carter and Pollard before them, at the cutting edge of bibliography. Without the trade, old books would quite literally have no value. I am particularly obliged to Brian Cassidy and Anthony Smithson for talking fakes with me, and to Adam Douglas for an illuminating lesson on spotting dodgy autographs. Last year's York Antiquarian Book Seminar showed me that, under the next generation of booksellers, the trade will be in safe hands for decades to come. It is to that next generation, no less than the generations that came before, that this book is dedicated.

My last and greatest debt is, however, to my heroic wife Melissa, who listened to draft after draft of chapters-in-progress, gamely nodding along or pointing out where I had lost my way. And, of course, to Tristan and Olive, who make everything better.

Notes

Quotations have been taken from a variety of primary and secondary sources, both in print and in manuscript. I have, on occasion, taken the liberty of transposing reported speech into direct speech. All instances of this are properly signified in the notes. From time to time I have tweaked the formatting or spelling of quotations for reasons of grammar, clarity, and consistency: expanding or contracting honorifics, numerals, and so on. The following standard abbreviations for libraries and frequently cited texts have been used.

BL	British Library, London.
Bodl.	Bodleian Libraries, Oxford.
Carter	John Carter, *Taste and Technique in Book Collecting*, rev. edn (London, 1970).
Centenary Studies	William B. Todd, ed., *Thomas J. Wise: Centenary Studies* (Austin, TX, 1960).
Collins	John Collins, *The Two Forgers: A Biography of Harry Buxton Forman and Thomas James Wise* (Aldershot, 1992).
CUL	Cambridge University Library, Cambridge.
Dickinson	Donald C. Dickinson, *John Carter: The Taste and Technique of a Bookman* (New Castle, DE, 2004).
Enquiry	John Carter and Graham Pollard, *An Enquiry into the Nature of Certain*

NOTES

	Nineteenth Century Pamphlets (London, 1934).
Foxon	D. F. Foxon, *Thomas J. Wise and the Pre-Restoration Drama: A Study in Theft and Sophistication* (London, 1959).
HRC	Harry Ransom Center, Austin, TX.
Letters	Fannie Elizabeth Ratchford, ed., *Letters of Thomas J. Wise to John Henry Wrenn* (New York, 1944).
Muir	Percy Muir, *Minding My Own Business* (London, 1956).
ODNB	*Oxford Dictionary of National Biography.*
Partington	Wilfred Partington, *Thomas J. Wise in the Original Cloth* (London, 1946).
Schimmel	Sale of the Stuart B. Schimmel Forgery Collection, 23 May 2012, Bonhams, London.
Sequel	Nicolas Barker and John Collins, *A Sequel to an Enquiry into the Nature of Certain Nineteenth Century Pamphlets* (London, 1983).
TLS	*Times Literary Supplement.*
TNA	The National Archives, Kew.

PEOPLE

AFP	Albert Frederick Pollard
CSP	Catherine Susanna Pollard
DLS	Dorothy L. Sayers
EWG	Edmund William Gosse
HBF	Harry Buxton Forman
HEG	Herbert Edwin Gorfin
HGP	[Henry] Graham Pollard
JHW	John Henry Wrenn
JWC	John Waynfleet Carter
MBF	Maurice Buxton Forman
TJW	Thomas James Wise

NOTES

PROLOGUE

2 'Great ... made' Qtd. in Collins, 238.

1. INNOCENT FANCY

3 'Why ... Society?' *Note-Book of the Shelley Society* (London, 1888), 33.

4 'By Jove! I will' Ibid.

4 'no ... should' *The Shelley Society First Annual Report* (London, 1887), 2.

5 'We cannot ... Shelley?' Edward Freeman, 'Literature and Language', *Contemporary Review*, 52 (1887), 549–67 at 549.

5 'irregular ... vain' Matthew Arnold, 'Shelley', *The Nineteenth Century* (Jan. 1888), 36–9.

5 'the foul ... imagination' 'The Cenci at the Grand', *Bell's Life in London and Sporting Chronicle*, 3781 (8 May 1886), 2.

5 'Next ... opinion' *The Shelley Society First Annual Report* (London, 1887), 5.

6 'bright ... command' Robert Browning, *Alma Murray: Portrait as Beatrice Cenci* (London, 1891), 10.

6 'tall ... beard' Doris Arthur Jones, *The Life and Letters of Henry Arthur Jones* (London, 1930), 221.

6 'inveterate ... discussion' Qtd. in Partington, 315.

6 'pious ... vegetarian' Qtd. ibid., 316.

6 'Three ... out' Jones, *Life and Letters*, 221.

7 'snobbish ... artists' 'The Cenci at the Grand', 2.

7 'face ... Society' Stopford A. Brooke, 'Inaugural Address to the Shelley Society', *The Shelley Society's Papers, Part I* (London, 1888), 2.

7 'I do not ... examples' Ibid.

8 'slim ... graduate' Qtd. in Partington, 316.

8 'Rather ... today' TJW to JHW, 10 Apr. 1904, in *Letters*, 364.

8 'simpler form' Ibid.

9 'The true ... worthless' John Herbert Slater, *Round and About the Book-Stalls* (London, 1891), 1.

12 'Had I ... moment to pass' TJW, *A Browning Library* (London, 1929), xxvi–xxvii.

12 **Campbell** The copy presented to Campbell was inscribed by Browning and is now in HRC, PR 4217 .A1 1833. As one would expect, it is a beautifully clean copy.

275

NOTES

13 **facsimile reprint** The *Pauline* facsimile is, in truth, not particularly good when compared side by side with the original. Although the layout is closely matched, the typeface is some way off. The numerals are all wrong, as is the paper. The surviving proof sheets have been annotated by Wise (HRC, MS 4564/4.2) but the annotations bear no relation to the finished book, which makes very little sense. I leave this puzzle to some enterprising future scholar.

14 'concession ... Society' Qtd. in Partington, 45.

14 'By ... highly' TJW to HBF, 7 Jan. 1886, in *Sequel*, 270.

14 'The line ... hurry' HBF to TJW, 11 Jan. 1886, ibid., 270–1.

15 'In all ... it' TJW, 'Prefatory Note' to Robert Browning, *Pauline: A Fragment of a Confession*, ed. TJW (London, 1886), x.

15 'as exact ... retained' TJW, 'Prefatory Note' to Percy Bysshe Shelley, *Hellas: A Lyrical Drama*, ed. TJW (London, 1886), viii.

15 'perhaps ... time' Browning, *Alma Murray*, 5.

17 'He ... aid' *The Shelley Society First Annual Report* (London, 1887), 15.

17 'expressed dissent' TJW, *A Shelley Library* (London, 1924), 82.

18 **Philadelphia Historical Society** This detail was added only when Wise was correcting the proofs: see William Andrews Clark Memorial Library, PR5422.P651*.

18 'When ... prince' Edward Dowden to TJW, Aug. 1888, in *Sequel*, 133.

2. COMMUNISM WITH BIBLIOGRAPHY

22 'notorious ... homosexual' Evelyn Waugh, *A Little Learning* (Boston, 1964), 179.

22 'their tongues ... tonsils' Tom Driberg, *Ruling Passions* (London, 1978), 55.

22 'The premises ... aesthetes' Qtd. in 'Anthony Powell: A Symposium', *Summary*, 1 (Autumn 1970), 34–139 at 117.

22 'the last ... noticed' Evelyn Waugh, *Put Out More Flags*, 2nd edn (London, 1967), 58.

22 'unashamedly ... glories' Maurice Bowra, *Memories: 1898–1939* (London, 1966), 154.

22 'One ... subject' 'Shrewsbury School Mid-Term Report', [June 1920], Bodl., MS Pollard 418, fol. 41r.

23 'I am sorry ... care for' J. B. Oldham to AFP, 25 July 1917, Bodl., MS Pollard 418, fol. 57. One mortifying report card from the headmaster states: 'the flesh is very weak. He is too fond of regarding himself as an interesting physiological study' (ibid., fol. 38r). What he meant by this I dread to think.

NOTES

23   'too voluble ... criticism' Arthur Lionel Smith to AFP, 22 Dec. 1920, Bodl., MS Pollard 418, fols. 116–18.

23   'I do not ... Paper' HGP to AFP, 18 July 1920, Bodl., MS Pollard 417, fol. 35v.

23   'I regret ... out' HGP to AFP, 15 Jan. 1921, Bodl., MS Pollard 417, fol. 39r.

23   'we elected ... father!' Senior Bursar to AFP, 20 Jan. 1921, Bodl., MS Pollard 418, fol. 121r.

25   'My dear ... Pollard' HGP to AFP, 20 Apr. 1921, Bodl., MS Pollard 417, fol. 40.

25   'I am sure ... life' HGP to AFP, 21 Apr. 1921, Bodl., MS Pollard 417, fols. 40–4.

26   'splendid onion omelettes' HGP to CSP, [1924?], Bodl., MS Pollard 417, fol. 96r.

26   'thoroughly good fellow' HGP to CSP, 2 Oct. 1921, Bodl., MS Pollard 417, fol. 54r.

26   'water ... hair' HGP to AFP, [1922?], Bodl., MS Pollard 417, fol. 65r.

27   'spinning across the river' HGP to CSP, 18 Mar. 1922, Bodl., MS Pollard 417, fols. 75–6.

27   'I was done' HGP to CSP, 18 Mar. 1922, Bodl., MS Pollard 417, fols. 75–6.

27   'Goya pilgrimage' John Crawford Flitch, *An Idler in Spain: The Record of a Goya Pilgrimage* (New York, 1914).

27   'perfectly ... think' HGP to CSP, [1922?], Bodl., MS Pollard 417, fol. 74v.

28   'I was ... term' A. L. Rowse, *A Cornishman at Oxford* (London, 1965), 67.

28   'bamboozle tradesmen' HGP to CSP, [1924?], Bodl., MS Pollard 417, fol. 95v.

28   'I had ... setting up' HGP to CSP, 8 Feb. 1923, Bodl., MS Pollard 417, fol. 86r.

29   'the Jesus ... society' JWC, 'Graham Pollard', in R. W. Hunt, I. G. Philip, and R. J. Roberts, eds., *Studies in the Book Trade: In Honour of Graham Pollard* (Oxford, 1975), 1–9 at 3.

29   'I have ... hope not' HGP to CSP, 19 May 1922, Bodl., MS Pollard 417, fol. 80r.

29   'in a most ... sleep' Rowse, *Cornishman*, 81.

29   'tousled ... bibliography' Waugh, *A Little Learning*, 183.

30   'learned ... required' Henry Taunt, *Oxford Illustrated by Camera and Pen* (Oxford, 1911), 222.

NOTES

30 'old ... workhouse' Joseph Wells, *The Charm of Oxford* (London, 1920), 9.

30 'big ... shop' Rowse, *Cornishman*, 82.

31 'poems ... books' Ibid.

31 'already ... books' Anthony Powell, *Infants of the Spring* (London, 1976), 155.

31 'cull ... sell' Qtd. in Nicolas Barker, 'Forgery: The New Enquiry, Part 2', *Book Collector*, 32 (1983), 8.

31 'well ... here' HGP to CSP, [1922?], Bodl., MS Pollard 417, fol. 74r.

31 'I bought ... bargain' HGP to CSP, 19 June 1922, Bodl., MS Pollard 417, fol. 84.

31 'I have ... folios' HGP to CSP, [1924?], Bodl., MS Pollard 417, fol. 96v.

31 'They must ... should think' HGP to CSP, [1924?], Bodl., MS Pollard 417, fol. 96v.

31 'I am ... bookshops' HGP to AFP, 15 Dec. 1923, Bodl., MS Pollard 417, fol. 88v.

32 'Donne's ... Holywell Press' *New Oxford*, 14 (28 Oct. 1922), 7.

32 'There is ... are here' [HGP], 'Bibliographical Notes', Ibid., 15 (11 Nov. 1922), 11.

32 'I am ... Hodgson's' HGP to CSP, [1924?], Bodl., MS Pollard 417, fol. 97v.

33 'when ... sale' Peter Quennell, *The Marble Foot* (New York, 1976), 126.

33 'fat old ladies' HGP to CSP, [1924?], Bodl., MS Pollard 417, fol. 90r.

33 'between ... frowns' HGP to CSP, [1924?], Bodl., MS Pollard 417, fol. 90r.

33 'one ... book-collectors' Giles Barber, 'Libraries', in Brian Harrison, ed., *The History of the University of Oxford*, 8 vols. (Oxford, 1994), VIII. 471–84 at 477.

34 'Pray ... ashamed of' Bodl., Don.d.7.

35 reproved him HGP tells the story in Bodl., MS Pollard 361, fol. 13r.

3. FORGING AHEAD

38 'faked up' TJW, 'Two Shelley Forgeries', *Bookman's Journal*, 9 (1924), 219.

38 'I once ... comfortable quarters' John Herbert Slater, *Early Editions* (London, 1894), 46–7.

39 **Joseph Smeeton** On Smeeton, see David McKitterick, *Old Books, New Technologies: The Representation, Conservation and Transformation*

	of Books since 1700 (Cambridge, 2013), 88–90; A. T. Hazen, 'Type-Facsimiles', *Modern Philology*, 44 (1947), 209–17.
39	'doctored . . . books' TJW, 'Two Shelley Forgeries', 219.
39	'all respects . . . exactly' TJW, 'Prefatory Note' to Browning, *Pauline*, x.
40	'Murray . . . book' Edward Berdoe, *The Browning Cyclopædia* (London, 1898), 300.
41	'By God . . . consequence' William Henry Ireland, *The Confessions of William-Henry Ireland* (London, 1805), 30–2.
42	'I beheld . . . satisfaction' James Boden, *A Letter to George Steevens* (London, 1796), 2.
42	'How happy . . . peace' Ireland, *Confessions*, 96.
42	'Missteerree . . . poottaattoooeesse' *Telegraph* (14 Jan. 1796).
43	'some . . . groans' Joseph Farington, *The Farington Diary*, ed. James Greig, 8 vols. (London, 1922–28), I. 145.
46	near-identical . . . imprint See Thomas Hobbes, *Leviathan*, ed. Noel Malcolm, 3 vols. (Oxford, 2012), I. 209–71; Christopher N. Warren et al., 'Canst Thou Draw Out Leviathan with Computational Bibliography? New Angles on Printing Thomas Hobbes' "Ornaments" Edition', *Eighteenth-Century Studies*, 54 (2021), 827–59.
47	inspection . . . 1790 A. T. Hazen, *A Bibliography of the Strawberry Hill Press* (New Haven, 1942), 24–9.
48	'He was . . . excitement' Georgiana Burne-Jones, *Memorials of Edward Burne-Jones*, 2 vols. (London, 1906–12), I. 215.
49	'Theodore . . . tricks' Qtd. in Partington, 318.
49	Quotations are taken from TJW's account of the meeting in his *A Swinburne Library* (London, 1925), xi–xiii.
51	'I did not . . . ephemeral' Swinburne to TJW, 25 April 1888, in *The Letters of Algernon Charles Swinburne*, eds. EWG and TJW, 2 vols. (London, 1918), II. 188.
51	'I am almost . . . ambiguous' Swinburne to TJW, 27 April 1888, in *The Letters of Algernon Charles Swinburne*, II. 189.

4. BIRRELL AND GARNETT

53	excess stock His books begin to appear in the Birrell and Garnett stock ledger from April 1924: BL, Add. MS 52862, fols. 23v–25v.
53	'enormous cockney housekeeper' David Garnett, *The Flowers of the Forest* (London, 1955), 208.
53	'put up cheap deal shelves' Ibid., 205.
53	'two or three shelves' Ibid.

NOTES

54 'like lichen on a rock face' Frances Partridge, *Memories* (London, 1982), 74.

54 'meeting-place . . . arts' Garnett, *Flowers*, 193.

54 'Frankie's . . . fingerprints' Ibid., 204.

54 'I refused . . . discovery' Ibid., 207.

55 'It was . . . enticing items' Ashley Montagu, 'The Nonesuch Press', *Princeton University Library Chronicle*, 44 (1983), 127–34 at 127.

56 'Those . . . other things' Qtd. in Sue Bruley, *Leninism, Stalinism, and the Women's Movement in Britain, 1920–1939*, 2nd edn (Abingdon, 2013), 136.

57 'adviser . . . newspaper work' HGP to AFP, 16 Dec. 1926, Bodl., MS Pollard 417, fol. 104r.

57 'The general . . . anarchy' Stanley Baldwin, 'A Message from the Prime Minister', *British Gazette*, 2 (6 May 1926), 1.

57 'It is . . . people' Qtd. in G. A. Phillips, *The General Strike: The Politics of Industrial Conflict* (London, 1976), 124.

58 'knots . . . bags' Partridge, *Memories*, 113.

59 'The officer . . . dislikes' TNA, KV4/227, 17.

59 'one . . . agents' TNA, KV4/227, 17.

60 'My . . . contrary' TNA, KV4/227, 19.

60 M/1 The identification of HGP as M/1 was made by Henry Hemming in his book *M: Maxwell Knight, MI5's Greatest Spymaster* (London, 2017).

61 'new weapon . . . battle' *Workers' Life* (20 Dec. 1929), 1.

5. NOTHING SURREPTITIOUS

66 'I never . . . affair' Browning to TJW, 1 Aug. 1888, in *Letters of Robert Browning*, ed. TJW and Thurman L. Hood (New Haven, 1933), 298.

66 'for . . . Atlantic' [TJW and HBF], 'Advertisement', in Elizabeth Barrett Browning, *The Runaway Slave* (London, 1849 [i.e. 1888]).

66 'Dear . . . Browning' Robert Browning to TJW, 3 Aug. 1888, in *Letters of Robert Browning*, ed. TJW and Thurman L. Hood (New Haven, 1933), 298.

67 **design of the book** Not only do both books have cream wrappers with the title page framed by a double rule (the inner thin and the outer thick); the main pages of each are also and quite unusually framed by a single rule with a running header in capitals.

68 'so acute . . . result' TJW, *A Bibliography of the Writings in Prose and Verse of Algernon Charles Swinburne* (London, 1919), 73.

- 69 'care ... nothing' Swinburne to TJW, July 1887, in *Swinburne Library*, 41.
- 69 'skilfully fabricated' Quoted in *Centenary Studies*, 28.
- 69 'There ... market' Slater, *Early Editions*, 294.
- 70 series of notes and bibliographies Flora V. Livingston, *Swinburne's Proof Sheets and American First Editions* (Cambridge, MA, 1920), 18.
- 70 new title page Three proof sheets for the title page were found in the library of Wise's friend Walter B. Slater (now HRC STARK SS 68 STK), raising the intriguing possibility that he knew something of the book.
- 71 blank page *Sequel*, 249–50.
- 71 'This book ... possession' Quoted in Fannie E. Ratchford, 'Idylls of the Hearth: Wise's Forgery of *Enoch Arden*', *Southwest Review*, 26 (1941), 317–25 at 322–3.
- 71 'excessively rare trial issue' Maggs Bros., *English Literature of the 19th & 20th Centuries* (London, 1923), 525.
- 72 Forman had bought See JWC and HGP, *Precis of Paden* (Oxford, 1967).
- 72 The New Timon This overprinting was probably done by William Bowden and not by Clay's (*Sequel*, 107). In conception and execution, this curious forgery comes much closer to the benign mischief of Forman than the profiteering deceptions of Wise.
- 72 'far more ... find' Quoted in W. D. Paden, 'Tennyson's *The Lover's Tale*, R. H. Shepherd, and T. J. Wise', *Studies in Bibliography*, 18 (1965), 111–45 at 137.
- 73 'This is ... second printing' Quoted in *Centenary Studies*, 70–71.
- 75 'George ... Wise' Quoted in Collins, 93.
- 75 'It has ... author's' William G. Kingsland, 'Ruskin on Wages: Unpublished Letters', *Poet Lore*, 3 (1891), 360–2.
- 76 'reserved for private distribution only' TJW and James P. Smart, *A Complete Bibliography of the Writings in Prose and Verse of John Ruskin* (London, 1889–93), 147–8.
- 76 'First and only Edition' TJW, *The Illustrations to the Bibliography of the Writings of John Ruskin* (London, 1893), no. 139 [i.e. fig. 6].
- 77 'The enclosed ... exactitude' HBF to TJW, 6 May 1889, in *Sequel*, 276.
- 77 passed off as genuine See R. H. Super, 'The Authenticity of the First Edition of Arnold's *Alaric at Rome* (1840)', *Huntington Library Quarterly*, 19 (1956), 306–9.

NOTES

6. THE BIBLIO BOYS

My portrayal of the Elkin Mathews staff and shop and of the events that transpired at the sherry parties draws largely on Percy Muir's wonderful memoir.

- 80 gothic tracery Muir, 77.
- 80 'beautifully clothed' Ibid., 78.
- 80 'oozed ... pores' Ibid., 64.
- 80 'albeit ... maledictions' Ibid., 56.
- 81 'more ... customers' *33 Conduit Street, London, W.1.* (London, 1928), 9–10. I am grateful to Richard Ford for supplying me with a photocopy of this pamphlet.
- 81 'leaving ... street' Muir, 89.
- 81 'He was ... tolerated' Ibid.
- 82 'In his ... display' Ibid.
- 82 'informal, convivial, disrespectful' Qtd in Dickinson, 77.
- 83 'As he ... trouser crease' Lord Maud, 'Eulogy for John Carter', King's College, Cambridge, GBR/0272/JWC/2.
- 83 'Knowledge ... head' A. E. Housman, 'The Application of Thought to Textual Criticism', in *Selected Prose*, ed. JWC (Cambridge, 1962), 131–50 at 150.
- 83 'but what ... think again' JWC, *Taste and Technique in Book Collecting*, rev. edn (Pinner, 1970), 218.
- 85 'I enjoy ... hugely' JWC to HGP, [9 Mar. 1932?], Bodl., MS Pollard 131, fol. 112r.
- 85 'A dry ... world' JWC, *The Dry Martini* (London, 1963), [2–3].
- 86 'fashionable ... extra bid' Carter, 131.
- 86 'The result ... means' 'Notes on Rare Books', *New York Times* (20 Jan. 1929), 14.
- 86 'WITHOUT ... AUCTION' *The Library of Jerome Kern*, 2 vols. (New York, 1929), II. 348.
- 86 'FIRST ... issued' Ibid., I. 24.
- 87 'withdrawn ... misunderstanding' Ibid., II. 369.
- 87 'GENUINE ... COPY' Ibid., II. 388.
- 87 $1.7 million Thompson, 'Birth', 135.
- 87 'You asked ... attract them' HGP to JWC, 11 Feb. 1931, Bodl., MS Pollard 131, fol. 103r. See the list of books 'Wanted by Carter' (fol. 106r), which includes works by Nietzsche, Marx, Schopenhauer, Spinoza, Montesquieu, Rousseau, Descartes, and Napier.

88	'a keen reader' JWC, 'Introduction', in Dorothy Glover and Graham Greene, *Victorian Detective Fiction* (London, 1966), ix–xv at ix.
88	'It is notorious ... public' JWC, 'Detective Fiction', in *New Paths in Book Collecting* (London, 1934), 31–63 at 33–4.
88	'read ... stories' George Orwell, 'Bookshop Memories', in *The Collected Essays, Journalism and Letters of George Orwell*, eds. Ian Angus and Sonia Orwell, 4 vols. (London, 1968), I. 242–6 at 244.
89	'very ... thrilling' Muir, 88.
90	modern ... room *TLS*, 1501 (6 Nov. 1930), 924.
90	Dobell's latest catalogue Ibid., 1502 (13 Nov. 1930), 948.
90	Byron manuscript Ibid., 1503 (20 Nov. 1930), 996.
90	£18,000 ... price Ibid., 1504 (27 Nov. 1930), 1020.
90	Harzof He ought to have known a fake when he saw it, for Harzof was himself responsible for numerous fakes: see William E. Colburn, 'The Vizetelly Extracts', *Princeton University Library Chronicle*, 23 (1962), 54–9; Schimmel, lots 31 and 32.
90	'something funny' Muir, 90.
90	'vaguely phoney' Ibid.
90	'beautifully clean state' Ibid.
91	'When ... facts' Ibid., 91.
91	'somewhat ... exercise' *The Works of John Ruskin*, eds. E. T. Cook and Alexander Wedderburn, 39 vols. (London, 1903–12), I. 288.
92	'certainly ... Ruskin' Ibid., II. 102.
92	'This pamphlet ... condition' Ibid., XVIII. 14.
92	'I've had ... others' Muir, 91.

7. MAKING A MARKET

95	My account of Wrenn's visit draws from Ratchford's introduction to *Letters*, 8–9.
96	'only ... books' Ibid.
97	'At the ... difficulty' Slater, *Round*, 13.
97	'I feel ... Browning' Ibid., 52–53.
98	'The craze ... miniature' William Roberts, 'The First Edition Mania', *Fortnightly Review*, 55 (Mar. 1894), 347–54 at 347.
98	'typographical ... beauty' Ibid.
98	'the first ... thought' Ibid.
98	'too-zealous ... masterpiece' Ibid., 349.
99	'among ... treasures' TJW, 'Early Editions', *Bookman*, 6 (May 1894), 48–50.

NOTES

99   'among ... gold' William Sharp, *Life of Robert Browning* (London, 1890), 173.

99   'Time ... contentment' Barton Wood Currie, *Fishers of Books*, 2 vols. (Boston, 1931), II. 199.

100   'to the ... dailies' Ibid.

100   'sport of money kings' Joseph Jackson, 'The Sport of Money Kings', *World's Work* 25 (Nov. 1912), 80–4.

100   'disturbing ... doomed' Currie, *Fishers*, II. 200.

101   'My copy ... much' William Harris Arnold, *First Report of a Book-Collector* (New York, 1898), 61.

101   bewhiskered bon viveur Compare the portrait of Bangs by Harry Furniss, now in the National Portrait Gallery, ref. D16458.

101   Rumour ... perusal Dickinson, 26.

101   Book Row For a useful guide, see Marvin Mondlin and Roy Meador, *Book Row: An Anecdotal and Pictorial History of the Antiquarian Book Trade* (New York, 2004).

101   'It is ... dealer' Arnold, *First Report*, 80.

102   'It seems ... occurrences' Ibid., 82.

102   'not only ... bargain' Ibid., 92. On Bowden's character, see Fannie E. Ratchford, 'A Review of Reviews, Part II', *Library Chronicle of the University of Texas*, 2 (1946), 21–55 at 50.

103   carelessly printed ... $400 R. H. Super, 'The Authenticity of the First Edition of Arnold's *Alaric at Rome*'.

103   'charmingly exorbitant' 'Scarce First Editions Appreciated', *New York Times* (24 Nov. 1894), 2.

103   'So little ... catalogue' Arnold, *First Report*, 39.

103   'Through the ... collectors' William Henry Arnold, *Ventures in Book Collecting* (New York, 1923), 14.

104   'miserable ... know about' TJW to JHW, 14 Dec. 1896, in *Letters*, 125.

104   'Upon ... this one' TJW to JHW, 13 Jan. 1897, Ibid., 127.

104   'I do ... for it' TJW to JHW, 17 Apr. 1897, Ibid., 130.

105   'very cheap' TJW to HBF, 24 June 1894, in *Sequel*, 279.

105   'one of ... acquisition' TJW to JHW, 17 Apr. 1897, in *Letters*, 131.

105   'As ... bought it' TJW to JHW, 17 May 1897, Ibid., 132.

105   'Pray ... have it' TJW to JHW, 17 May 1897, Ibid.

106   'It is ... golden day' Sharp, *Life*, 148.

107   spring of 1893 After which the type used for the *Sonnets* (Clay's Long Primer No. 3) was replaced by a new set (Miller and Richard's 17 Long Primer), for which see *Enquiry*, 64.

107	'NOT ... BY E.B.B.' Elizabeth Barrett Browning, *Sonnets* (Reading [i.e. London], 1847 [i.e. 1893]).
108	'hot buttered ... *Sonnets*' TJW, *A Browning Library* (London, 1929), xxx.
109	'held him ... own room' EWG, *Critical Kit-Kats* (London, 1896), 2.
109	'As he ... *by e.b.b.*' Ibid., 2–3.
110	'It will ... public' William G. Kingsland, 'Browning Rarities', *Poet Lore*, 6 (1894), at 264–8 at 266.
110	'It is not ... this form' Ibid.

8. A BOOK WE DON'T MUCH CARE FOR

113	'I can ... questions' Muir, 90.
113	Natalie Blair Dickinson, 96.
114	Clark ... facsimile Collins, 232–5.
114	'What ... sonnets?' TJW to William Andrews Clark, Feb. 1928, in Collins, 235.
114	price of $1,250 *Enquiry*, 167.
114	Edgar Wells ... fishy business Muir, 90.
115	all the ... America *Enquiry*, 363–8.
115	Maggs ... monastic library See the images printed in *The Mediaeval Bookchambers at Thirty-Four & Thirty-Five Conduit Street* ([London, 1923?]).
115	'would ... generals' 'Obituary: Mr Bernard Quaritch', *The Times*, 36016 (19 Dec. 1899), 6.
116	well-proportioned ... glass doors I am grateful to the staff at Maggs for sharing old photographs of the shop on Grafton Street.
117	'It's not ... out of him' JWC, 'How We Got Wise', *Sunday Times*, 7658 (8 Mar. 1970), 38–44(S) at 42. Details of this meeting are taken from JWC's account.
117	'Browning ... before 1901' Muir, 90–1.
117	'Now ... delightful' Ibid., 91–2.
118	'Have ... see it' Ibid., 92.
118	textual criticism ... Roman texts See Anthony Grafton, *Forgers and Critics: Creativity and Duplicity in Western Scholarship* (Princeton, 1990).
118	Richard Bentley ... spurious allusions See *inter alia* Joseph M. Levine, *The Battle of the Books: History and Literature in the Augustan Age* (Ithaca, NY, 1991); Kristine Louise Haugen, *Richard Bentley: Poetry and Enlightenment* (Cambridge, MA, 2011).

NOTES

119   'Unless ... outside' W. W. Greg, 'The Present Position of Bibliography', *The Library*, 4th ser., 11 (1930), 241–62 at 241.

119   'amateur ... scholar' Ibid., 247.

119   'And you ... prowess' Ibid., 259–60.

119   **independent scholar** After marrying his cousin in 1907, Greg resigned his post as librarian of Trinity College, Cambridge, and lived on the income provided by his shares in *The Economist* newspaper, which had been founded by his grandfather. See F. P. Wilson and H. R. Woudhuysen, 'Greg, Sir Walter Wilson (1875–1959)', *ODNB*.

120   'mere prostitution ... pretty books' Greg, 'Present Position', 258–9.

120   'Upon ... mature science' Ibid. 258.

120   'amiable game' Ibid.

120   'curious similarity' W. W. Greg, 'On Certain False Dates in Shakespearian Quartos', *The Library*, 2nd ser., 9 (1908), 113–31 at 116.

121   **William Jaggard** Greg did apportion some blame to Pavier, though the current scholarship leans towards Jaggard as primary mover. See Zachary Lesser's terrific book *Ghosts, Holes, Rips and Scrapes: Shakespeare in 1619, Bibliography in the Longue Durée* (Philadelphia, PA, 2021); Adam G. Hooks, *Selling Shakespeare: Biography, Bibliography, and the Book Trade* (Cambridge, 2016), 112–24.

121   **1619 injunction** See Hooks, *Selling*, 113–14 and 123.

122   'stolen and surreptitious copies' *Mr William Shakespeares Comedies, Histories, & Tragedies* (London, 1623), sig. πA3r.

122   **untangle ... two fakes** [HGP], *Birrell and Garnett Catalogue of Secondhand Books* [no. 20] (1928), 8 (item 72). Unfortunately, Pollard's guess of a 1675 date for the 'ornaments' edition was twenty years off.

122   'clue to the mystery' W. W. Greg, *Collected Papers*, ed. J. C. Maxwell (Oxford, 1966), 54.

122   'our chain ... puzzle' Quoted in Laurie E. Maguire, *Shakespearean Suspect Texts: The 'Bad' Quartos and Their Contexts* (Cambridge, 1996), 66. The following paragraph draws on Maguire's account (66–8).

122   'same ... *Lear*' F. P. Wilson, 'Sir Walter Wilson Greg 1875–1959', *Proceedings of the British Academy*, 45 (1959), 307–34 at 331.

122   'intuitive ... Holmes' Review of W. W. Greg, *Principles of Emendation in Shakespeare* (London, 1928), *Life and Letters*, 1 (June 1928), 526–7.

122   'distinguish ... tobacco' Arthur Conan Doyle, *A Study in Scarlet*, ed. Owen Dudley Jones (Oxford, 2009), 35.

122   'detective mind ... puzzles' Greg, *Collected Papers*, 176.

123 **Holmes ... bookman** Material from this section draws on Madeleine B. Stern, 'Sherlock Holmes: Rare Book Collector', *The Papers of the Bibliographical Society of America*, 47 (1953), 133–55.

123 **'just ... efficient'** Arthur Conan Doyle, *Memoirs of Sherlock Holmes*, ed. Christopher Roden (Oxford, 2009), 116.

123 **Clementson** Cf. Stern, 'Holmes', 137–8.

123 **'This is ... 1642'** Doyle, *Study*, 44.

124 **'weather-beaten'** Arthur Conan Doyle, *Through the Magic Door* (London, 1907), 162. Holmes's fictional tome was evidently based on a real book picked up by Doyle in Edinburgh, as described here.

124 **'Charles's ... off'** Doyle, *Study*, 44.

124 **'remnant box'** Doyle, *Through*, 162.

9. THE MORAL POSITION

125 **'not more ... edition'** BL, Ashley 2102. A photograph of the page is included in Collins, 120. Alternatively, is it possible that Strahan himself was duped into inscribing the book? Wise assumed Strahan to have been dead at the time, but in 1904 discovered that 'he is still very much alive, 74 years of age, & quite lively. He is coming to spend an evening & talk Tennyson in a few days' (TJW to HBF, 30 Jan. 1904, qtd. in HRC, MS 4564/23.6).

125 **Maggs later sold a copy** Maggs Bros., *First Editions of the Esteemed Authors of the 19th and 20th Centuries*, no. 367 (London, 1918), 193.

125 **cluster of fakes** Between 1907 and 1909, the fakes often appeared at auction en bloc alongside other 'privately printed' Wise pamphlets and editions: for instance, twenty-seven suspect books at Hodgson's on 27 Feb. 1908 and another eleven on 6 July 1909. Frustratingly, the extant Hodgson's account books, naming vendors, don't begin until 1915 (BL, Add. MS 45619).

126 *The Falcon* On this ploy, see Collins, 227.

126 **'It is said ... example'** W. Robertson Nicoll and TJW, eds., *Literary Anecdotes of the Nineteenth Century*, 2 vols (London, 1896), ii. 355.

127 **'gentleman ... crop up'** TJW to EWG, 6 Feb. 1897, in *Centenary Studies*, 31–2.

127 **'household gods'** From the bookplate of HBF.

127 **portrait of Shelley** Terry L. Meyers, '"A Magnificent Find, If Genuine": A Possible Portrait of Shelley—From the Workshop of Harry Buxton Forman?', *Keats-Shelley Journal*, 38 (1989), 82–102 at 98.

127 **'relics ... wide'** From the bookplate of HBF.

NOTES

128	'scurvy ... Well!' HBF to TJW, 29 Sept. 1896, in *Sequel*, 281–2.
128	'appearance ... twelve' HBF to TJW, 29 Sept. 1896, Ibid., 282.
129	'Quite so ... *same!*' TJW to HBF, [30 Sept.?] 1896, Ibid., 284.
130	'Do ... reprint' Sydney Cockerell to HBF, 8 Sept. 1897, Ibid., 155.
130	'For ... acceptace' HBF to Cockerell, [10?] Sept. 1897, Ibid.
130	'I could ... so' HBF, *The Books of William Morris* (London, 1897), 125.
130	'I shall ... 1860' Cockerell to HBF, 11 Sept. 1897, in *Sequel*, 155.
130	'I will ... for me' HBF to Cockerell, 16 Sept. 1897, Ibid., 156.
131	'I think ... quantity' HBF to Cockerell, 16 Sept. 1897, Ibid.
131	'If ... think?' Cockerell to HBF, 17 Sept. 1897, Ibid., 156–7.
131	'As executors ... Copyright Act' F. S. Ellis and Cockerell, 'A Warning to Collectors', *Athenæum*, 3656 (20 Nov. 1897), 709.
131	'It appears ... illegal' Thomas and Archibald Constable [and TJW?], 'Some College Memories', Ibid., 3663 (8 Jan. 1898), 53.
132	'several ... correspondents' TJW, 'Some College Memories', Ibid., 3667 (5 Feb. 1898), 184.
132	'There is ... lately' Quoted in *Centenary Studies*, 5.
132	**spiralling demand for modern firsts** The best study is Madeleine Myfanwy Thompson, 'Birth of the First: Authenticity and the Collecting of Modern First Editions, 1890–1930' (unpublished doctoral thesis, Indiana University, 2013).
132	'Does ... fabricated' Quoted in *Centenary Studies*, 5.
133	'**in the realms of gold**' John Keats, 'On First Looking into Chapman's Homer' (1816) in *John Keats*, ed. John Barnard (Oxford, 2017), 10.
133	**fanciful backstory** In a letter dated 8 Dec. 1897, TJW had informed Arnold that a copy of the *Sonnets* belonged to William Axon, the former secretary of the Manchester Literary Club (and, more controversially, a notable proponent of vegetarianism). When TJW later sold a copy to Arnold, he claimed that it was Axon's copy and that it had previously been accompanied by a letter of authenticity written by Mary Russell Mitford. See the letter quoted in *Enquiry*, 23.
133	'It is rarely ... money' 'The Arnold Sale', *New York Times* (11 May 1901), 343.
133	'I had ... indeed' TJW to JHW, 23 May 1901 in *Letters*, 209.
134	'Collectors ... insurance' Leon H. Vincent, 'The Collector's Point of View', in *A Record of Books and Letters Collected by William Harris Arnold* (New York, 1901), vii–xvi at viii.
134	'an event ... editions' 'Books and Men', *New York Times* (12 April 1902), 26.

135	'I am ... tell you' TJW to JHW, 17 Jan. 1901, in *Letters*, 194.
136	'horribly rare' TJW to JHW, 17 Apr. 1897, Ibid., 132.
136	'had the cheek ... copy' TJW to JHW, 17 Jan. 1898, Ibid., 147–8.
136	'At this ... value' TJW to JHW, 23 Mar. 1898, Ibid., 151.
137	'four little ... books' TJW to JHW, 23 Nov. 1900, Ibid., 186–7.
137	'very rare trial issue' TJW to JHW, 22 Mar. 1899, Ibid., 164.
137	'Dolby ... property' TJW to JHW, 9 Apr. 1901, Ibid., 200.
138	'considerable ... collation' Partington, 135.
138	another man The divorce file names Lionel Rogers as a co-respondent: TNA, J 77/618/18874.
138	marriage documentation Partington, 144.
138	'book-hunting expeditions' TJW to JHW, 7 Feb. 1904, in *Letters*, 354.
139	'It is ... here' TJW to JHW, 26 August 1903, Ibid., 325.
139	'We shall ... sort' TJW to JHW, 4 June 1905, Ibid., 415.
139	give the baby a kiss TJW to JHW, 13 May 1911, Ibid., 577.
139	daughter of her own TJW to JHW, 26 Mar. 1911, Ibid., 575.
139	'second rate ... grapes' TJW to JHW, 23 May 1901, Ibid., 209.

10. THE KERNLESS F AND THE CURIOUS ?

141	Brice's JWC, 'Pollard', 5. The detail of the burgundy followed by coffee is of my own invention, but given the menu at Brice's and the tastes of the JWC and HGP, it seems likely enough that they split a bottle.
141	'Catalogue ... Gorfin' Herbert E. Gorfin, *Catalogue of a Miscellaneous Collection of Books* (London, 1930), t.p.
142	New York According to immigration documents, JWC arrived in New York on 6 Feb. 1932.
142	'Efforts ... party' 'Spies and Touts', *Daily Worker* (29 Mar. 1932).
143	'Zanoff' TNA, KV 2/1595/114Ba.
143	sitting tight with Bishop TNA, KV 2/1595/121A.
143	'interview ... plays' TNA, KV 2/1595/121b.
143	Red Army ... agents TNA, KV 2/1595/120a: 'SPRINGHALL, as you are aware, soon after his return spent a considerable time in the N[orth] E[ast] coast district. He is supposed to be organising Seamen and Dockers. When a Lenin student SPRINGHALL did not spend a lot of his time with the <u>Far-Eastern</u> Russian Red Army to train him to come back to this country and organise Seamen and Dockers [...]

NOTES

students from the Lenin courses are definitely allotted jobs of the utmost importance to the U.S.S.R. upon their return to this country.'

143 'Springhall . . . East' TNA, KV 2/1595/121b.

144 leaving for Russia TNA, KV 2/1599, unfoliated.

144 'took . . . still there' TNA, KV 2/1599, unfoliated.

144 'Detective . . . prove them' Maxwell Knight, *Be a Nature Detective* (London, 1968), 2.

145 account books BL, Add. MS 52864, fol. 149r. Dozens of her letters to Pollard on the finer points of Wilkie Collins bibliography are in Bodl., MS Pollard 130, fols. 141–218.

145 'dark . . . house' Gladys Mitchell, *Dead Men's Morris* (London, 1936), 163–4.

146 not being circumcised i.e. *Whose Body?* (1923).

146 tube of oil paint i.e. *The Five Red Herrings* (1931).

146 'Enough . . . drugs' DLS, *The Unpleasantness at the Bellona Club* (New York, 1963), 46.

146 infiltrate . . . wardroom DLS, *Whose Body?* (New York, 1923), 235. On Wimsey's earlier career in intelligence, see Philip L. Sowcroft, 'Espionage and Lord Peter Wimsey', *Sidelights on Sayers*, 13 (1985), 9–12.

147 Sayers . . . marriage Cf. Martin Edwards, *The Golden Age of Murder* (London, 2015). I am indebted to Edwards's vibrant account of both the Detection Club and of Sayers's double life.

147 letters to librarians i.e. Ethel Roberts to JWC, 3 Mar. 1933, MS 4564/19.3.

148 friends of Gosse Cf. 'I cannot at this distance of time be certain whether I had direct authority in stating that Browning's story about the *Sonnets from the Portuguese* was told to Gosse himself' (Frederic George Kenyon to JWC, 13 Jan. 1933, HRC, MS 4564/18.2).

148 'sole . . . table' Quoted in Partington, 49.

148 'In making . . . troubling you' JWC to TJW, 19 Dec. 1932, HRC, MS 4564/18.2.

148 Wise simply directed TJW to JWC, 20 Dec. 1932, HRC, MS 4564/18.2.

148 'only so much . . . materialism' DLS, 'Introduction', in DLS, ed., *Great Short Stories of Detection*, 3 vols. (London, 1928–34), i. 11–18 at 15–16.

149 'The detection . . . type' Arthur Conan Doyle, *The Hound of the Baskervilles*, ed. W. W. Robson (Oxford, 2008), 32.

NOTES

149   **'magnificent form'** TJW to William Andrews Clark, Feb. 1928, in Collins, 235. On Pollard's use of the photo-facsimile, see *Enquiry*, 38.

150   **clubbable wit** See 'Mr Stanley Morison', *The Times*, 57070 (12 Oct. 1967), 10.

150   **hole in the crown** John Barr, *Stanley Morison: A Portrait* (London, 1971), 63.

150   **simple ... differentiate** Cf. *Enquiry*, 39.

151   **which part ... recall** Cf. Ibid.

151   **'kern'** For a useful primer on kerning, on which I draw here, see Robert Bringhurst, *The Elements of Typographic Style*, 3rd edn (Point Roberts, WA, 2004), 50.

151   **broken-backed** Stanley Morison to HGP, 31 Jan. 1933, in Barr, *Morison*, no. 138.

152   **accidentally been punched upright** HGP suspected this had been deliberate: 'when Clay's broke or lost the matrix for the roman question mark proper to Shanks's Long Primer No. 20, they in fact supplied the deficiency by casting the italic question mark of the next smaller size (bourgeois or nine point) upright on a long primer or ten-point body' (HGP quoted in *Sequel*, 67). HGP was wrong. In fact, the errant question mark came from Miller and Richard's Long Primer No. 28 (*Sequel*, 79). It does look a bit odd, but that is a quirk of design and not a fault in manufacture.

152   **'I may ... 1847'** Stanley Morison to HGP, 31 Jan. 1933, in Barr, *Morison*, no. 138. Morison is often credited with spotting the kernless 'j' that also features in this font. Because there is no mention of the 'j' in his letter, I have chosen not to mention it in this chapter.

153   **run itself** This is not strictly true. Jane Norton was running the shop and by all accounts doing an expert job.

153   **larger premises south of the river** See Robin Myers, *The Stationers' Company: A History of the Later Years, 1800–2000* (Chichester, 2001), 147.

153   **catalogue of examples** This was HGP's *Catalogue of Typefounders' Specimens* (London, 1928), a work of enduring scholarly importance.

154   **1883** HGP thought the font was first introduced in 1883. In fact, it was introduced in 1877 (Collins, 246), though this doesn't make much difference to the story and for that reason I have decided to keep things as HGP saw them at the time.

154   **'How often ... Apply them'** Arthur Conan Doyle, *Sherlock Holmes: Selected Stories*, ed. Barry McCrea (Oxford, 2014), 35.

NOTES

155 **swap in a similar example** Though this was the working theory, it was not correct; the impostor question mark was simply lifted from Miller and Richard's Long Primer No. 28 (*Sequel*, 79).
155 'direct clue' *Enquiry*, 63.
155 **The broken-backed ... mark** Ibid., 64.
155 'Printed by ... WISE' Matthew Arnold, *Alaric at Rome*, ed. TJW (London, 1893), t.p.

11. STICKY FINGERS

160 'Magic ... truth!' Max Schweidler, *The Restoration of Engravings, Drawings, Books, and Other Works on Paper*, trans. Roy Perkinson (Los Angeles, CA, 2006), 118–19. On false watermarks, see ibid., 118–20, 258–63.
160 **chlorinated lime** Ibid., 64–5.
160 **handful of artisans** To this list might be added the firm of Kelly and Sons, who specialised in so-called 'Kelligram' bindings, gaudily inlaid with pictorial leather decoration. So far as I am aware, and in a rare demonstration of good taste, Wise never employed Kelly.
160 **Riviere ... stream** Cf. Collins, 278.
160 'hospital copies' See McKitterick, *Old Books*, 45.
161 'I think ... there' Frank Maggs to Maurice Pariser, HRC, MS 4564/22.3.
161 'it was ... detect them' [William Roberts], 'Notes on Sales: John Harris, Facsimilist', *TLS*, 888 (23 Jan. 1919), 48.
162 'condemning ... outrage' Robert Cowtan, *Memories of the British Museum* (London, 1872), 227.
162 'He was ... punished' Ibid.
162 'abstracted' Ibid.
162 **1845 statute** i.e. 8 and 9 Vict. cap. 44: see *The Statutes of the United Kingdom of Great Britain and Ireland* (London, 1845), xvii. 745.
163 'a scholar ... mate' Quoted in P. R. Harris, *The Reading Room* (London, 1979), 20.
163 **north room** Access to the north room was controlled by the superintendent: see *A Guide to the Use of the Reading Room* (London, 1919), 21.
163 'nothing would be simpler' Foxon, 3.
164 'This young ... success' TJW to JHW, 6 June 1903, in *Letters*, 318.
164 'play of ... cost to him' TJW to JHW, 6 June 1903, Ibid., 317.
165 'soiled and slightly torn' TJW to JHW, 8 Apr. 1903, Ibid., 307.
165 'If only ... bibliographies!!!' TJW to JHW, 8 Apr. 1903, Ibid., 308.

- 165 **another of Wise's masks** Ratchford (*Letters*, 75) and Barker and Collins (*Sequel*, 152) suspect that 'Calder' was a pseudonym for Gorfin. This seems unlikely. After all, most of the books coming from 'Calder' were made up with Museum leaves stolen by Wise himself.
- 165 **Pope ... title page** David Foxon, 'Two Cruces in Pope Bibliography', *TLS*, 2917 (24 Jan. 1958), 52.
- 165 **museum stamp had bled** The book containing the stolen leaves is BL, Ashley 5211; the orphaned title page is 644.m.14(2). The scraping away of the stamp bleed is clearly visible over transmitted light.
- 165 **'I had ... any kind'** TJW to JHW, 17 Apr. 1903, in *Letters*, 310.
- 165 **damaged ... stealing** Foxon, 22–3. A further two stolen leaves were transplanted into a copy for another American collector, George Aitken, while a fifth leaf was held back by Wise and remained among his collection of hospital leaves at his death. I am currently writing an article about the leftovers of Wise's book hospital, where I hope to expand on this story.
- 166 **'fair ... market copies'** TJW to JHW, 18 Mar. 1906, in *Letters*, 442.
- 166 **Sotheran ... thousand dollars** See TJW to JHW, 16 Apr. 1901, Ibid., 202 (cf. 20). For the 'reputation', see TJW to JHW, 15 June 1901, Ibid., 213.
- 166 **shipped over ... rebound** See Foxon, 7.
- 168 **'For ... Wise'** This copy of Wise's *A Landor Library* (1928) was recently offered for sale by Kay Craddock, antiquarian bookseller in Melbourne: see catalogue no. 242, item 21.
- 168 **'He steals ... Wise'** David Foxon to JWC, 13 Oct. 1956, HRC, MS 4564/17.3. When Foxon asked to quote this binder (who was called Philips) in his study of the thefts, he was refused: 'he has been very unwilling to blacken any one's name or to be quoted himself'. I think enough time has now passed for this evidence to see light of day. A few names require some blackening.
- 168 **'THOMAS JAMES WISE. HIS BOOK.'** A reproduction of the bookplate can be found in Collins, 240.

12. CHEMICAL WOOD, TRACES OF RAG

- 171 **in places** *Enquiry*, 63.
- 171 **the foreman's letter** Dated 28 Apr. 1933 (*Enquiry*, 64).
- 172 **no arguing with the facts** 'When we laid these facts before Messrs Clay, they admitted readily enough that the facts which we have just set out proved that they had printed the pamphlets' (*Enquiry*, 65).

NOTES

173 **American inventor** This was Benjamin Chew Tilghman: see R. S. Kellogg, *Pulpwood and Wood Pulp in North America* (London, 1923).

174 **discouragingly impressionistic** Cf. 'I shall only mention printing wet and dry in passing. The paper is substantially the same question and much more definite to the outside world' (HGP, 'Sundry Observations on the Plan of the Book', HRC, MS 4564/18.2).

175 **series of publications** For instance, in *Swinburne's Proof Sheets and American First Editions* (Cambridge, MA, 1920) and *Bibliography of the Works of Rudyard Kipling* (New York, 1927).

175 **'hopelessly ... misleading'** TJW, *A Swinburne Library*, 93.

175 **'I have ... enough'** Flora V. Livingston to JWC, 6 Apr. 1933, HRC, MS 4564/22.1.

176 **paper samples** The chemists' report (Cross and Bevan to HGP, 22 May 1934, HRC, MS 4564/19.3) includes all the items from the list of pamphlets lent by Gorfin earlier that month (HRC, MS 4564/15.7), suggesting that this was the purpose for which they were lent. Though we have not yet encountered Gorfin, it makes narrative sense to discuss the paper chemistry here. I beg the reader's forgiveness for defying the strict chronology of events.

177 **'a tall ... books'** Partington, 200. This and the following paragraph draw on Partington's vivid account of Shepherd.

178 **provoked the ire of the poet laureate** For a full account of the legal proceedings, see W. D. Paden, 'Tennyson's *The Lover's Tale*, R. H. Shepherd, and T. J. Wise', *Studies in Bibliography*, 18 (1965), 111–45.

179 **less likely it all seemed** For reasons against Shepherd's involvement, see *Enquiry*, 122.

179 **'we are ... Shepherd'** Cecil Clay to JWC, 3 July 1934, HRC, MS 4564/19.3.

180 **letter from Browning to Leigh Hunt** [Percy Lubbock], 'Browning in His Letters', *TLS*, 1652 (28 Sept. 1933), 647.

180 **'Gosse's ... antecedents'** JWC, 'Conclusion' (Jan. 1933), HRC, MS 4564/18.2.

181 **'I agree ... else?'** Quaritch to JWC, 11 Jan. 1933, HRC, MS 4564/18.2.

181 **'Even ... them'** HGP to JWC, 17 Mar. 1933, HRC, MS 4564/18.2.

13. PUTTING ON THE RITZ

183 **morning coat** 'I fear that at the last Roxburghe Club dinner I must have shocked you by my strange get-up. The simple fact is, I was late and changed in a hurry, and in my haste snatched up a morning coat

instead of a dress coat. This to my horror I noticed when I arrived at the Ritz—too late to do anything' (TJW to Sydney Cockerell, 20 Aug. 1928, HRC MS 4564/20.2[5]). The dinner took place on 27 June 1928 (Eton College Library, P.Rox.1920[3]).

183 **To 'ritz' ... verb** See *OED* 'ritz' *v.* 1b.
184 **'the cause ... world'** See Nicolas Barker, *The Roxburghe Club: A Bicentenary History* (London, 2012); and the potted history on the Roxburghe Club website (https://www.roxburgheclub.org.uk/history/).
184 **27 June 1928** Eton College Library, P.Rox.1920(3).
184 **'No man ... life'** TJW to Sydney Cockerell, 12 Dec. 1926, HRC, MS 4564/20.2[3].
185 **'From the first ... flawless'** David Nichol Smith, 'Introduction to Volume Eight', *Introductions to the Catalogue of the Ashley Library* (New York, 1934), 46–51 at 46.
186 **'Open my ... door'** A. Edward Newton, 'Introduction to Volume Six', in *Introductions*, 33–8 at 36.
186 **'in the front ... conquistadores'** [R. W. Chapman], 'The Ashley Library', *TLS*, 1112 (10 May 1923), 312.
186 **'Mr Wise ... them out'** [R. W. Chapman], 'The Ashley Library', *TLS*, 1165 (15 May 1924), 303.
186 **'great work ... epic poem'** [R. W. Chapman], 'Mr Gosse's Library', *TLS*, 1153 (21 Feb. 1924), 106.
186 **bound uniformly by Riviere** Richard Curle, 'Introduction to Volume One', in *Introductions*, 1–8 at 4.
186 **'He considers ... posterity'** Ibid. Cf. the blushing author of one unsolicited note: 'A total stranger must apologise for addressing you but a collector of your fame has almost ceased to be a private individual' (qtd. in Collins, 230–1).
186 **book of special beauty** A full description of the volume is given in TJW, *A Browning Library* (London, 1929), 85–8. It is now in the British Library, Ashley 4715. The whole thing is, as Collins points out, in very poor taste.
187 **'I do not ... generations'** Seymour de Ricci, *English Collectors of Books and Manuscripts* (Cambridge, 1930), 186–7.
188 **summoning ... book trade** See Partington, 235.
188 **scoundrels, thieves, and liars** See, for instance, TJW to 'Mr Nordau', 3 Aug. 1930, in Schimmel, lot 129.
188 **'I immediately ... property'** Partington, 236. For the identification of Partington's '*******' with Spencer, cf. Walter T. Spencer, *Forty Years in My Bookshop* (London, 1923), 273.

NOTES

188   'In detecting ... terrier' EWG, 'More Frauds of the Book Forger', *Bookman's Journal*, 3 (7 Jan. 1921), 177.

188   **the subject of Wise himself** Cf. Partington, 237–8.

188   'I visited ... followed' Qtd. Ibid., 238.

189   'He ... about him' [?] to JWC, 12 Nov. 1966, HRC MS 4564/15.2.

189   'The gloom ... poets' TJW to JHW, 11 Apr. 1909, in *Letters*, 512.

190   **right of first refusal** TJW to EWG, 10 May 1909, in Collins, 184.

191   'It appears ... pen' TJW, *A Bibliography of the Writings in Prose and Verse of Algernon Charles Swinburne*, 2 vols. (London, 1919–20), I. xii. This paragraph draws on TJW's account on pages xi–xiv.

191   'the mere ... prolific' Ibid., I. xiv.

192   'mystic ... poem' Algernon Charles Swinburne to William Michael Rossetti, 6 Oct. 1869, in *The Swinburne Letters*, ed. by Cecil Y. Lang, 6 vols. (New Haven, CT, 1959–62), II. 45.

192   'How could ... left it' TJW to EWG, 5 July 1909, in Collins, 185.

192   'I lose ... thousands' EWG to TJW, 6 Oct. 1909, Ibid., 187.

193   'gilt-edged security' TJW to EWG, [July 1909?], in Partington, 163.

193   'Would not ... printing' TJW to EWG, 15 Dec. 1909, in Collins, 188–9.

194   **three times that sum** i.e. around £10,000: see Partington, 179.

194   **thousand pounds a year** Collins, 190.

194   **personal work on company time** Cf. Ibid., 158.

194   **signing ... various names** There is a receipt for a copy of Tennyson's *Morte d'Arthur* made out to Wise signed 'Walter Harrison' and dated 27 Mar. 1899 (HRC, MS 4564/28.4). Ratchford alleges this is in HEG's hand, albeit written with an uncharacteristically sharp nib. JWC disagreed.

195   **library ... Smart** Collins, 189.

195   **large numbers of forgeries** For details of the books bought by Gorfin, including all the forgeries, see *Enquiry*, 371–8.

195   **vanishingly rare** Cf. Charles P. Johnson, 'To be Read at Dusk, by Charles Dickens', *Athenæum*, 3316 (16 May 1891), 636: 'I fear that the pamphlet is only interesting to the bibliographer, as the collector can hardly hope to possess a volume so rare as I believe this to be.'

195   **found in an old publisher's warehouse** For this version of the yarn, see Partington, 209.

196   'keep ... bed' Collins, 190.

196   **more distant** Cf. Ibid., 195.

196   '**My dear Harry Buxton F!**' TJW to HBF, [1914?], Ibid., 204.

- 196 **'I do not ... *about*'** HBF to TJW, Dec. 1913, in Collins, 200. My italics.
- 196 **'I hurry ... present'** HBF to TJW, April 1913, in *Centenary Studies*, 12.
- 197 **lukewarm obituary** *The Times*, 4508 (19 June 1917), 5.
- 197 **'I see ... manuscripts'** EWG to TJW, June 1917, in Collins, 205.
- 198 **sage-green levant** This was the same copy sold at the Kern sale in 1929, which also records that Wise offered Forman £1,000 for the book, but was unsuccessful (*Library of Jerome Kern*, II. 348).
- 198 **'Were you ... had it'** Quoted in Collins, 206.

14. FROM PILLAR TO POST

- 199 **train out** There is some confusion about the dates. JWC and HGP seem to have acquired copies of the forgeries from HEG in March and in May (HRC, MS 4564/15.7), which were then used for the paper chemistry tests. However, they later claimed to have been shown the incriminating notebook and cheque stubs 'in the summer of 1933' (*Gorfin's Stock*, 1). My guess is that the initial meeting took place in March and that 'summer' is a slip for an unseasonably warm 'spring'.
- 200 **assistant to a grocer** JWC and HGP, *Gorfin's Stock*, 12.
- 201 **skulking in a nearby café** Partington, 105.
- 201 **assure Gorfin** When a copy of Tennyson's *Lover's Tale* (1870) sold for $112.50 in the Forman sale, TJW contacted HEG to tell him that he had three 'spare copies' and that HEG should 'report them at once to three people in America for £5.5.0. each'. Next to which HEG has written, in pencil, 'I had previously bought "all" of these from TJW' (HRC MS 4564/4.8).
- 201 **back out ... buyer** Partington, 209–10.
- 202 **'The moment ... tool'** Ibid., 210.
- 202 **'Look ... own?'** Ibid., 209.
- 202 **sold ... Quaritch** JWC's list of items 'Purchased from Gorfin at various times by Quaritch' includes headings for each of these authors (HRC, MS 4564/18.2).
- 203 **sell on commission** The list is in *Enquiry*, 376.
- 203 **more than a dozen** 'Maggs says he used *regularly* to buy the book [i.e. *Sonnets*] from Gorfin, who got them from Wise; usual price £20, later £40 to sell at £60. Has sold at least a dozen copies, but none recently' (JWC notes in HRC, MS 4564/18.2). Cf. 'all three [copies of the *Sonnets*] came from a book-seller who at one time was private

NOTES

secretary of T. J. Wise' (Flora Livingston to JWC, 16 Jan. 1933, HRC, MS 4564/18.2).

204 **reporting on communist activities** See, for instance, 'Personal M/1', 25 Sept. 1933, TNA, KV 2/1599/[1932].

205 **Pollard contacted** HGP had tried unsuccessfully to make an appointment with Wise in August, which his nurse refused on grounds of ill health: see HGP to E. Woolhorse, 23 Aug. 1933, HRC, MS 4564/14.4.

205 **'You must not excite him'** Collins, 246.

206 **'cruel, porcine eyes'** [?] to JWC, 12 Nov. 1966, HRC, MS 4564/15.2.

206 **'as though ... page'** Augustus Muir quoted in Partington, 237.

206 **'Those eyes ... secrets'** Ibid., 237.

206 **'I am ... can'** Wise quoted Ibid., 285 (converted into direct speech).

207 **'They cost ... received'** Wise quoted Ibid., 285 (converted into direct speech).

207 **shook her head ... shouting** Collins, 246.

208 **subservient office boy** Cf. JWC quoted Ibid., 249.

208 **'Gorfin told ... make'** JWC and HGP, *Gorfin's Stock*, 12.

208 **'Trouble ... £30'** HEG, 'Gorfin's Declaration II', HRC, MS 4564/17.4, 1 (converted into direct speech).

15. GIVING YOURSELF AWAY

211 **nasty fall** TJW to William Andrews Clark, 1 Dec. 1932, WAC, Clarkive.Pres-1934, box 9/19; cf. Partington, 278.

211 **'bibliographer-like ... demonstration'** Ibid.

212 **long walks** Dorothea Braby qtd. in *Sequel*, 185.

212 **his way of repaying Wise** Newman I. White qtd. in Fannie E. Ratchford, 'A Review of Reviews, Part II', *Library Chronicle of the University of Texas*, 2 (1946), 21–55 at 36.

213 **Richard Herne Shepherd?** There is a strong possibility that Wise may have been setting up Shepherd as the 'fall guy' from an early stage. Thirty years earlier, he wrote, 'That Shepherd was quite equal to the sin of printing the tracts in later years, and adding an earlier date to its title is perfectly true—provided he could have induced some small and evil minded printer to act as his dupe' (TJW to Luther Livingston, 20 Sept. 1905, HRC, MS 4564/5.1).

215 **'Those monstrous ... away'** Qtd. in Partington, 268: 'Clay, describing the interview, gave me the following verbatim report of what was said.'

- 215 'full facts ... think best' HEG, 'Gorfin's Declaration II', HRC, MS 4564/17.4, 1–2.
- 217 'It is so unfortunate ... want you' HEG, 'Gorfin's Declaration II', HRC, MS 4564/17.4, 2–4 (converted to direct speech).

16. WISECRACKING

- 221 **unassuming first-floor bistro** Muir, 100.
- 222 **'Although ... business'** HEG to TJW, 29 Oct. 1933, HRC, MS 4564/18.2.
- 222 **note to Leigh Hunt** See [Percy Lubbock], 'Browning in His Letters', *TLS*, 1652 (28 Sept. 1933), 647.
- 222 **'I enclose ... ever told'** Flora V. Livingston to JWC, 11 Dec. 1933, HRC, MS 4564/22.1.
- 222 **'Wisecracking ... title'** JWC, late draft book proposal, summer 1933, HRC, MS 18.2.
- 223 **'You'll ... verbal'** JWC to David Randall, 4 Dec. 1933, University of Delaware Library, MS 0601/I, box 3, folder 129. The draft preface for a revised edition of the *Enquiry* explicitly called the book 'a detective story' (JWC, 'Draft for Preface to Enquiry Mk II', HRC MS 4564/18.5).
- 223 **'position ... questions'** *Enquiry*, 123.
- 223 **'There was ... work'** Ibid., 109.
- 224 **'inflicted ... felt'** Ibid., 141.
- 224 **On facing pages** Ibid., btw. 64–5.
- 224 **'a careful ... honest man'** James P. R. Lyell, 'Re. Literary Forgeries', HRC, MS 4564/18.2, 1–4.
- 226 **'Mark ... pie!'** TJW to Coulson Kernahan, qtd in JWC, 'Supplement to An Enquiry: Chapter 1. The counter-attack that failed', HRC, MS 4564/18.6, 18.
- 226 **'As a Briton ... suggestion'** HGP to AFP, 2 Nov. 1933, Bodl., MS Pollard 417, fol. 136r (converted to direct speech).
- 226 **'I have ... cads'** TJW to Cockerell, 18 Jan. 1934, HRC, MS 4564/20.2. TJW considered HGP to be more of a cad than JWC. In a conciliatory letter to Frederick Page, he wrote: 'I feel no ill will against Carter, for I am convinced that he is not the one responsible for the—shall we say unusual?—tone in which it is written. That, I feel sure, is the effect produced by another hand. All I have ever heard regarding Carter has been to his credit, and I consider his skill and his work to be good' (TJW to Page, 12 July 1934, HRC MS 4564/14.4).

NOTES

227 'Is it true ... old chap' Richard Curle to Michael Sadleir, 27 Jan. 1934, HRC, MS 4564/18.2.

227 'It was ... undertake' JWC to Richard Curle, 9 Feb. 1934, HRC, MS 4564/18.2.

227 'It occurred ... about it' Richard Curle to JWC, 16 Mar. 1934, HRC, MS 4564/18.2.

227 put up to it Cf. TJW to Richard Curle, 26 May 1934, HRC, MS 4564/4.7: 'I still think the little book must be genuine.'

228 'May ... generous' Richard Curle to JWC, 7 Apr. 1934, HRC, MS 4564/18.2.

228 'Auntie Page ... in 1847' Ralph Binfield, 'The Case Against Wise', *TLS*, 3179 (1 Feb. 1963), 77.

229 'I will ... boast of' TJW [and Frederick Page], 'Mrs Browning's Sonnets, 1847', *TLS*, 1686 (24 May 1934), 380.

229 'hot buttered ... hurried' TJW, *A Browning Library*, xxx.

230 'A detailed ... weeks' HGP, 'Mrs Browning's Sonnets, 1847', *TLS*, 1687 (31 May 1934), 396.

231 'First ... state' *A Catalogue of the Library of Rare and Choice English Books Formed by the Late H. T. Butler, Esq.* (London, 1934), t.p. and 59.

231 'bore ... touched' JWC to Michael Sadleir, 9 Jun. 1934, HRC, MS 4564/18.2.

231 closer to thirty The following lots from the Butler sale are confirmed forgeries: 556–7, 559–60, 564–7, 579–80, 591–3, 603, 735, 742, 752, 755, 764, 781, 792–9, 817, 821, 827, 829.

231 'I want ... unwise' Michael Sadleir to JWC, 8 Jun. 1934, HRC, MS 4564/18.2.

232 'If this book ... any fiction' DLS, 'Authenticity of Famous First Editions', *Sunday Times*, 5803 (1 July 1934), 11. R. Austin Freeman agreed: 'I have seldom met with a book which I have enjoyed so much' (Freeman to JWC, 4 Feb. 1938, HRC MS 4563/17.3).

232 'tireless ... reasoning' 'First Edition Forgeries: An Essay in Detection', *The Times*, 46793 (29 June 1934).

232 'The reader ... humour' Harold Nicolson, 'A Literary Bombshell', *Daily Telegraph*, 24682 (2 July 1934).

17. A DELICATE MISSION

233 'You know ... motor-spanner' Partington, 290.

233 'I asked ... killing' Schimmel, lot 70.

NOTES

234 'All my ... Shepherd' 'Forged Books Sensation', *Daily Herald* (30 June 1934).

234 'personal statement ... duped' TJW, 'Certain Nineteenth-Century Pamphlets: A Personal Statement', HRC, MS 4564/4.1, 2–3. Into the typed phrase, 'I have been duped', TJW inserted the following in pen: 'in common with my contemporaries'.

235 'crush ... two moves' Frederick Page to TJW, 20 July 1934, in *Letters*, 52–3. A dignified silence was also the suggestion of Wise's American friend Gabriel Wells: 'the wisest course in the circumstances is to maintain a dignified silence ... To know oneself to be innocent, and to have disinterested, loyal friends believe so, that should be sufficient' (Wells to Louise Wise, 20 Sept. 1934, HRC, MS 4564/28.2).

235 'I regret ... do so' Frances Louise Wise, 'Mr T. J. Wise', *TLS*, 1700 (30 Aug. 1934), 589.

236 'angry ... man' Ralph Binfield, 'The Case Against Wise', *TLS*, 3179 (1 Feb. 1963), 77. JWC expressed his relief in a letter to Page: 'I am glad that you have decided to relinquish your brief in this matter, which I realise was imposing a gradually increasing strain both on your friendly relations with Mr Wise, and on your scholarly regard for the truth. I am sorry that we should only have met under rather disagreeable circumstances, but I hope we part without ill feeling' (24 July 1934, HRC, MS 4564/21.3).

236 'Book ... where it is' Lord Esher, 'Nineteenth-Century Forgeries', *TLS*, 1699 (23 Aug. 1934), 577. JWC advised on the typescript before Esher sent it off (HRC, MS 4564/16.5).

236 'It seems ... list' Lansdowne to Hornby, 18 Oct. 1934, HRC, MS 4564/20.2(13).

236 'This makes ... Wise' Lansdowne to Mersey, 8 Aug. 1934, HRC, MS 4564/20.2(11).

237 'I regret ... possibly do' TJW to Aldenham, 26 Nov. 1934, HRC, MS 4564/20.2(33).

237 'no dog ... resign' Sir Frederic Kenyon to Hornby, 14 Nov. 1934, HRC, MS 4564/20.2(28).

237 **Aldenham most feared** Aldenham to Crawford, 7 Nov. 1934, HRC, MS 4564/20.2(18).

237 'l'affaire de Wise' Lansdowne to Hornby, 14 Nov. 1934, HRC, MS 4564/20.2(27).

237 'concealed ... premises' Lansdowne to Hornby, 1 Dec. 1934, HRC, MS 4564/20.2(37). At this point in his transcript of the letter, Carter places an exclamation mark in the margin.

NOTES

237 'We were ... at once' 'Extracts from Sir Sydney Cockerell's Diary', HRC, MS 4564/20.2(43). The following account of Cockerell's mission draws on his version of events.

238 'The tea-party ... over' Qtd. in Tim Munby to JWC, 26 May 1964, HRC, MS 4564/20.2(43). On the reverse of this account JWC has inscribed: 'O for a verbatim record'. O indeed.

239 the librarian at the Bodleian i.e. Falconer Madan: see HGP to AFP, 11 Nov. 1934, Bodl., MS Pollard 417, fol. 147v.

239 'It is ... inked' *Centenary Studies*, 68–9.

240 'I think ... before' HGP to AFP, 11 Nov. 1934, Bodl., MS Pollard 417, fol. 147v; cf. JWC to Flora Livingston, 15 Nov. 1934, HRC, MS 4564/21.2.

241 £9,500 Purchased from Sotheby's in the Carysfort sale on 2 July 1923 (item 1). See Eric White, 'From Mainz to Austin: Carl H. Pforzheimer's Gutenberg Bible', Pforzheimer Lecture, Harry Ransom Center, Austin, 9 Feb. 2017.

241 attention ... Wells Collins, 266.

241 'Quite so ... same!' TJW to HBF, [30 Sept.?] 1896, in *Sequel*, 284.

241 invited by Pforzheimer JWC published his own account of the meeting in 'Thomas J. Wise and His Forgeries', *Atlantic* (Feb. 1945), 93–100.

242 'constitutional ... week' JWC to HGP, 22 Dec. 1936, in Bodl., MS Pollard 371, fol. 94r.

243 '1. Because ... suppressed' JWC to William A. Jackson, 23 Dec. 1936, in Bodl., MS Pollard 371, fol. 92r.

243 'I did ... opportunity' William A. Jackson to JWC, 18 Apr. 1937, in Bodl., MS Pollard 371, fol. 101r.

243 'Once ... result' JWC to Carl Pforzheimer, 14 Feb. 1936, HRC MS 4564/21.3.

18. WHAT A LOT OF BOOKS

245 'It's all ... now' Collins, 267.

245 'Children! ... for that!' Partington, 134.

245 'Exposed ... Museum' Qtd. in Collins, 272.

245 'Wise ... perspective' 'The Ashley Library', *The Times*, 47787 (11 Sept. 1937), 11.

246 revised edition There is a document headed 'Tentative Synopsis of *The Enquiry Concluded*' in JWC's hand, dated 3 Mar. 1936 (HRC, MS 4564/15.2).

246 **Sayers had stopped by the shop** HGP to DLS, 15 June 1934, Bodl., MS Pollard 130, fol. 192r.

246 **corrections and hints** See DLS to HGP, 18 June 1934, Bodl., MS Pollard 130, fol. 193r.

246 **'Chatterton? ... other day?'** DLS, *Gaudy Night* (1935), 259.

247 **'BRISTOL ... 1816'** *An Account of Lord Mortimer Wimsey* (Bristol [i.e. London], 1816 [i.e. 1937]).

247 **'I have ... not do'** HGP to DLS, 17 Dec. 1937, Bodl., MS Pollard 130, fol. 210r.

247 **'I must ... used'** HGP to DLS, 12 Jan 1938, Bodl., MS Pollard 130, fol. 217c.

247 **house party** See Ernestine Carter, *With Tongue in Chic* (1974), 39.

248 **'She is ... years'** Philip Hofer to Percy Muir, 24 Jan. 1937, qtd. in Dickinson, 133.

248 **'I *am* very happy'** JWC to HGP, [Dec. 1936?], Bodl., MS Pollard 130, fol. 99r.

248 **Zaehnsdorf ... morocco** This copy was last sold at Christie's New York, 28 June 2005, lot 1112. Cf. 'I hope one day to acquire a copy myself—the book has meant a good deal to me, and I should like to have one' (JWC to James H. Pershing, 29 Feb. 1936, HRC MS 4564/19.3).

249 **wardrobes ... motorcar** Warmington & Co., '*Kirkstead*' ... *Catalogue of the Whole of the Well-Made Household Furniture and Effects* (1939), t.p.

249 **'thinnest veneer'** Collins, 272.

249 **bundle of pages** Collins, 275. The remnants of the book hospital were later donated to the British Library by Quaritch. They remain uncatalogued.

250 **'gas masks ... realities'** Dickinson, 129.

250 **'England ... books'** JWC qtd. Ibid., 137.

250 **'I look very odd with a rifle!'** JWC to Charles Scribner III, 12 July 1940, Princeton University Library, C0101, Box 1001/1.

250 **makeshift bomb shelter** JWC, 'A Bookseller's Day in London', *Publishers Weekly* (2 Nov. 1940), 1764.

250 **'I'm sick ... afterward'** JWC to Percy Muir, 21 Apr. 1941, qtd in Dickinson, 139.

251 **Ashley collection ... intact** See P. R. Harris, 'Acquisitions in the Department of Printed Books, 1935–50, and the Effects of the War', *British Library Journal*, 12 (1986), 119–44.

NOTES

251 **David Foxon** On Foxon's intelligence career and how it influenced his bibliographical work, see James McLaverty, 'David Foxon, Humanist Bibliographer', *Studies in Bibliography*, 54 (2001), 81–113. Medical tests would later reveal Foxon to have abnormally high levels of adrenalin in his bloodstream, which helped explain his periods of exceptional productivity and subsequent exhaustion.

253 'His fictions . . . happy?' Qtd. in Partington, 319.

254 'Clearly . . . work' Foxon, 5.

254 'nerves . . . drugs' Holbrook Jackson, *The Anatomy of Bibliomania* (1930; 3rd edn 1932), 9.

254 'Some . . . mad' Ibid., 665.

254 'Bibliomania . . . them' Ibid., 667.

254 'seizes . . . race' Frederic Harrison, *The Choice of Books* (1907), 87.

254 'and was . . . blanket' Jackson, *Bibliomania*, 666.

255 **Flaubert** For good analysis, see Gerry Max, 'Gustave Flaubert: The Book as Artifact and Idea', *Dalhousie French Studies*, 22 (1992), 9–22.

255 **purportedly true** Although the story was reported as true in the French newspapers, there is no actual evidence for the crime in Spanish records.

256 **Fullford of Pentonville Road** For a decent overview of Fullford's business and specialities, see *Illustrated London and Its Representatives of Commerce* (1893), 199. The sign text is qtd. in Partington, 31.

256 **paper** The following, including the bibliographical details of different paper stocks, draws on JWC, 'Thomas J. Wise's *Verses*, 1882/1883', *The Library*, v, 24 (1969), 246–9.

257 **vellum** Technically, not 'vellum' but parchment, though 'vellum' is what the bibliophiles call it.

257 'neither . . . printer' JWC, 'Wise's *Verses*', 249.

257 'Thoughts . . . chamber' TJW, *Verses* (1882), t.p.

EPILOGUE

261 'distasteful . . . bizarre' Collins, 165.

262 **paragon . . . capitalism** John Sutherland makes the same point in 'Well Done, You Forgers', *LRB*, 15.1 (7 Jan. 1993).

262 **awkward statement** Bodl., MS Pollard 420, fols. 45–52.

262 **Biblio Boys** Bodl., MS Pollard 371, fol. 168r.

262 **Gutenberg Bible** Dickinson, 145–9.

263 **Life as an attaché** See Ibid., 154–6.

263 **reverse ... fiction** HRC, MS 4564/18.5.
263 **'Pollard's pace'** JWC, 'Graham Pollard', in Hunt et al., *Studies*, 1–9 at 7.
263 **'John ... support'** HGP to Ernestine Carter, Mar. 1975, qtd. in Dickinson, xiii.

Index

Acton, Harold 22
Aitken, George 161
Aldenham, Alban Gibbs, 2nd
    Baron 236, 237, 239
Aldus Manutius 97
Allen, George 75, 76
American Book Collector
    (periodical) 234, 235
Anderson Galleries, New York
    85–6
Arnold, Matthew 5, 7, 195,
    203, 231
  Alaric at Rome 77–8, 103, 155,
    172, 240
Arnold, William Harris 100, 101–2,
    103–4, 105, 133
  catalogue 133, 134
Ashley Library 96, 115, 125, 168,
    169, 175, 185–8, 192, 193,
    195, 205–6, 214, 226, 236,
    245, 249–52, 259–61
Ashley Road (No. 52), London 95,
    104, 106, 137, 138
Athenæum, The (weekly)
    131–2
Aveling, Edward Bibbins 6

Bacon, Francis 33
  New Atlantis 31
  Sylva Sylvarum 31
Baldwin, Stanley 57
Balliol College, Oxford 23, 26
Bangs, Lemuel W. 101
Bangs and Co. (auctioneer) 101,
    103, 132
Barnes Common: 'Branksea' 24,
    25–6
Bateson, F. W.: *Cambridge
    Bibliography* 91
Beauchamp, Joan 24, 26
Beauchamp, Kathleen (Kay)
    see Pollard, Kathleen
Beauchamp, Muriel 24, 26
Beaumont and Fletcher 31–2
Beeton's Christmas Annual 1
Bennett, Dr William Cox 108, 178,
    179, 181, 229–30
Bennoch, Francis: 'Books bring me
    friends . . .' 169
Bentley, Richard 118
Berwick Salome, Oxfordshire 248
Bevan, Edward John *see* Cross,
    Charles Frederick
bibles 259
  Gutenberg Bible 241, 262
Biblio Boys 82, 89, 221, 262
  see also Gathorne-Hardy, Eddie;
    Muir, Percy

INDEX

Bibliographical Society of London 2, 34, 119, 185, 203
bibliomania 254–5
binderies 71, 159–61, 167–8
Binfield, Ralph 228, 229, 236
Birrell, Francis 54
Birrell and Garnett Ltd (booksellers) 53–4, 55, 84, 145, 149, 150, 246, 250
Bishop, Reginald 143, 144
Blackwell, Basil 30
Blackwell's Bookshop, Oxford 30, 31, 32
Blair, Natalie 113, 115
Bletchley Park, Buckinghamshire 251–2
Blind, Mathilde 6, 49
Boccaccio, Giovanni 26
  Decameron 50
Boden, James 42
Bodleian Library, Oxford 83, 239–40
Bonham's auction house 261
Bookman magazine 69, 92, 97, 98–9, 135
bookplates 37, 127, 168–9
Boswell, James 42, 44
Bowden, Alfred James 102, 132, 133, 139
Bowden, William 72
Bowra, Maurice 22
Bowring, Sir John 96
Brasenose College, Oxford 29
Brawn and Brawn (printers) 179
Brice's bistro, Soho 141
British Library 259–60
  see British Museum
British Monotype Corporation 57
British Museum 4, 40, 55, 73, 74, 103, 123, 148, 155, 161, 177, 226, 228, 233, 243, 245, 249, 251, 253, 259
  as bibliographical authority 73, 103
  security arrangements 162–4
  theft of leaves from 164–8
  purchase of the Ashley Library 245–6
Brooke, Rev. Stopford 7–8, 10, 44, 108
Brown, Ford Madox 49
Browning, Robert: courtship and marriage to Elizabeth 106–7; Wise's embellishment thereof 109–10, 180; and Furnivall 3–4; on Alma Murray 6, 15–16; and Wise's missed chance of a copy of *Pauline* 12–13; uncomfortable with reprint of *Pauline* 14; duped by Wise 65–8; his books in Wise's collection 96; death 106; and Sharp's biography 99, 106–7, 109; and Forman's contributions to *Literary Anecdotes* 128; forgeries of his works 90, 132, 171, 203, 206, 207; Wise's bibliography 135; Shepherd's unauthorised printings 177; Wise's 'Memento' 186–7, 260–61; and Wise's tales 187, 188; and Wise's *Verses* 256
  works and correspondence
  Cleon 99
  correspondence 222, 229
  De Gustibus 185–6
  Gold Hair 99

Pauline 12–14, 15, 38, 39, 99, 134, 166
The Ring and the Book 133
The Statue and the Bust 99
Browning, Elizabeth Barrett 106–7, 109, 110, 133, 148, 180, 186, 187, 229, 260–61
  works
  Poems see Sonnets from the Portuguese
  The Runaway Slave 65–8, 74, 86, 103
  Sonnets from the Portuguese 92–3, 106–11, 113–18, 123, 126, 133–4, 147–8, 149, 150–55, 174–7, 180–81, 186–7, 196, 226–30, 261; as 'Reading' *Sonnets* 107–8, 113, 148, 178–9, 187, 192, 203, 222, 223–4, 226, 228, 230, 231, 248
Browning Society 3, 11, 13, 39, 47, 108, 172–3
Bryan, Mary 247
Burne-Jones, Georgiana 48
Butler, Herbert T. 231, 232
Byron, George Byron, Lord 39, 90, 97
'Byron, Major' *see* Gibler, George de Byron, Robert 22

'Calder, William' 164, 165
  see Wise, Thomas James
Calkin, Arthur 167–8
Cambridge University Press 84
Campbell, James Dykes 12, 13
Carter, Ernestine (*née* Fantl) 247–8, 250, 263
Carter, John: appearance 82, 84; background 82–4, 183; personality 85, 146; joins Scribner's 84; knife-edge trouser-crease 83; meets Pollard 82, 84–5; in New York 85; and Jerome Kern auction 85–6, 87; asks Pollard for new ideas on book collecting 87–9; at meeting of Biblio Boys 89–92; has suspicions of foul play concerning 'Reading' *Sonnets* 92–3, 113–15, 116–17, 118; at Bibliographical Society of London 119; and Walter W. Greg 119, 122; joins with Pollard in listing suspicious books 141–2; continues to investigate the 'Reading' *Sonnets* and other 'first editions' 147–8, 150, 171–3, 175–6, 179–80; decides on Wise as forger 180–82; confirms his suspicions 199–201; what to do next? 203–4, 205; told of Pollard's interview with Wise 208, and Wise's invitation to Gorfin 208, 209–10; and Cecil Clay's meeting with Wise 214–15; updates the Biblio Boys 221–2; and Pollard's *An Enquiry into the Nature of Certain Nineteenth Century Pamphlets* 222–6, 230, 232; undaunted by Wise's attempts at intimidation 226–7; and Richard Curle 227; and sale of Herbert

INDEX

Carter, John: – *cont.*
Butler's library 231;
delighted by Dorothy Sayers's
review of the *Enquiry* 232;
and Wise's fight back 233–6,
and resignation from
Roxburghe Club 236–9;
fails to secure Pforzheimer
document 241–4; compiles
materials for revised edition
of the *Enquiry* 246, 263;
marriage 247–8; his personal
copy of *Sonnets* 248, 261;
and Wise's death 246; in the
war 250–51, 262; after the
war 262–3; publishes *ABC
for Book Collectors* 263;
death 263
Caxton, William: Chaucer 259
Chapman, George: translations of
Homer 133
Chaucer, Geoffrey 3, 32, 259
Chaundy, F. W. 30
Chaundy's bookshop 29–30
Chesterton, G. K. 145
Chez Victor, Wardour Street,
London 55
Christie, Agatha 89, 145, 147
Christie's auction house 261
Clairmont, Jane 96
Clark, William Andrews
114, 149
Clay, Cecil 171, 172, 179, 214, 215,
224, 235
Clay and Sons (printers) 15, 18, 19,
46, 49, 67, 70, 72, 74, 77,
107, 155, 161, 171–2, 176,
179, 205, 214, 215, 223,
224, 235, 240
Clementson, Alfred B. 123

Cockerell, Sir Sydney 130–31, 184,
226, 237–8, 239
Coleridge, Samuel Taylor 133
Collier, John Payne 43–4, 223
Collins, John 261
Collins, Wilkie 88, 145
Comintern 61
Communist, The 57, 61
Communist Party of Great Britain
27–8, 56, 58, 59, 60, 61–2,
63, 142
Constable (Archibald and Thomas)
and Co. 131–2, 222
Cook, Edward Tyas 91
(with Alexander Wedderburn)
*Complete Works of
Ruskin* 91
Cornhill Magazine 59
Cotton, Charles: *Poems* 32
Cowley, Arthur 83
Crabbe, George 34
Inebriety 34–5, 53
Crawford, David Lindsay, 27th Earl
of 237
Crawley, Frederick 75
Cross (Charles Edward) and Bevan
(Edward John) 174, 175, 176
Curle, Richard 227–8
Currie, Barton Wood 99, 100

Daily Herald 234
Daily Mail 57
Daily Telegraph 232
Daily Worker 60, 61, 62, 142, 143
Davenant, Sir William: *Plays and
Poems* 32
David, Gustave: bookshop 83
Dekker, Thomas: *The Wonder of a
Kingdom* 164–5
Descartes, René 87

INDEX

Detection Club 145, 147, 232
Dickens, Charles 99, 137, 171
  To be Read at Dusk 195
Distributive Worker (magazine) 56
Dobell, Bertram: bookshop 10, 14, 32, 34, 90, 221
Dobell, Percy 221
Dolby, George 137–8
Donne, John 33
  Poems 32
Dowden, Edward: *The Life of Shelley* 17, 18
Downside Crescent (No. 23), London 139
Doyle, Sir Arthur Conan 88
  see also 'Holmes, Sherlock'
Driberg, Tom 22
Dryden, John 104, 135

Eliot, George, 171, 203
  Agatha 69, 73–4, 77, 103, 195
  Brother and Sister 195
  The Legend of Jubal (*Brother and Sister*) 68, 69, 74
Elizabeth I 41
Elkin Matthews (bookselling firm) 79–80, 81–2, 84, 88–9, 90, 113, 221
Ellis, F. S. 6, 131
Elzevir (printer) 97
Esdaile, Arundell 233
Evans, A. W. 80, 81, 88, 89, 221
Examiner, The (periodical) 126–7

facsimile printing 7, 13–14, 15, 16, 18, 19, 46, 47, 77–8, 92, 155, 158, 161, 167, 172–3, 240, 261
'faking up' 38–9, 126, 240
Ferguson, F. S. 116

Fitzgerald, F. Scott 231
Flaubert, Gustave:
  Bibliomania 255
Fleming, Ian 89
Flitch, John Crawford 27
Foote, Charles B. 103
Forman, Harry Buxton: and the printing of Horne's *Galatea* 45; early dealings with Wise 14–15, 17, 45–6; works on forgeries with Wise 67, 68, 70, 71, 72, 74, 105; has no desire to sell the books 72, 77; as an unwilling participant 76–7; corrects Wise's errors 77–8; and Shelley's *Queen Mab* 86; and Elizabeth Browning's *Sonnets* 107, 108; increasingly piqued by Wise's dishonesty 127–9, 132; questioned by Cockerell 129–31; relations with Wise 131, 137, 196–7; death and obituary 197; his library searched by Wise 197; blame shifted on to him 213–14, 217, 230, 234, 235; Wise incriminates himself in their correspondence 241–2
Forman, Maurice Buxton 197, 212–14, 218, 226, 230
Forman, Simon 43
Forster, E. M. 53
Fortnightly Review 98
Foxon, David 251–3, 254
Freeman, Edward Augustus 5
Freeman, R. Austin 88
Frick, Henry Clay 100
Fullford, William 256, 257

Furnivall, Dr Frederick James:
founds Shelley Society 3–4, 5–6; at inaugural meeting 6, 7; sets out programme of facsimile printing 7; takes Wise under his wing 11–12; introduces him to Browning 12, 13, 188; recruits him into the Shelley Society 13, 19; recommends his reprint of *Adonais* to Forman 14; finds him difficult to control 17; gives Clay & Sons commissions 172–3; on Murray and Shelley forgery 40; feeds Wise with scandalous tales about Swinburne 49–50; and Wrenn's visit 139

Galsworthy, John 80
Garnett, David ('Bunny') 53, 54, 55
  see also Birrell and Garnett Ltd
Gathorne-Hardy, Eddie 80, 81–2, 88–9, 90, 92–3, 117, 118, 141
General Strike (1926) 57–8, 59
Gibbon, Edward 33
  Decline and Fall 31
Gibler, George de 39–40
Gibson, Strickland 34
Gill, Eric: Gill Sans 57
Gladstone, William E. 4, 30
Goldsmith, Oliver: *The Vicar of Wakefield* 104
Gorfin, Herbert E.: works for Wise 194–5, 201–3; sets up as an independent bookseller 195, 199–200; becomes a stooge for Wise's forgeries 195–6, 200–1, 202–3; discovered by Carter and Pollard 141–2, 199–203, 205; final meetings with Wise 208–10, 211, 215–19; refuses to shift blame on to Forman 217, 221–2
Gosse, Edmund 108, 109, 110, 127, 139, 148, 180, 192, 193, 197
Graham, Alastair Hugh 22
Grand Theatre, Islington 15–16
Grant, Duncan 53
Gray, Olga 60
Gray, Thomas: *Odes* 46–7
Greenidge, Terence 21, 22, 29
Greg, Sir Walter Wilson 34, 119–21, 122–3
Grolier Club, Manhattan 100
Gutenberg Bible 241, 262

Halsey, Frederick Robert 103
Hancock-Nunn, Vivian 60
Hardy, Thomas 231
Harris, John 161
'Hartley, Mr' 165
  see Wise, Thomas James
Harzof, Max 90–91, 92–3, 113, 233
Heywood, Thomas 158
Hobbes, Thomas: *Leviathan* 46, 122
Hodgson's auction house 32–3, 54, 55, 67, 132, 231
'Holmes, Sherlock' vii, 1, 88, 122–4, 149, 154, 173
Holywell Press 28
Hornby, Charles St John Hornby, Lord 236, 237, 239
Horne, Richard Hengist (*formerly* Henry) 45, 128, 137

INDEX

Galatea Secunda 45–6
'hospital copies' 160–61, 249–50
Hotten, John Camden 49, 51, 240
Housman, A. E. 83
Howes, Mr (bicycle shop owner) 21
Hunt, Leigh 180, 222
Huntington, Henry E. 100
Huntington Library, California 240
Hypocrites Club 21–2, 28

Inquiry into the Genuineness of the Manuscript Corrections in Mr J. Payne Collier's Annotated Shakespeare, An 223
Ireland, Samuel 41, 42
Ireland, William Henry 41–4, 47, 223

Jackson, Holbrook 254, 255
Jackson, William 241, 242–3
Jaggard, William 121–2
Jennings, Richard 68
Jesus College, Oxford 23–4, 29, 30–31, 83, 185
Johnson, Samuel: *A Journey to the Western Islands of Scotland* 100–1
Johnson Club 4
Jones, Henry Arthur 6–7
Jonson, Ben 158
    The Case is Alter'd 252
    hypothetical quarto 158, 159

Keats, John 11, 127, 133, 212
    Poems 133
Kelmscott Press 128
Kenyon, Sir Frederic 237, 238, 239
Kern, Jerome: sale of books 85–7
Kerr and Richardson (booksellers) 11

Keynes, Dr Geoffrey 119
King's College, London 240
Kingsland, William G. 75, 110
Kipling, Rudyard 175, 176, 231
Knight, Maxwell ('M') 59–61, 142, 143, 144–5, 153, 204, 205

Lamb, Charles 86
Langstone Monotype Company 57, 149
Lansdowne, Henry Petty-Fitzmaurice, 6th Marquis of 236, 237
Lewisham: Lee High Road (No. 91) 199–201
Liberty Bell (magazine) 65, 66
Lincoln College, Oxford 30
Livingston, Flora 70, 175–6, 222, 262
Lovelace, Richard 33
Lyell, James 224–6

'M' *see* Knight, Maxwell
Madan, Falconer 34
Madden, Sir Frederic 73
Maggs, Frank 161
Maggs Bros. (bookseller) 71, 115, 125, 194
Malone, Edmond: *An Inquiry into the Authenticity of Certain Miscellaneous Papers* 42–3, 223
Marlow, Mr (book restorer) 160
Marlowe, Christopher 158
    The Jew of Malta 166, 167
Marlowe, Thomas 57
Marx, Eleanor 6
Marx, Karl 7, 26, 27
Maund, Mona 60

INDEX

Maxwell, George T. 103
Meredith, George 231
Mersey, Charles Clive Bigham, 2nd Viscount 236
Meynell, Francis 56–7, 61
MI5 59, 60, 61, 62
  see also Knight, Maxwell
Middleton, Thomas 158
Midsomer Norton, Somerset 24, 25, 26
Milton, John 135
  Paradise Lost 37, 104–5
miners' strike (1926) 57, 58
Mitford, Mary Russell 107, 108, 109–10, 178–9, 181, 229
Moore, Thomas: *The Epicurean* 10
Morgan, John Pierpont 100, 150
Morison, Stanley 57, 150, 151–2, 174, 262
Morris, William 6, 30, 129–30, 131, 184, 231, 256
  The Pilgrims of Hope 130
  Sir Galahad 130
  Socialists at Play 129
Moxon, Edward 39, 40, 65, 66, 67, 70, 137
Mudie, Charles Edward 116–17, 181, 197–8
Muir, Percy 80, 81, 82, 88–9, 221, 250
Murray, Alma 6, 15
Murray, John 39, 40

Nabbes, Thomas: *The Bride* 165
National Amalgamated Union of Shop Assistants, Warehousemen and Clerks 56
National Gallery, London 74, 75
National Library of Wales, Aberystwyth 251
National Secular Society 6
New Oxford (periodical) 28, 29, 30–31, 32, 56
New York Times 86, 103, 133, 134
Newton, A. Edward 80–81, 185–6, 233
  This Book-Collecting Game 81
Nicolson, Harold 232
Nonesuch Press 55, 56, 61
Nowell-Smith, Simon 221

Ogden and Co. (printers) 179
Oldham, James Basil (schoolmaster) 23, 29
Orwell, George 88
Oxford Bibliographical Society 34
Oxford English Dictionary 3
Oxford University Labour Club 27
Oxford University Press 228

Page, Frederick 228–9, 234, 235, 236
paper 8, 15, 16, 31, 37–9, 47, 69, 71, 129, 149, 158, 159–60, 193, 207, 229, 230, 240, 252, 256, 257; chemical composition of 173–6; coloured 11, 129, 256; watermarked 77, 120, 121; heavy Whatman 256, 257
Pares, Richard 28
Parker's Bookshop, Oxford 30, 31
Partington, Wilfred 233
Partridge, Frances 54, 58, 62
Perkins, Thomas 43

INDEX

Pforzheimer, Carl 241, 242, 243–4, 246

Phalaris: *Epistles* 118

'Philadelphia Historical Society' 18

Pierpont Morgan Library, New York 150, 151

Pines, The, Putney 48, 49–51, 60–61, 95, 190, 192, 193, 194

Poe, Edgar Allan 88, 134

Poet Lore (magazine) 75, 110

'Poirot, Hercule' 1–2, 148, 149

Pollard, Professor Albert Frederick 23, 24–6; Graham Pollard's letters to 31–2

Pollard, Henry Graham: background 22–4; character and personality 22, 29, 33, 62–3, 183, 263; meets Kay Beauchamp 24–6; at Oxford 26–9, 30–31, 53, 185; introduces corduroy trousers to polite society 29; shambolic appearance 29, 33, 84, 171; love of books 29–34, 84–5; meets Wise 34–5; buys stake in Birrell and Garnett 53, 54–5; marries Kay Beauchamp 56, 61–2; as political activist 56, 57, 58, 61–2; recruited to MI5 60, 61, 62–3; friendship with John Carter 82, 84, 87, 89, 92, 262, 263; with the Biblio Boys 79, 82, 89, 91, 92; becomes interested in the 'Reading' *Sonnets* 117, 118; at Bibliographical Society of London 119; follows in W. W. Greg's footsteps in identifying fakes 122; joins Carter in listing books worthy of investigation 141–2; continues his work for MI5 142–5; relationship with Dorothy L. Sayers 146, 147; continues to investigate suspect books 148, 149, 150, 152–5; visits Cecil Clay 171–3, 214–15; examines the paper used in the *Sonnets* 174, 176; cautious about naming Wise as forger 181–2; gets evidence from Gorfin 199–203; takes inspiration from 'M' 204–5; interviews Wise 205–8; persuades Gorfin to see Wise 208–10; updates Biblio Boys 221–2; and Carter's *Enquiry* 223, 224, 225, 226; and Wise's counter-attack 226–7; writes to *Times Literary Supplement* on Wise's bibliographical competence 230; and Wise's fight back 233–6; and Wise's resignation from Roxburghe Club 236–9; investigates the forged Swinburne *Siena* 240; fails to secure Pforzheimer document 241–4; and news of Wise's death 246; produces forgery with Sayers 247; and Carter's marriage 248; and sale of Wise's secret 'book hospital' 249–50; in the war 262; death 263

INDEX

Pollard, Kathleen (Kay) (*née* Beauchamp) 24, 25, 26, 56, 57–8, 61–2, 63
Pope, Alexander 135, 165, 259–60
  An Essay on Man 165
Powell, Anthony 22, 31
Punchard, Charles 34

Quaritch, Bernard 115–16
Quaritch (bookselling firm) 90, 115, 116, 150, 181, 197, 203
Quennell, Peter 33

Ricci, Seymour de 187, 226
Ritz Hotel, London 183–4
Riviere and Son 71, 151, 160, 167, 168, 192, 194, 260
Roberts, William 98
Rossetti, Christina 4, 231
Rossetti, Dante Gabriel 4, 49, 74, 169, 187, 190, 231, 256
  Sister Helen 77
Rossetti, William Michael 4, 17, 18–19
Rowse, A. L. 28, 29, 30, 31
Roxburghe Club, the 184–5, 189, 203, 236, 237, 238, 239
Rubeck (Herman) and Co. 9, 76, 194, 195, 201
Rubeck, Otto 64
Ruskin, John 30, 74–5, 75, 91–2, 99, 171, 187
  works
    Catalogue of the Turner Sketches 75
    essay on Samuel Prout 75
    fake pamphlets 74, 117, 118, 213
    The Future of England 75
    Leoni 68, 75–6, 91, 92
    The National Gallery 92
    The Queen's Gardens 75, 92
    The Scythian Guest 91–2
Ruskin Society of London 75
Russia *see* Soviet Union
Rutland, John Henry Montague, 9th Duke of 236

Sadleir, Michael 221, 222, 224, 227, 231
St Bride Foundation Library 153, 154
St Paul's Cathedral 243
Sandys, Frederick 59
Sangorski and Sutcliffe 160, 168, 186
Sawyer's bookshop 90
Sayers, Dorothy L. 88, 89, 145, 146–7, 148–9, 232, 246, 247
  Gaudy Night 246
  see also 'Wimsey, Lord Peter'
Schimmel collection 261
Schlengemann (trader) 74
Scott, Sir Walter 97
Scott, William Bell 127
Scribner, Charles 101
Scribner's (Charles) Sons 84, 87, 88, 113, 248, 250
'Seymour, Charles Alfred' 18
Shakespeare, William 3, 40, 41, 43–4, 120–22, 223, 259; first folio 38, 90; second folio 43; fake love letter 41
  works
    Cymbeline 43
    Henry II (fake) 41–3
    King Lear 41–3, 120, 122
    Macbeth 43
    The Merchant of Venice 120

316

A Midsummer Night's Dream
  120, 121
  Pavier (i.e. Jaggard) quartos
  120–22
  Vortigern and Rowena (fake)
  41–3
  The Winter's Tale 43
Shanks, P. M. (type foundry) 172
Sharp, William 99
  Life of Robert Browning 106–7,
  109
Shaw, George Bernard 6–7, 8, 16,
  49, 253
Shelley, Mary, Lady 17, 96
Shelley, Percy Bysshe 3, 4, 5, 6, 7–8,
  9, 11, 14, 15, 38, 44, 49, 65,
  97, 127, 135, 256
  works and correspondence
    Adonais 11, 14, 15, 96, 261
    Alastor 15
    The Cenci 10–11, 15
    Hellas 15, 95–6
    letters 18–19, 39–40, 96, 188
    The Necessity of Atheism 16
    Oedipus Tyrannus 96
    Poems and Sonnets 17–18
    *A Proposal for Putting Reform
    to the Vote* 68
    Queen Mab 86, 198
    Revolt of Islam 54
Shelley, Sir Percy 14, 16, 48
Shelley Society 3–6, 13, 14, 16, 18,
  19, 24, 39, 40, 46, 47, 76,
  108, 172–3, 188; inaugural
  meeting (1886) 6–8, 44; first
  Annual General Meeting 17;
  Wise's facsimiles 13–19,
  38–40, 46, 47, 48, 69, 261
Shepherd, Richard Herne 72,
  177–9, 213, 234

Shirley, James 253
Shrewsbury School 22–3, 29
Simpson, Percy 34
Slack, Henry J. 18
Slater, John Herbert 9–10, 38
  *Early Editions of Some Popular
  Modern Authors* 69,
  97–8, 99
  *Round and About the Book-
  Stalls* 96–7
Smart, James P. 75, 91
Smart, Thomas Burnett 195
Smeeton, Joseph 39
Smith, David Nichol 34, 185
Smith, George D. 132
Socialist League 6
Society of Antiquaries 4
Sotheby's auction house 117,
  132, 226
Sotheran (Henry) and Co. 104,
  166, 203
Southampton, Henry Wriothesley,
  3rd Earl of 41
Soviet Union 58, 61, 143–4
Sparrow, John 232
Spectator, The 232
Speechley, Mrs (housekeeper) 53
Spencer, Walter T. 68, 188
Springhall, Douglas 143–4
Stevenson, Robert Louis 131–2,
  175, 231
  The Story of a Lie 86–7
Strangeways and Walden (printers)
  179
Stratford-upon-Avon 40–41
Strawberry Hill, nr
  Twickenham 47
Strong, Mr (book restorer) 168
Sunday Times 232
Sweet, Henry 3

Swinburne, Algernon Charles: on
Wise's hit list 48; his life
saved by Theodore Watts-
Dunton 48–9; tea with
Mathilde Blind and Wise
49–50, 95, 188; invites Wise
to call again 50–51; accepts
Wise's copy of *Cleopatra*
51–2, 68; Wise donates fakes
of his works to the British
Museum 74; his booklets of
verse feel 'vaguely phoney'
90; Wise shows off titles
purportedly from his private
collection 96; fakes of his
works sell for hundreds of
dollars 132, 133; Wise
publishes his bibliography
135; and Flora Livingston's
research 175, 222; and
Richard Herne Shepherd
177; death 189; leaves
everything to Watts-Dunton
189; his books and
manuscripts bought by Wise
189–94, 213; first editions
sold by Gorfin 202; Pollard
and Carter find gaps in
provenance of his pamphlets
206, 207; his 'first editions'
in Herbert Butler
sale 231; fakes still to be
found 261
works
  Cleopatra 49, 51–2, 74, 99
  Dead Love 68, 74, 87
  The Devil's Due 126–7
  Hertha 192
  Siena 69–70, 73, 77, 99,
   239–40

Taunt, Henry 30
Tennyson, Alfred, Lord: first
editions 97; and Moxon 65;
Wise's forgeries 74, 90, 99,
103–4, 132, 133, 135,
139–40, 171, 195, 206, 222;
and Richard Herne Shepherd
177, 178
works
  The Cup 132, 203
  Enoch Arden 70–71
  The Falcon 126, 203
  Idylls of the Hearth 70, 71,
   74, 105
  The Last Tournament 125,
   129, 132, 241
  The Lover's Tale
   178, 179
  minor poems 71–2
  Morte d'Arthur 137, 222
  The Promise of May 105, 136,
   203
Thackeray, William Makepeace
132, 137
Thompson, Edward Maunde 73
Thornton's Bookshop, Oxford 30
Times, The 57, 115–16, 149, 173,
197, 245–6
Times Literary Supplement (TLS)
186, 221, 229, 230, 231, 235,
236
Times New Roman 57
*TLS see Times Literary
Supplement*
trade unionism 58
Trades Union Congress 57
Trelawny, Edward 96
Trout Inn, Godstow, Oxford
26–7
Tupper, Martin 257

typefaces/typography 57, 149, 150–55, 172, 179, 180, 214, 224, 229, 230, 240, 256

University College London 24
  Botany Theatre 3, 6, 24

Vanderbilt, William Henry 100
vellum 16, 42, 257
Vinchelés Payen-Payne, James Bertrand de 188–9

Wade, Henry 88
Wade, Thomas 128
Wadham College, Oxford 30
Walpole, Horace 47
watermarks 37, 38, 39, 42, 47, 77–8, 120, 121, 129, 160, 240
Watts-Dunton, Theodore 48–9, 50, 189–93, 213
Waugh, Evelyn 21–2, 29
Wedderburn, Alexander *see* Cook, Edward T.
Wells, Edgar 114
Wells, Gabriel 241
'Westmacott, Mary' *see* Christie, Agatha
Wheatley, Dennis 89
White, William 39–40
Wilde, Oscar 16
Wilkinson, Cyril 33–4
Williams, Mr (farmer) 41
'Wimsey, Lord Peter' 1–2, 145–7, 246, 247
Wise, Frances Louise (Louie) (*née* Greenhaigh): as Thomas Wise's second wife 138–9, 157, 183, 245; on trips with the Wrenns 139; and Pollard's interview with her husband 205–6, 207; and Gorfin's visits 208, 215–16, 217, 218, 219; and Maurice Forman 213; writes to *Times Literary Supplement* 235; at Wise's tea party with Cockerell and Kenyon 238; death 249
Wise, Selina (*née* Smith) 95, 138
Wise, Thomas James 2; appearance and voice 8, 11, 18, 34, 82; background 8–9; and printing of his *Verses* 255–7; becomes addicted to book-collecting 9–11; meets Dr Furnivall 11; is introduced to Browning 12; fails to get a copy of Browning's *Pauline* 12–13; recruited into the Shelley Society 8, 13; becomes responsible for facsimile reprints of rare editions 13; oversees reprint of *Pauline* 13–14, 15; in touch with Harry Buxton Forman over reprint of *Adonais* 14–15; supervises reprints of other Shelley titles 15; at production of *The Cenci* 16; starts on his forging career 16–19, 38–40; meets Pollard 34–5, 53; learns from Forman 45–6; decides to produce new 'rarities' 46–8, starting with Swinburne's *Cleopatra* 48–52; fakes Elizabeth Browning's *The Runaway*

INDEX

Wise, Thomas James – *cont.*
Slave 65–8; further forgeries 68–78; relationship with Forman suffers 76–8; and the Biblio Boys 81–2; and Jerome Kern sale 86–7; and Ruskin editors' suspicions 91–2; moves house with new bride 95; and Slater's handbook for book-hunters 96–9; interests Wrenn in his library 95–6, 106; his reputation 102; and the American market 102–4; sets trap for Wrenn 104–6; fakes Elizabeth Browning's *Sonnets* 107–11, 114, 115, 118, 133–4; and W. W. Greg 119; steps up pace of production 125; buys own lots at auction 125–6; as editor of *Literary Anecdotes of the Nineteenth Century* 126–7, 128, 130, 241; rift grows between him and Forman 127–9; authenticity of his forgeries begins to be questioned 131–2; as an expert on Swinburne and Browning 134–5; further dealings with Wrenn 135–8, 139–40; wife leaves him 138; second marriage 138–9, 157, 245; and Carter and Pollard's investigation into his fakes 147–8, 149, 155, 175–6, 178–82; becomes interested in playbooks of Shakespeare's contemporaries 157–62; steals from the British Museum 162–9, 249, 253; as member of the Roxburghe Club 183–5; his Ashley Library 185–8; after Swinburne's death 189–94; and Wrenn's death 194; and Herbert Gorfin 194–6, 200–3; and Harry Forman's death 296–8; unmasked by Carter and Pollard 203–10, 211–12; gets Maurice Forman on his side 212–14; has unsuccessful interview with Cecil Clay 214–15; final meetings with Gorfin 215–19, 221–2; and Carter and Pollard's *Enquiry* 222–7, 230, 231, 232; plots counter-attack 226; exploits Frederick Page's friendship 228–9; defends himself in *Times Literary Supplement* 229–30; found in Hastings by reporters 233–4; chooses to remain silent 234–6, 249; resigns from the Roxburghe Club 236–9; new forgeries come to light 239–41; incriminates himself 241–4; death and will 245–6; his forgeries 253–5, 260–61; his character in retrospect 253–4, 262, 263; *see also* Ashley Library
Woolf, Leonard 53
Woolf, Virginia 53
Woolhorse, Mrs, 211, 212
Worcester College, Oxford 33, 34, 185, 226

Wordsworth, William 65, 171
'On the Projected Kendal and
Windermere Railway' 67
Worthington, Greville 90–91, 92–3, 113, 117
Wrenn, Harold 139
Wrenn, John Henry 99; visits Wise at Ashley Road 95–6, 104, 137; trapped 104–6; strikes a deal with Wise 135–8; their relationship 135, 138, 139–40; duped by Wise and receives stolen material 164–5, 166–7; his bookplate 169; accompanies Wise on pilgrimage to The Pines 193; death 194
Wright, Ralph 55
Wyse, Sir Thomas 8

Young Communist League 28

Zaehnsdorf bindery, Covent Garden 160, 168, 248
Zouch, Richard: *De Jure Inter Gentes* 123–4

penguin.co.uk/vintage